C000125756

THE MEDICINE PATH

Hearthlight Publishing, Calgary, Alberta, Canada.

© 2014 Jaki Y. Daniels

All rights reserved.

Except for brief passages quoted for the purposes of a review, no part of this publication may be reproduced or transmitted in any form or by any means—electronic or mechanical, including photocopying, recording or any information storage and retrieval system—without permission in writing from the publisher.

While the events described in this book are real and historically accurate, the names of some people and places have been changed to protect the privacy of individuals and sacred sites.

EXCERPTS: *from* SACRED PLANT MEDICINE: The Wisdom in Native American Herbalism. © *2006 by Stephen Harrod Buhner. Used by permission of Bear & Company, an imprint of Inner Traditions • Bear & Company.* www.innertraditions.com.

First Softcover Edition March 2014
Library and Archives Canada Cataloguing in Publication Data

Daniels, Jaki Y. 1957–

The Medicine Path: a return to the healing ways of our indigenous ancestors / Jaki Daniels

ISBN: 978-0-9784636-1-8 (softcover)

EDITING AND PROOFREADING: Miranda Buchanan, Marilyn Geddes, Chris Daniels, & Barbara Higgins, Calgary, Alberta.

TYPESETTING & PRE-PRESS PRODUCTION: Chris Daniels

FINAL EDITING: Sandy Gough, Calgary, Alberta.

Cover Drawing (Drum): Jonathon Daniels

COVER DESIGN: Jaki & Chris Daniels

www.jakidaniels.com

THE MEDICINE PATH

A return to the healing ways of our
indigenous ancestors

JAKI DANIELS

Hearthlight Publishing
CALGARY, ALBERTA

I am truly humbled
by the footsteps that have walked before me,
created through the lineage
of indigenous medicine men and women
from around the globe,
who,
for thousands of years
listened to the earth,
studied the sky,
and followed their guidance.

These teachings are their teachings,
only in a different time and place.

This book is dedicated to them.

"Jaki's garden is a garden of lost souls. She plants them carefully and tends them with great attention. Some may wither and die, but oh so many flourish. In turn, each of these reaches out a cultivating hand to another and another. And so it goes. And so it goes." (Marilyn Geddes)

Acknowledgements

For me, writing a book is a very solitary process. I take what I know inside, gather it into themes, type it out, and craft it into story. As the thoughts turn into words and the words create sentences, paragraphs, pages, and chapters, it becomes possible for someone else to have access—a format evolves and it becomes readable. Then a refinement process begins: a polishing of the rough and raw into something smooth and appealing. Once the foundation has been laid, the risk must be taken—the manuscript needs to be read by others. This is the hardest part. In many ways it is like passing over an infant child into the arms of a stranger. One moment you hold something most precious and dear, close to your heart where it is safe and sound. In the next you are trusting someone else to know the value of what is being offered, and willing to hold it with the same regard.

In that way I have been fortunate beyond measure. I have been blessed with a team of initial reviewers and editors who know me, know how deeply personal the story is, how sensitive I am to criticism, and yet also understand that I want the book to be the best it could possibly be, and I can't do that alone. Feedback is not only important, it is necessary.

I would like to thank Mica (Miranda Buchanan), an apprentice, friend, and spiritual sister, who so considerately and graciously walked beside me through all the steps of this book's creation, from being the first reader of the initial manuscript through months of edits and content changes. She held the highest regard for how sensitive I was about the story, how accurately and respectfully I needed to represent the Mountain, and how difficult some of the proposed changes might be for me to hear. Despite her own commitments and responsibilities she never failed to make herself available for a review reading, a meeting, or a fire ceremony to discuss content.

The second reader was my husband Chris, my best friend and lifelong companion. Chris is a philosopher and a scholar and so naturally takes a hard and critical look at what I am saying. He won't let me get away with blanket statements or flimsy explanations. He doesn't walk the same spiritual path and is quick to point out where I haven't made myself clear. There is no one else who cares as much about the quality of this book, because he knows how important it is to me.

Thirdly I would like to thank Barb Higgins, a friend, student, colleague, and advisor, for her bold and critical appraisal of what I was offering and how it could be received, with the result that whole sections ended up in the waste basket and others revealed more about me than I imagined I was willing to tell.

I would also like to thank Marilyn Geddes, my dear friend and colleague, who has the greatest respect for who I am and the work that I do. She is an accomplished editor and writer herself yet always encourages me to speak with my own voice. She is also an avid reader and I trust her perceptions and opinions. If she tells me the book is worthy of publishing, I believe her, despite my own fears and reservations.

And finally I would like to thank Sandy Gough, who performed the final edit before publication. It was not easy for me to reach out to an editor when I knew the content of this manuscript could challenge some people's beliefs. Sandy edited my first book, so she already knew about the Mountain. I surmised that she could openly receive these additional features of my world. In the end, I had nothing to worry about. Sandy accepted the manuscript on its own terms, without judgement, and offered her services professionally, with great care and attention to what the reader was being, introduced to.

Beyond that, I extend gratitude to the patients who were willing to have their healing journeys told – many of them for the first time, the students who helped me discern what was important to teach and how to teach it well, and the apprentices who trusted me with their spiritual training and were willing to make a commitment to this path, even when they knew I was still carving my own. Their dedication has been humbling indeed.

To respect the privacy of those individuals, groups, land-owners and business-owners who are included in this story, I have shielded their true identities. In each patient story, the names have been changed or their initials used with permission. In the sharing of my personal stories some names are real and included with permission, others have been changed. In the rare case that I no longer had contact information for a patient or person featured in a chapter, I have changed the name and other possible identifying characteristics as respectfully and considerately as possible.

Every story in this book is true. In some chapters I have changed small details slightly, such as location, gender of the person involved, or background information to protect anonymity. These details have been chosen carefully so as not to change the tone, integrity, or accuracy of the story.

Contents

Foreword

by Chris Daniels, Ph.D

A number of years ago, while working towards a Master's degree specializing in Philosophy of Religions, I became particularly enthralled by the works of a 20th century philosopher—Alfred North Whitehead. Whitehead was a Harvard mathematical physicist who had taken on the challenge of making sense of the diversity of human experience in light of the findings of the new physicists such as Albert Einstein, Neils Bohr, and Werner Heisenberg. If these scientists were correct, thought Whitehead, our whole understanding of how the everyday world worked, and our place in it, must change. We could no longer accept the mechanistic worldview that saw reality as fundamentally composed of "things" or "substances" that endured unchanged through time and space. We must reject the legacy we inherited from the Greeks and European intellectuals such as René Descartes and Sir Isaac Newton. Rather, we must begin to view the world as a process of experiential events which are fundamentally constituted by relationships. We are not "things" that *have* relationships, we are constituted *by* our relationships, as is the rest of creation. That is what quantum physics appeared to be telling us.

Well that changed everything for me. The consequence of viewing reality as fundamentally relational is that many human experiences which seem completely incommensurable with the popular Western understanding of reality can actually be accommodated! I soon realized that such a way of understanding the world is consistent with a plethora of diverse cultural traditions and perspectives that seemed like mystical fantasy when viewed through a typical Western mechanistic lens. In particular I thought it seemed remarkably consistent with what I understood to be the experience of Indigenous peoples as expressed in their narratives, ceremonies, dances, songs, and traditional relationship with the natural world. So much so, in fact, that my Masters studies turned into a Ph.D comparing the Indigenous worldview and ways of gaining knowledge with those articulated in Whitehead's philosophy.

At the same time I was doing my doctoral research and writing, my wife Jaki was writing *The Medicine Path*. Her first book, *Heeding the Call*, documented her struggle to come to terms with a particularly moving experience with nature that did not fit neatly into her previously held view of the world as a secular atheist. It was the type of experience I would later define in my dissertation as "indigenous." Although when applied to people "Indigenous" is one of those words that have been co-opted for a wide variety of different uses—political, economic, anthropological, sociological, and religious—at its most basic it is about "being born of the land." Indigenous practices, beliefs, and experiences come directly from the land, developed by and for the people who live on the land. Indigenous people are those that have such practices, beliefs, and experiences. I did not quite realize to what extent that definition described Jaki even though I had lived through those formative years and knew *Heeding the Call* to be an accurate portrayal of that period of her life. This became abundantly clear however, when we exchanged her book and my dissertation manuscripts for our usual round of editing—me with her writing and her with mine. We were both surprised and a bit shocked to discover to what extent I was philosophically explaining her actual lived experience of the world!

Once Jaki had come to terms with that first indigenous experience, her life and healing practice took on a whole new dimension. From that point on it seemed like a day didn't go by that the lives of her clients weren't transformed in some way. The healings were diverse in nature—some physical, some emotional, and some spiritual—but almost all were life-altering. Although Jaki often describes her work as subtle, many clients left her small office in the basement with the deep conviction that, after falling through the cracks of the conventional medical system, Jaki had literally saved their lives. But that was only half of it! Because of these seemingly miraculous successes, and her growing connection to the natural world and the divine, a small community of like-minded people had gathered to learn more about this way of living. Through ceremony, ritual, and teaching, Jaki was also reaching out to others who felt the need for shared community with each other, creation, and creator. More lives were transformed, if in a somewhat different manner than with her regular clients. What had become increasingly clear was that her whole life was ceremony, whether in her clinical practice, her personal meditations, or her connection to her community, both human and non-human. All of this was possible because of her profound relationship with a mountain, and through the mountain, the rest of creation. She had surely *become* Indigenous.

This then was what we realized as we read each other's manuscripts. Jaki was relating her experiences, her ways-of-knowing, and the often dramatic consequences that stemmed from her deepening relationship with the natural world, while I was philosophically attempting to interpret and explain a relational worldview that could accommodate such a life. I believe we were both successful. The substance-based model of reality the rest of us take for granted, despite our own quantum scientists increasingly finding it inadequate, has placed both humanity and the earth in peril. It does not accommodate many of our most fundamental experiences, it does not serve those who are wounded and require healing, and it has brought the world to the brink of ecological disaster.

Jaki's alternative understanding is not new. It encapsulates a paradigm that the world's Indigenous peoples have unceasingly held in trust in the face of unthinkable and relentless oppression and opposition. It is indeed "a return to the healing ways of our indigenous ancestors." If we look back far enough we all had ancestors that related to the land in an indigenous way. By becoming Indigenous, even though she is not "Native," Jaki represents the human re-indigenization that may be necessary for this world to survive.

The Medicine Path is not merely Jaki's personal story. It is a vision of what this way of life and understanding can mean, and the healings that can result. Although I, as yet, do not share this path with Jaki, even though I accept the worldview it pre-supposes, I have once again lived through her latest story as it unfolded and know the efficacy of the methods she relates. No matter what imagery, narrative, or interpretation of experience expresses this relational understanding, I have seen first-hand the results of her remarkable journey. Another famous philosopher, William James, once said "The truth is what works." If so, then this book, and the world it envisions, is indeed true.

Dr. Chris Daniels Ph.D (Religious Studies)
Calgary, Alberta, March 2014

Preface

It is a beautiful morning. The sun has risen to reveal a decidedly blue sky and to lighten the dew drops on the plants in the forest, as if touching them with a fairy wand and bringing them to life. The birds are chirping and the squirrels are busy, as always. The season is autumn and there are nests to prepare and harvests to store.

I too, as part of the natural world, embrace the season. I am preparing my nest for the winter, a writing sanctuary in the forest. It is also a time of harvest, a time to bring forward another eight years of my life's journey, to craft it into story.

In appreciating the beauty and my place within it, I stand where I can see the four directions. I light some copal resin and as the smoke rises to the sky, I offer my prayers:

To the grandmothers and grandfathers of the four sacred directions,
mother earth,
father sky,
to the stone people,
the plant people,
the animal people,
to the wing-ed ones and the weather beings,
to father sun and mother moon,
to all my relations,
welcome,
to this beautiful day.

I call out to the sacred Mountain, my Teacher and Guide. I wait patiently until I can see the Mountain Spirit Beings in my field of inner vision. They appear busy, attending to their tasks. I realize we all have our work to do and the Mountain is no different. I am struck by how, at this point in time, their work is my work—that the Mountain Spirit Beings are also preparing for a harvest, for the manifestation of this book. They are working in the background and I am working in the foreground. I sense a smile from Grandmother Mountain as if confirming my understanding. As I glance toward her, she is gathering something in her arms. I look closer. It is wood she is carrying, perhaps to build a fire. Returning my gaze, she corrects me with her eyes. The wood is for the paper I am using and will be using. And then I see the trees on the Mountain. I see them all standing in line, waiting to be next. I realize they are willing to sacrifice their flesh—that the giving of their lives is important if the medicine gifts of the natural world are to be revealed, if they are to be shared.

I feel the enormity of all the forces coming together to support me in my work but then quickly realize it is OUR work. As a human being it is so easy to turn to the place of burden, responsibility, and being 'in this' alone. I have just been reminded that none of these are true. WE are bringing forward the teachings at this time. As always, I am simply the voice of the Mountain, its voice in the physical world. Together, we prepare to tell the story . . .

PART I:

The Introductions

Introducing myself, the Mountain, and the Medicines

Chapter One

How I Came To Be Here

There is a beautiful tradition among the First Nations Cree people, as introduced to me by my Cree Elder and Teacher, Pauline Johnson, also known by her 'Indian'[1] name, Fishwoman. Whenever you are hosting a ceremony, whenever the people have gathered and are turning to you as guide, you must help them understand how you came to be here, how you came to be holding this sacred pipe, and the events of your life's journey that have led you to this time and place.

I never asked Pauline why it is done this way. In working with her, I have always understood that asking is not the way to learn. Spending time with the Elder, with Spirit,[2] and with Nature, participating in the ceremonies, that is the way to learn.

When we were first working together I was still in a natural period of adjustment. I had never spent time with native peoples before. I had very

---

[1] I use this term because Pauline refers to herself that way. I recognize that in other contexts it could be deemed offensive.

[2] When used with a capital 'S' this term refers to the Great Mystery, both in the multiplicity and unity of its expressions. With a small 's' it is descriptive of the 'spiritual' aspect of all things, which references the nature of, but is not identical to, Spirit.

limited exposure to ceremony. Pauline took the protocol of sharing with the people who you are and how you came to be here, very seriously. So seriously, in fact, I was often embarrassed to be present. Pauline had endured a difficult life. The ease with which she shared the details was sometimes hard for me to hear. To her, it was all part of the ceremony. The people needed to know who was lifting the pipe on their behalf, who had been honoured with the privilege of doing so. The people needed to know that she was just another human being, that they were of the same stock. By baring her heart and soul, the people could move to a place of trust and beyond any personal resistance. They could enter into the ceremony with an open heart. Pauline's honesty created a backdrop of mutual compassion and understanding that set the tone for a shared spiritual experience.

At the time of this writing I have been apprenticing with Fishwoman for fourteen years. She has been willing to teach me, a white person, something she tells me her own mother would never have agreed to. She has honoured and accepted my calling to this path through being chosen by a mountain to be its voice in the world, to be its student in the ways of spirit, energy, and matter, and she has accepted that while I am alone in receiving those teachings, she has the skills and tools to keep me safe and grounded in my work on this land in Alberta, Canada. She has brought forward some of the most treasured aspects of her spiritual tradition—the ceremonies, the songs, the ways of making offerings to Spirit—and given me the gift of participating within it. She has prayed to the Great Spirit and received my true name: One Who Walks With Eagle Mountain. I have been blessed.

As each of us progresses from student to teacher, and from teacher to Elder, we bring something of ourselves forward, and the protocols change slightly. Before Pauline and I ever met, the Mountain appeared to her in a dream. She understood that she was being asked by Creator to guide me and was willing to step outside her ancestral ways to do so. Now I am the one who must forge my own path. Pauline would not be comfortable sharing the nature of the medicines she works with or the spiritual gifts she has received. To her, that type of knowledge is best kept private. Yet the teachings I receive from the Mountain and Spirit can be shared, because in so doing the true nature of reality is exposed and the Mountain's story is told. To Pauline, and others still honouring the traditional ways, this reality is already understood. For me, it is an introduction I have been asked to make. The people are ready to learn about the healing ways of Spirit, as these medicines are sorely needed. Many of us here in the West live in material abundance but our souls are longing for something more. Developing a relationship with Nature and Spirit is one way to bring that meaning and purpose into our lives, and the medicine gifts can offer healing and support along the way.

As I embark upon this journey, then, to invite you into the world of my spiritual experiences, my patients, and my growing understanding of the vast array of medicine gifts that are available for our healing, I humbly share how I came to be here, how I was introduced to these medicines, and how I prepared myself to carry them forward.

Chapter Two

Healing and Spirit

I began my career in the healing arts in 1988 when I was 30 years old. But even before my Master Herbalist diploma was hanging on the wall, people had begun asking for my help. My unwavering enthusiasm for all things natural—foods, health, and medicines—had already been evident to everyone who knew me, for at least eight years. I started out with a part-time practice in a small rental home, and while there were some definite stops and starts in those early days as life offered its varied adventures and challenges, my passion never waned. As I worked to help people recover from illness, I continued my studies, developing skills in relating diet to health, becoming certified in aromatherapy, and eventually teaching others.

When I had been in practice for about a decade, I was able to draw upon the wisdom of experience to review the efficacy of my methods and medicines. One of my concerns was that some patients, despite my best efforts, were unable to get well. While their conditions had improved, they could not gain independence from the herbs and other remedies. If they stopped taking them, their symptoms reappeared. I took this quite seriously, repeatedly asking myself, "What am I missing?"

In time I discovered that what I was missing was actually something I couldn't address. Some people were wounded on the inside. While their 'dis-ease' symptoms were physical, the root cause came from deep within and my physical remedies could not help them to heal.

It was around that time I read Eliot Cowan's book, *Plant Spirit Medicine*. True to my herbalist nature it was the part about plants and the part about medicine that appealed to me; I actually ignored the word 'spirit'. Looking back, I can see how I read the entire book through coloured glasses, tinted with the hue of my beliefs and assumptions that led me only in the directions I was willing to be taken. His was a book about a different kind of healing, using a medicine that was drawn from the spirit of plants, not their physical bodies. I didn't notice. Within weeks of finishing the book I took one of the boldest moves of my life and signed up for his two-year training program in rural Massachusetts. This was a medicine that healed people by addressing the invisible wounds created by their life experiences. This was what I needed to help my patients. This was the missing piece. It was exciting beyond words.

The first week of training shook me to the core. The program was about spiritual healing, but not in the way I had been exposed to, not in the way of prayer and faith. This program was about using medicines that had their source in the realm of Spirit. I didn't believe in Spirit! Fortunately there was a fascinating technical component which satisfied my inner scientist. The theoretical framework was based on Classical Chinese Five Element Medicine. Eliot had been trained as an acupuncturist in that healing tradition and had developed an innovative method of treatment that used plants, actually the spirits of plants, instead of the more commonly used needles. The restoration of health was accomplished via accessing the meridian system of the body and optimizing the quality and quantity of the flow of life force energy it carried. Now that was something I could sink my teeth into!

During the training however, the word 'spirit' kept coming up over and over and I found myself in a very awkward position. Eliot talked about 'spirit' as if it were tangible and real. While I had some relative comfort using the word 'spiritual,' and had entertained the possibility that there may be a creative, intelligent force that underlay the foundation of the physical world—a force that some may refer to as God—the idea of spirits, spirit teachers and guides, animal spirits and plant spirits . . . well, that was just plain nonsense. If there were such a thing as Spirit, it was an over-riding, elusive, and intangible force—certainly not one that would respond to our whims!

The idea that there may be a form of healing that could reach into *our* spirit—our hidden inner world—seemed reasonable, but not that the source of such healing would be the spirit *of* something, like a plant. That was an entirely different premise. If I was going to embrace a philosophy of Spirit it had to make sense. Eliot was stating outright that we would be talking to plant spirits and they would be talking back! I actually didn't know what to do with that. On the fourth night of the training I called my husband Chris and told him of the precarious position I now found myself in. Not only was Eliot talking about spirits, when I looked around the room everyone else seemed to be taking it in stride, behaving like this was a normal topic of conversation. While Chris was supportive, there was nothing he could do or say to help. I had two more days to go before this first class was over and I was in the middle of nowhere. I hadn't rented a car and there were no taxis or shuttle service nearby. I was stuck. I had stepped out on a limb and committed to two years of training—in another country! A distinct unease started to well up inside me. I thought about the resources it had taken to get me there. I was spending more money on this one project than anything else I had ever done during my marriage. I thought about how right it had seemed in the beginning. And then I remembered why I was there. I couldn't give up what I knew I needed. I calmed myself down and reasoned that if I could believe it *just enough*, I could learn the medicine and return home to help others. I was willing to give it a try.

It was literally only a few weeks later, on a hot summer day, while hiking in the mountains with a friend, that I discovered first-hand there was indeed a world of Spirit and that there was more to reality than what I could see, hear, taste, touch and smell. The call to accept that realm came forward in a way that was so much bigger than me, so much stronger, it was no longer possible to deny it. It was time to accept and begin the journey to learn what it all meant.

Chapter Three

The Mountain

I can think of no better way to introduce you to the special mountain in my life than the one I offered in my first book, *Heeding the Call*. It is the diary of events that changed my life forever.

Excerpts from *Heeding the Call*, Chapters 1 and 2:

It was a beautiful spring day. The kind of day when I remembered why Alberta is known as 'blue sky country'. In the midst of the Rocky Mountains, the peaks themselves were the only interruption to that vast expanse of blue, dotted with occasional white clouds. Hiking with a friend, meandering our way around one curve, then another, we slowly zigzagged our ascent of the mountain trail. It seemed like any other day, except that I was especially grateful to be outdoors, to be in the mountains, and under the warm shining sun.

I was quiet, lost in my own thoughts. My friend Donna is one of those people who are comfortable with silence. I felt no need to fill the empty spaces with idle chatter. Watching my feet, taking care with each step to avoid any loose shale or protruding tree roots, I became acutely aware of the many hundreds of small stones and pebbles that dotted the trail. Marvelling at their subtle yet undeniable beauty and individuality, I contemplated picking some up or stopping to get a closer look, yet our pace was solid and I didn't want to disrupt it. We continued on. I looked up at the trail ahead, looked down at the carpet of stones, over and over. At one point, something in my awareness must have shifted. I don't know how. But the next time I looked down, I heard words echoing in my head like whispers, "I have a story to tell. I have a story to tell." At first, it was difficult to know if those were my thoughts, as they seemed to be coming from both the inside and outside of me at the same time. But when I looked again at the stones, I could almost detect them waiting... waiting to know my response. A small flutter rippled through my stomach as I realized something out of the ordinary was happening. Curious to determine if the state I found myself in was real or imagined, I tried experimenting by closing my eyes briefly then opening them again. I watched carefully to see if the stones reverted back to normal. They didn't. I noticed that my senses were heightened, everything around me appeared brighter than usual. The trees seemed to be reaching their branches toward me as they swayed in the breeze, the green of their leaves more vibrant than ever. It was as if the rhythm of my step had been altered, tuned to fit with another, more primal rhythm.

At the time, at the height of the experience, it seemed impossible not to accept it as real. It was real. But gradually it started to fade, and a few minutes later when I began to reflect on what had just happened, I wasn't so sure. I knew I had experienced something. I could still feel the remnants of it, a gentle alertness that carried with it a profound sense of peace and calm. But talking stones? Perhaps I got carried away. To be certain, I decided to share it with Donna. She listened, grunted something unintelligible under her breath, and continued on. After hearing how it sounded when I said it out loud, I decided not to pursue it any further.

About an hour later, a little wearier and thirstier for our trek, we were approaching the end of the trail. Not having been there before it was hard to know exactly where that would be, but I could see that the treeline was very close. Soon we would be able to see over the top and capture the entire vista of the landscape. A few more turns, a steep straight path, and in a step there it was. We had arrived at a clearing where we could see for miles, to the tops of the other mountains, the lake below, the highway winding into the forest like a footpath, and directly in front of us, a massive expanse of rock that was this mountain's peak. It was close enough that with a few more steps we could reach out and touch it. Yet suddenly, I wasn't in any shape to do so.

In the same instant that I glanced upward from the trail that had held me captive, and set my gaze ahead at the mountain summit, I heard something both silent and thunderous, a low, resounding voice that seemed to speak directly to my bones, "I HAVE A STORY TO TELL." This was nothing compared to the gentle whisper of the stones that had tried to warn me on my ascent. As I felt these echoes reverberating through my body, I started to stagger, losing my footing. I reached out, groping for a tree to steady me. It was like reaching into infinity; I had lost my bearings in the world around me. The realization that I needed to sit down was a welcome burst of sanity. As I slowly eased my way to the ground I noticed my breathing had become rapid; my heart was pounding in my chest. My head felt light and waves of 'something' seemed to move right through me, adding to the surreal nature of the experience. I tried to concentrate on the solidness of the earth beneath me, and after a few minutes, the disorientation started to fade. But as my body settled and my mind cleared, the inevitable question rose to the surface, "What was I supposed to do now? What does a person do when a mountain speaks to them?"

╱ ╱ ╱ ╱ ╱ ╱ ╱

Over the year I had known Eliot [Cowan] I had come to trust him considerably. I also learned that he was not just a man who had developed a new healing methodology, he was also a shaman in the tradition of the Huichol people, indigenous to Central Mexico. This type of shamanism was never discussed in class. It was kept to late evenings by the fire. I had been to several of these fires, and heard some of the stories of Eliot's training, his teacher, and his shamanic work. Eliot certainly gave the impression that this was serious and not to be embarked upon lightly . . .

On the basis of that trust, I approached him in the spring of 2000 to ask if we might speak in private after class. He agreed. Feeling slightly nervous, I mustered the courage to tell the strange and engrossing tale of the mountain, and its effect on me. He listened attentively, never interrupting, nodding occasionally. When I was finished, he took off his glasses, looked at me intently, then closed his eyes. He stayed like that for some time. When he opened them, he started talking. Luckily, I had planned ahead and brought a pen and paper along. I scrambled to write as quickly as he spoke.

"You must go to this mountain, alone. Spend three days and three nights there. At night, do a fire vigil by lighting a fire and staying up with it all night. You may doze, but never let the fire go out, until morning after daybreak. You must fast for the first 24 hours, taking no food or water, after that you may eat sparingly, just to keep up your strength. Spend each day with the mountain, all day, at the place where it spoke to you. At night, be with the fire. You must be absolutely alone; no one else can be present. At the end of the third day, you may ask, politely, that the mountain share the story with you. I suspect you won't get the story all at once. It will take time for it all to unfold."

///////

It was now the third and final day and having survived the

three nights unscathed offered some sense of relief and accomplishment. I started to relax a little. I had the whole day in front of me, but before nightfall I would head down the mountain, pack up my camping gear and be home safe in my own bed by midnight. That realization shifted something. As I sat in my usual spot, leaning against the tree, staring at the mountain and wondering if and when anything was going to happen, it struck me, the role I needed to play. If I could just get beyond the physicality of my struggle, if I could reach out to the mountain instead of passively waiting, I might receive something in return. All of a sudden it seemed so simple. I had to be willing and able to receive what I was searching for. It wasn't going to tap me on the shoulder to announce its impending arrival.

That was the first insight. The next step was how to accomplish it. There were only two experiences I could recall that might be relevant, starting with the hike when the mountain first spoke to me. I thought about how I felt at the time, happy, relaxed, open. The other was a part of the training I was taking with Eliot. He had been teaching us the age-old method of tuning in to the plant world, of sitting with the plants as medicine-people, literally sitting with them until we started to experience the world as they did, started to get a sense of what each plant was about, culminating in understanding how to use that plant as food or medicine. While this had not come easily, I had been practicing, and now had enough experience sharing the results with my classmates to know that I was on the right track. This was a skill I could draw upon that might be appropriate here.

So I changed my way of being. I settled into that spot and started to focus on the rock face of the mountain. I drew it in my notebook, every crack and crevice. I screened out everything else; the mountain alone was the object of my attention. I was prepared to wait for hours if need be, to receive my first sign of connection. But once I had it figured out, it didn't take long.

Staring at the mountain peak, I started by clearing my mind, concentrating on listening, to being still inside, and as receptive as I could possibly be. I tried to re-create the feeling of calm that had swept over me one year ago when the mountain first whispered its call. A few minutes later, words started to form in my head, words with a quality that helped me to know they were not mine. I started to write them down. The next thing I knew I was back in my usual conscious awareness, and had several pages of haphazardly scribbled notes, barely legible, in front of me. Not knowing how much time had elapsed I struggled to continue writing while maintaining the connection with the mountain that I had finally found, but it gradually faded and was gone. I turned back to the notes I had written, to review them. It was then I realized that the mountain had just introduced itself.

It is hard to describe the feeling that was welling up inside me as the meaning of the words sunk in. What I do know is that I wanted time to stand still once more, so that whatever the feeling was, it could last forever. If my mind had been active, it would have been desperately trying to make sense of it all, but it was calm, content to just be part of all that had happened. Looking down at the notes once more, I was amazed at how much information I had received, and the detail, yet it was the content that was so captivating. A mountain had just introduced itself to me! It was undeniable. Even if I suspected that I had made it all up, I would never have been able to imagine the scope of what this mountain had just revealed about its true nature. One thing I knew for certain, I would never look at mountains the same way again...

Finally back home I was still in a somewhat altered state. I knew I had established some kind of bond with the mountain and I didn't want to let that feeling go. I wanted, in fact, to go deeper, to explore this new relationship more fully. It was then I realized I had another new-found skill from my classes with

Eliot to call upon—the shamanic journey.[3] A journey would allow me to be with the mountain in yet another way, one that was outside the ordinary realms and didn't require me to be physically close. Still a novice, I knew that I needed to get started as soon as possible, while the connection I felt was still tangible and before my everyday life was back in full swing. So I closed my eyes, entered into a journey state asking the mountain to be with me, and the wonder of all that had unfolded that day continued.

As the journey ended and my full awareness gently returned, I lay as still as possible, lingering in a sensation of subtle vibrations coursing through my body. The clarity and strength of the knowing received in this journey far surpassed anything I had experienced before. I was taken beyond my usual awareness and my inner senses were acutely clear. The mountain had reached out and taken me inside itself. Once there, it offered me a gift, a healing gift. I had known for some time that there was more I wanted to offer the clients in my practice, and here was something beyond anything I could have imagined. Thinking it through, replaying the journey in my mind, I was overcome with humility and hoped with all my heart that I was worthy of such a gift. As I started to think about the practicalities of how I might introduce this into my work, I realized how very late it was and that I was exhausted. It had been an incredible three days and it would take many more for me to digest all that had happened, but I needed sleep. I snuggled further under the blankets, immensely grateful for their warmth and relishing their softness. I tried to stop my mind from going over everything again and again so I could drift off to sleep. In the last moments of wakefulness I found myself wondering, "Was this the story the mountain wants to tell?"

⸌ ⸌ ⸌ ⸌ ⸌ ⸌ ⸌

---

[3] My first book, *Heeding the Call*, contains a detailed description of the shamanic journey process, including a complete program of instruction and audio tracks.

I began the spiritual journey of my life that day, though I couldn't have said it so clearly and succinctly at the time. The words the mountain spoke were received by my soul with no context to place them in. The only thing I knew was that this experience was so far out of the ordinary it demanded my attention. The ensuing four to five years became a quest for understanding what it means when a mountain speaks to you, and an acknowledgement that Nature is not only alive, it is conscious. It was a time of coming to know that there is more to this world than what we can physically perceive and once we break through the barriers of fear, resistance, and skepticism, we find another layer to our existence that is equally real, and infinitely beautiful.

The call of the mountain touched me in a way I never thought possible. Slowly, and quite tentatively on my part, we developed a relationship. The mountain offered to be my Teacher of the ancient ways and I accepted. It taught me how to learn from the land, how to access the stories of time and place, how to feel colour, light, and energy; and it helped me to heal and grow into the person I needed and wanted to be.

Chapter Four

The Medicines

There is an entire world of healing agents that you may not have known existed. These medicines are not accepted within our current medical systems, either allopathic or naturopathic, yet they are real. I know this because they are the medicines I use in my healing practice every day and they help my patients to get well. In fact, these medicines are so far outside our present day awareness of what healing agents are, that in order to understand them, we must learn about the ancient ways of our indigenous ancestors.[4]

The medicines I want to share with you heal us from the inside out, unlike most of the medicines you may be familiar with, whether pharmaceutical or herbal, that heal from the outside in. These medicines not only change the course of your illness but the course of your life. These medicines will reveal the wounds that have not yet healed, even the ones you have forgotten. These are the medicines of Spirit and they reach directly into your spirit and initiate changes there. These changes can be dramatic, though often they are subtle,

---

[4] I use the term 'indigenous' here to refer to our biological ancestors who by necessity, lived in close relationship to the Earth. No matter what our current culture or racial background, we can trace our heritage back to a time in human history when the land was the source of our livelihood, informing our ways of living and being.

sometimes even indiscernible. But over time they build, layer upon layer, until you begin to feel well, whole, functional, happy, and abundantly alive.

Each of us has experience with some of the common and gentle forms of these medicines, the ones we all have the ability to give and receive: the hugs, the smiles, the thoughtful surprises or the tender caress. There are many things we do each day to help others feel loved, appreciated, and supported. These deeds, in turn, contribute significantly to their sense of health and well-being. When we feel safe and accepted for who we are, creative expression and joy spring forth naturally. We don't often consider acts of love and kindness as medicine, yet there is no doubt they make us feel better! In this sense, a medicine is an agent that helps us heal and grow in our bodies, in our minds, and in our spirits. A medicine helps us recover from the woundings that have afflicted our lives and brings us to a greater understanding of who we are and how we are to serve.

For a medicine to be effective it must be chosen wisely. For a medicine to be safe it must meet the need with precision. If you scrape your knee, it is a simple matter to clean the area and dress it. If you have a bad cold you can rest in bed for a few days. You don't need to know anything about antibodies, white blood cells, cellular repair, or waste elimination. Your body knows what to do. For deeper cuts you may need to apply a salve to the wound, a healing balm that offers support beyond what the body can handle on its own. Sometimes our wounding goes deeper than what can easily be reached, affecting our ability to function. Sometimes, through our pain and suffering, we have closed ourselves off, and these gentle medicines cannot break through the barriers. Sometimes our hearts have been broken. In these cases a stronger medicine is required. To use the stronger medicines safely and effectively you need expert guidance and care.

Our indigenous ancestors were specialists in this type of medicine. They lived during a time when the raw materials of the earth provided all the necessities of life. There were no other resources to draw from. To live well, and to ensure health and survival, the earth had to be *known*. This process of 'coming to know' takes time and dedication, just as the people we know best are the ones we live with, the ones we invest our emotional and physical lives with.

Investing in someone or something can bring great rewards. Have you ever met a gardener who excelled in growing beautiful plants and who seemed to know what the plants needed to thrive? Have you ever met a dog owner who seemed to possess an uncanny bond with his animal,[5] so much so that their relationship and understanding of each other seemed to flow? We no longer think it strange that people talk to their plants, their gardens, or their pets. We don't even think it strange when people talk to their cars! "Come on Betsy, you can make it, we're almost home." But those people, the ones we say "have a way with plants" or "have a way with animals," those people don't just talk—they *listen*. They develop a connection, a spiritual connection, and through that intimate and invisible bond they form a relationship. Through that relationship an extraordinary form of communication becomes possible.

The spirituality of our earliest ancestors was born of the land. They studied the sky to learn about the weather, they studied the plants to learn about food and medicine. They studied the animals and the birds to learn about nature's changing patterns and the influence of the seasons on their environment. These notions are not difficult for us to accept. What we have lost track of however, is how these were accomplished. In our modern society we have become dependent upon outside sources: books, television, teachers, and the internet. Even the word 'study' now implies the strict use of our external senses. Indigenous societies placed equal value on the knowledge derived from internal and external perceptions, and furthermore, focused these perceptions to learn directly from the source.

If you want to get to know people, you can spend time with them, study them, observe them in their environment, but to know who they really are you will need a way to access what is on the inside. We do this through communication. Communication allows the invisible, and otherwise inaccessible, to be known. When working with Nature the process is the same but the method of communication is different. The earth's indigenous peoples embraced a natural theology, accepting that the divine is part of, and expressed through, the natural world. When you want to develop

---

[5] I will vary the use of gender terms throughout the book.

a relationship with Nature and Spirit—a relationship with the Great Mystery—you begin by doing two things: reaching out and reaching in.

Effective communication requires a congruency of connection. There must be a common ground for understanding, and ultimately knowledge, to flow. A person who specializes in spirit medicines has first learned to access her own spirit. When she knows her spirit well, it becomes possible to reach out and access Spirit in any of its forms. In the natural theology I'm introducing here, the entire natural world—the plants, the animals, the lakes, and the mountains—contain a spark of the divine. They all have Spirit and they can all become known.

Sadly, most of our species no longer know how to accomplish this. How do you listen to what doesn't speak? When you want to offer your patients a medicine that reaches beneath their symptoms, how do you come to know what it is they need? You come to know through spiritual connection—a connection that is deeper than what is available through sensory awareness of the external world, no matter how complex and finely tuned that awareness might be.

It was the land itself, and the features of the land, that held the medicines the indigenous peoples needed to be well. And it was through spiritual connection to these aspects of the land that the people learned how to use those medicines. The medicine people were chosen for their innate ability and passion. Their teachings were received through direct connection with the aspect of the land that they focused their attention on, a connection so pure that an alliance was formed, an agreement, between the agent that held the medicines and the person entrusted to their use.

Once an alliance is formed, it has the ability to grow and develop. As the medicine person works with the plants, for example, their relationship deepens. What is known about the medicines, and the people who can benefit from them, becomes greater. Sometimes, in an act of acknowledgement or need, such a practitioner is given medicines as a spiritual gift. At other times they are awarded through years of apprenticeship and dedication. These deeper and more powerful medicines require great skill in their application and a thorough knowledge of their effects. When their use becomes an art, it is possible that these medicines are able to restore patterns of function that have been distorted through illness. They are able to heal the deep emotional wounds that have left us vulnerable and afraid. They can restore a feeling of peace and calm when anxiety has become a way of life. They can uncover the causes, the root of the problem, and create the conditions that allow them to be shifted, to be changed. These medicines can weave their way inside you and find all the ways that you have been broken. Then the healing process can begin. The medicines know what to do. They can help you return to a full and meaningful life.

These are the medicines I speak about here. I believe them to be one of the most beautiful forms of healing possible. Their essence is spiritual but their effects are tangible and measurable, not only to the patients, but to everyone those patients share their lives with. They do not require any particular belief system, knowledge, or even understanding to be received, but they do require an openness and willingness on the part of the patient, accompanied by a sincere sense of gratitude.

These are the medicines of our indigenous ancestors. While there is a physical component, a plant for instance, the medicine itself is not. While the physical plant has properties that support its use as a healing agent, this potency is enhanced when combined with the knowledge of what the plant is. The healing agent received by the patient and delivered by the medicine person is invisible and untouchable. I'm not speaking about prayer or prayer-ful requests. What I am stating is that aspects of the natural world—plants, animals, and even mountains—have a potency of spirit, a connection to the divine that can be expressed and brought forward in a way that is not only predictable, measurable, and reproducible, it can also help us to heal. In this feature of their resulting effect, they are indeed medicine.

Chapter Five

The Medicine Person

In the truest sense of the term, a medicine man or woman is a person who works with the healing gifts they have been given from the world of Spirit. In our Western culture these people are sometimes called shamans, but an important distinction needs to be made.[6] Some modern day shamanism is taught in much the same way as other academic pursuits, from teacher to student via the mind, using information as the source. This approach tends to isolate healing methods from the land and the culture in which they were born and bypasses the deep relationship that is at the heart of the alliance. The healing work accomplished through this type of shamanism does not necessarily require the use of 'medicines' in the traditional, indigenous sense.

In my own journey I found this type of shamanic study very valuable. It helped me to understand ways of using internal rather than external senses and the focus on methods provided a foundation for the practical aspects of the work. Initially I drew heavily upon this style of teaching in my quest

---

[6] The term "shaman" refers to a traditional medicine person in Siberian/Mongol culture, yet the word has been artificially universalised to describe a similar role in all cultures.

to gain a context for what the Mountain was leading me to, and asking of me. Once I started working with the medicine gifts directly however, trusting the Mountain as my teacher and witnessing the effects of its healing gifts, I realized that for me, the shamanic teachings I had been exposed to were missing a critical component: a relationship with the land. I began to understand why Fishwoman and other native people I had spoken to were offended by the term shamanism. It is not their word. It is a word from another land and culture that has been applied to them by non-native people in the West. In the traditions I have been exposed to, some form of 'medicine person' is the descriptive phrase used. In addition, these people do not use the term as a title, nor do I, for the medicines do not belong to us. As Fishwoman says, "They are borrowed from Creator."

Those who carry spirit medicines in their medicine bundle also carry them in their soul. The physical tools—feathers, dried plants, stones—are only the material part, they are not the medicine itself. The medicine person, through their presence and the relationships they hold, infuses the physical tool with its spiritual essence when it is called into use, and thus a bridge is formed between the world of Spirit and the world of matter. The healing potential inherent in the spirit medicines can cross that bridge and affect change within a physical being, influencing its emotional, mental, and spiritual expressions, as well as how it experiences itself in the world.

To work with spirit medicines and be able to guide patients through their unique process of healing and growth requires skills that cannot be learned through the physical world and human teachers. Spirit medicine is a gift that is given from the world of Spirit. Therefore, Spirit is necessarily the Teacher.

Along the way, the medicine people who work with these healing agents need to live a style of life that is consistent with the honouring and respectful approach being taught. Many of us have received a good education but are still lacking in the wisdom of how to cultivate a beautiful and meaningful life. The spirit teachers recognize this and help along the way through their nudging, their teachings, and the experiences they lead us through. As we deepen our alliance and our commitment, these internal relations begin to affect us. Over time, they have the ability to change us. The intricacies of our relationship to each other, to the natural world, and to the divine, make up who we are. It is through these relationships that our identity develops. It is this style of living and the results that flow from it that this book will describe.

In our day and age walking a medicine path is an unusual approach to life, work, relationships, and God. I understand that. For many years it was not my path. I was raised, educated, and employed in the same Western style as most people in North America and Europe. I am not native, nor do I have any First Nations ancestry. But when the Mountain reached out and asked me to offer its medicines, I came to learn that accepting such a gift required a shift in how I thought, felt, and lived. I was willing to do whatever it took. I wanted to help people to heal.

Chapter Six

A Patient Story–A Young Boy With a Sad Heart

To work with spirit medicines in a professional capacity is a humbling experience. When I am first approached by potential patients and they describe their struggles, they are often looking for reassurance that I can indeed be of service. This is understandable. Yet from my perspective, all I can offer is my willingness to try. I can bring forward the medicines that have been entrusted to me. I can help create a healing environment in their bodies and their spirit. I can be on the lookout for factors that could compromise their goals. But I cannot know what the outcome of our time together will be. Every person, every illness, and every offering of the medicines is unique. The healing is in the hands of the Great Mystery.

The case of a young boy named Todd highlights the features of this approach. Todd's condition was serious and complex. In working with him I did what I always try to do: utilize every bit of knowledge and skill that could possibly support my efforts to help. I drew upon more than twenty years of experience working with people in my healing practice, and I called upon the medicines that had made themselves known and that I had developed an alliance with, sometimes plant, sometimes animal, and most important, the Mountain.

I share Todd's healing journey as an example of the work the Mountain led me to and an introduction to the ways in which Nature and Spirit medicines can heal.

In January 2009 I received this letter via email:

> Hello Jaki. Please let me introduce myself. My name is Molly. I have read your book and feel I have been guided by you as I embark upon my own journeys. I am drawn to you and your mountain—not for me but for my son. Todd is seven years old and suffering from vestibular seizures and daily dizziness that is triggered by movement. He is also suffering spiritually. We are not religious but through my reiki teacher and my own memories of how I felt and thought as a child, I have woken up spiritually. My son's energy and spirit is very blocked and he wonders if it would be better not to be here. He is seeing a psychologist and she is a very good doctor but she isn't touching on the essence of who he is and how his illness is affecting him. I believe that you and your mountain can. Deep down in my son is a darkness where there was once only light. He is trying so hard to find that light and I hope that you can guide him. My son is in the hands of the Children's Hospital's finest neurologist and he is very puzzled. I wonder if you would be willing to talk to me?

It was a few days before I had a chance to call Molly and receive some additional background on Todd's condition:

> My son has been throwing up since he was three months old. He has vomiting spells every few months where he vomits daily and nothing can control it. These can last for weeks. This has had an effect on him mentally. Also his balance is off. He can't walk down the street. He doesn't fall over but it makes him dizzy. He is on two different medications for seizures, which muddle his brain and make him tired. He is just utterly sad. He

has talked about suicide since the age of five. He is not being dramatic. He just doesn't like being here.

It would be a few weeks before I could begin a course of treatment with Todd. In the meantime I felt there were some physical supportive measures worth investigating. I recommended that he be assessed and treated by a NUCCA chiropractor[7] and that he undergo allergy testing.

On February 24th Molly emailed to say that the chiropractor had diagnosed Todd as being significantly out of alignment on his right side and that within several treatments, it had already improved more than 60%. Allergy tests revealed reactions to weeds, grasses, horses and cats, several different wheats, and milk protein. The finding about the cats was particularly difficult for the family. As Molly said, "We have three cats and have had them for Todd's whole life. Because of his fragile emotions he has a deep love and connection to them."

My first session with Todd was on March 2nd. I began by asking the Mountain if it would help me to connect with him and reveal his internal story. I sat beside him and touched him gently on the shoulder. Immediately I felt pressure inside his head, a surplus of saliva in his mouth, and nausea. I could feel his desire to stay quiet and not talk, as well as his discomfort at loud noises. His brain felt like it was swaying back and forth repeatedly, always on the verge of dizziness. Going deeper I could sense that below the discomfort was a clear mind with the ability to be articulate. But these capabilities were not part of Todd's day-to-day experience. I could sense his intelligence yet could also feel how much work it was for him to try to communicate through the muddle of his symptoms. In his spirit he was consumed with sadness. He had been fighting but was tired and depleted. Part of him desperately wanted to let go, to disconnect from life, but at the

---

[7] The National Upper Cervical Chiropractic Association provides this definition, "The focus of the NUCCA work is the relationship between the upper cervical spine (neck) and its influence on the central nervous system and brain stem function. It is this relationship that affects every aspect of human function from the feeling sensations in your fingers to regulating hormones, controlling movement, and providing the ability to hear, see, think, and breathe." www.nucca.org

same time there were bright spots in his world and they gave him a reason to keep going. This created an internal struggle which further contributed to his distress. In his experience of life, his body was not dependable. If he couldn't trust his own body, who and what could he trust?

Todd's healing journey with myself and the Mountain lasted approximately two years. The simple beginnings of restoring alignment to his body and removing the allergens from his home and diet created a significant difference. Along the way I offered him regular and frequent treatments with Chinese Five Element Healing, using carefully chosen spirit medicines. Initially the quality of the life force energy coursing through his meridians was erratic and unpredictable. There were many blockages to clear and the quantity of flow needed to be improved and balanced. This process worked to gradually restore as much physical, emotional, and spiritual functionality as those medicines could provide. There was a slow but definite pattern of improvement. It was exciting to be part of his return to wellness. The following are some of the significant landmarks along the way:

On March 29th Molly emailed, "He is coping better and going outside more. This makes three times in the past two weeks. Before this he hadn't been outside since November except to walk from the car to school—about 20 steps!"

By April 14th his dizziness had been reduced to lightheadedness, he was continuing to venture outside, and was coping better in normal day-to-day situations. His parents started working with his doctors to reduce his medication.

By May 6th he was able to go outside during school recess and start participating in physical education classes.

On June 22nd Molly reported that he had been taken off one medication completely with no adverse effects. He also started riding a bicycle!

On Sept 2nd, exactly six months since his first treatment, Todd returned to school after summer holidays and enrolled in some of the sports programs. At this session he declared that he was better and did not need to come for further treatments.

I understood. Todd's healing to date had been nothing short of remarkable. He now felt like a participant in his life, and his body now responded to his will. But, in truth, Todd had not yet achieved what I knew he was capable of. We had not yet restored the clear and articulate mental state that was shown to me in our first session. Yet I wanted to support his new-found confidence and independence. We agreed to take a break from regular treatments while he maintained the dietary changes and chiropractic. After a few months and the return of some of his symptoms, we began again, this time taking the work deeper until we were able to completely restore the functions of his brain and nervous system.[8] I will be honest and tell you it was not a smooth journey. The body and mind can be resistant to such a significant change after nine years of illness. But we persisted. The healing gifts that came forward for Todd were so gentle and respectful, yet created profound changes. He returned to wellness and embraced life as a healthy, happy, and completely functional young man. At the time of this writing he is in Grade 7, six foot tall, plays sports, is in the school band, enjoys people, makes his own decisions, and is a delight to be with.

---

[8] The bizarre details of the second phase of Todd's healing are revealed in Part II.

Chapter Seven

Where I Am Now

Looking back at the unfolding of this chapter in my life, it now seems divinely inspired. Helping my patients to heal—I can't think of anything else that could have compelled me to step outside my understanding of how the world worked, how I worked, and adopt such a radical change as to embrace the world of Spirit. It had to be something so alluring that I was willing to entertain the most bizarre ideas, just in case they turned out to be true. That first stage of my journey with the Mountain was not easy. Accepting the reality of Spirit and accepting it fully took several years. Only then was I ready to move forward.

Once I had released my previous limited framework and started using the medicines that had been entrusted to me, I began to realize how much my particular combination of skills had to offer. The first years of my career were dedicated to developing a naturopathic healing practice. I was trained in taking a medical history, assessing symptoms, identifying barriers or impediments to the healing process, and balancing what the plants could offer as remedy with what the patients were able to manage. With plant spirit medicine and Chinese Five Element Healing I had the tools to address one layer of the illness's root cause—its effect on our underlying life force and its systematic and intelligent flow throughout our bodies. With the Mountain I had a way to address yet another layer—revealing the original wounding and finding the story that was held deep inside. What's more, the Mountain could offer the medicine that was needed to heal. Combining them worked beautifully and synergistically. The new whole became greater than the sum of the parts. A truly holistic approach to wellness was now in my hands.

When the Mountain first spoke to me, it said, "I have a story to tell," and I believe that my stories have become part of the telling. The story in *Heeding the Call* was of my quest to find answers, to gain an understanding, to come to terms with the fact that there was indeed something we call Spirit. It was a journey that many of us go through. I am still the same person who hiked the trail that fateful day but I have entered into relationship with Nature and Spirit and in turn been blessed with a remarkable life; one in which miracles happen.

It has now been fourteen years since that day on the Mountain. I still live in the same small house in the same big city, but my understanding of *how* to live has changed. I still have the same husband and family, but the community of 'all my relations' extends further than I ever imagined it could. The world of Nature and Spirit, by being alive and conscious, interacts with me. The plants teach me how to use them for food and for medicine. The animals teach me how to use my senses, how to step outside the human framework, which is biased and self-serving, and see what is happening from a broader perspective. When I step back in, I realize more strongly the impact of our species and the changes that need to be made.

Today I am a healing arts practitioner who offers the medicine gifts of Nature and Spirit in the manner that has been asked of me. I am a teacher in the ways of healing and medicine. I am considered a Spiritual Elder by the small community I serve, and I am a writer.

Being in service, developing skills, nurturing relationships, and acquiring wisdom does not happen in a linear fashion. The three themes I am about to share with you are the foundation of my life's journey. They happen in one way or another every single day. I invite you to experience the medicine path in the same way. I only ask that when you pick up this book and read of the winding road that has led me forward, you acknowledge the risk I have taken. Everyone deserves to know what is held inside these pages, and each of you has the right to accept or reject these teachings. In order to offer you that choice, I have to take my soul's knowing and place it in your hands. My hope is that you will receive it in the spirit in which it is offered. I also realize I have no control over that. I'm willing to take the chance, just in case.

In case this is a story you need to hear.

PART II:

WALKING THE MEDICINE PATH

The three themes of Part II are denoted by:

 Personal stories of adventures, challenges, and growth.

 Teachings I received from totem animals or the Mountain.

Stories of patients who entrusted me with their care, features of my own personal healing, and the effects of the medicine gifts that have come forward.

Chapter Eight

The Trail Head

I had to begin by placing one foot in front of the other and seeing where they led me . . .

The journey to walk a medicine path began with my willingness to heed the call of the Mountain and bring into use the medicine gifts it had offered. It took several years after the Mountain first spoke to me before I was ready to trust that relationship enough to change the style of my healing practice and find the courage to share with my patients the stories that came forward. In the meantime I had travelled far and wide to find the answers I was looking for and to know that I could trust my ability to accurately receive what the Mountain was offering. Five years after the Mountain first issued its call, my desperate search for context and understanding had finally drawn to a close. I was ready to move forward. As it happened, the days that marked both that completion and the new beginning, were in Peru.

It was the summer of 2004 and Chris and I had ventured to Peru with a group of students and other teachers who were interested in shamanism and the indigenous ways. I had been particularly drawn to the Incan tradition because of their reverence for mountains, and their acceptance of them as teachers of the highest order. The ancient Incas fully recognized that mountains were holders of wisdom and knowledge. In Peru there was even a special designation for the medicine people who worked directly with mountains. They were called *alto-mesayaks* and were a rarity in modern times.

Near the end of our trip, on a sunny afternoon at Machu Picchu, our host convened a talking circle of sorts. Sitting there, on top of the world, we gathered together to share our experiences. I was careful not to rehearse my response, instead listening to what each person had to say. When it came my turn to speak, I realized that my sharing would not be like the others, but it came from my heart, and it was true.

We've been on a remarkable adventure in the incredible landscape of Peru. We have experienced the land from both a physical and ceremonial perspective. We have been guided by the indigenous people who have a deep reverence and understanding for the gifts that are available here, particularly from the mountains, but I find that when asked, I'm not thinking about this place, I'm thinking about what I left behind. It took a considerable amount of resources for Chris and I to come here, and it will take us a while to recover. I don't regret coming. I had a sense from the beginning that it was important, that something would happen here. What I can tell you now, amidst these amazing mountain teachers, medicine people, and villagers, is that what I need to focus on, the most important direction I can take in my life, is to bring forward the gifts I have received from the Mountain back home and to be in service with them. Never have I dedicated three weeks of my time to the Mountain in Alberta in the way that I have here. Never have I committed so much of our finances to focus on my training. I don't need to travel the world. Everything I need is back where it all began: my life, my work, my future and my destiny. It is time to start acknowledging the relationship between the land that I live on and the work I have been asked to do. I don't need to go anywhere else. Nothing is more important than what is being offered in my own backyard.

Returning home, it was exciting to feel the readiness that had eluded me for so long. I didn't have all the answers, but enough had fallen into place that I knew where I stood, what was expected of me, and most important, how to proceed. Just being true to who I was and trusting the Mountain were the key pieces, yet in many ways it was still scary. It would change my life—again—but now my resolve was coming from a much deeper place. I had become the person I needed to be to bring the Mountain's gifts to my people.

There is a saying, "When the student is ready, the teacher will appear." Having stepped solidly onto the path, I came across some writings that explained and validated what had happened to me. In some ways I wish I had found them sooner; it would have made my life easier. But perhaps if I had, I wouldn't have been ready to listen. It was from my new-found perspective of having a strong foundation and finally, a context to place my experiences in, that I understood what they meant.

In reading the introductory chapters of Stephen Harrod Buhner's book, *Sacred Plant Medicine: The Wisdom in Native American Herbalism*, I came across these passages. They were practically a formula for what had happened to me.

> Strong visionary experience is often accompanied by impera-
> tives for human conduct. Conveyed during contact with the
> sacred, these imperatives often require the person to whom they
> are given to act in a certain manner, engage in a specific life work,
> or make changes in lifestyle or behavior. (p.8)

／／／／／／

> Within Earth-centered cultures the stone and the tree are
> venerated as an expression of the sacred, a creation of God. Often-
> times, either through ritual or through direct manifestation of the
> sacred, the stone or tree begins to exhibit a totally other reality.
> It begins to manifest the sacred archetype of its kind. Far from
> being stone or tree or plant, it becomes STONE or TREE or
> PLANT, a pipeline to a deeper and more meaningful reality. And
> within Earth-centered religious practice, individuals spend many

years, sometimes a lifetime, in developing deep relationship with the aspect of the sacred that has revealed itself.

Within the lineage of Earth-centered spirituality, the individual will never choose which aspect of the sacred to focus on. In some manner, the sacred world indicates that the individual should focus on this or that aspect. (pp. 9-10)

⁄ ⁄ ⁄ ⁄ ⁄ ⁄ ⁄

For someone who is touched with the underlying reality of BEAR, the focus of spiritual life and power and communion with Spirit comes through the deeper archetype of the bear. The sacred and the archetype of the bear speak and convey knowledge and power to the person who has such deep contact with BEAR. Over time one is able to use this personal connection and knowledge of BEAR to manifest the archetype of BEAR into normal, secular reality and thereby effect change. Such a person is one of spiritual power but this power is specific in its scope and use. The power may be useable only when certain illnesses are present or certain ceremonies are necessary or the community faces certain crises. In other times and needs, the power of a specific archetype is not accessible or effective. (p.10)

It now seemed so simple. I had been called by a mountain and the nature of my experience, while originally outside my understanding, was not so unusual to the First Nations or other indigenous peoples who lived in close relation to the earth. I had been touched, and was held by, the underlying reality of MOUNTAIN. I had been asked to use this connection and the gifts that were being offered through it to effect change.

I could see in a new light how Fishwoman was such an ideal teacher for me. In the past I had been concerned that she couldn't offer me specific guidance about the Mountain teachings. She didn't do the same kind of work. She didn't have the same relationship with MOUNTAIN. I couldn't ask her questions about how to deliver the medicine or how to see and feel the rivers of light that ran through us. Now I realized that wasn't her role.

That wasn't why she was chosen for me and I for her. She didn't need to teach me about the teachings, she didn't need to know the details of my visions and guide me as to how I should interpret them. That was my job.

Instead, she brought me something much more valuable. After all my people had done to oppress hers, she was willing to open her arms and adopt me into her spiritual family, the component of her own life she held most dear. And she has lived up to the role of Elder, Teacher, and Guide every step of the way. Learning about shamanism and exploring its methods gave me the tools to understand the work that lay ahead, but Pauline provided the native spiritual ways that gave me a home.

A Journey to the Mountain

For one of the first times ever I was entering into a journey knowing that I had done everything the Mountain Spirit Beings had asked me to do and everything I said I would do. I felt like I had crossed a threshold. So many times I said I was ready—only to discover that I actually wasn't. As a result, I hadn't practiced the teachings or followed through.

As I go down the tunnel to the Lower World I have a sense of rushing, anxious to get to the Mountain. At first I think I am just in a hurry, but then realize the method I have been using is no longer needed. All I have to do is be at the Mountain, to place myself there, and I will be there. I may still go to the Lower World for other journeys but now I simply need to close my eyes and be with the Mountain Spirit Beings. Another first.

I greet the three aspects of the Mountain:[9] Grandfather Mountain, Grandmother Mountain, and Wizard of the Mountain. No words are spoken but as I glance around the circle I get a sense of acknowledgement from each one. Afterward I notice a very pleasant sensation in my physical body. I tell the Mountain Spirit Beings I am ready to keep going. They respond:

---

[9] As I developed a relationship with this sacred mountain, this is how it chose to present itself to me: three different aspects, each with their own teachings, knowledge, and gifts.

"We must continue, Little One. Now the true teachings will begin. From our perspective we have been laying the foundation, the groundwork. Now we need to step beyond... beyond the ordinary, beyond time and space and linearity, to move into the flow of what is outside your concepts of time and relevance. We must move into the heart of the matter, cross the boundaries of the dimensions, and make the shift, the leap. You are ready.

"Open up. Open as far and wide as you can possibly imagine— extend your awareness outside of your physical body. You have to be large to do this work, to encompass others and 'be' with it all at the same time."

I sensed the end of the journey and the beginning of the next phase of my training. The Mountain Spirit Beings retreated back into the Mountain, and so I returned.

I tried to prepare myself for the death—the passing of the old way of being and the birth of the new—but in the days when that understanding reached its peak the transition was still challenging. A resistance, a fear, rose within me. I imagined myself as a snake that had to shed its skin. Would the new one be as comfortable, would it protect as well? It all came to a head on one particular night. I had been in a state of unease and mild anxiety all day, culminating in a waterfall of tears, with Chris's arms holding and comforting me. I wasn't crying for what lay ahead, but what I would have to leave behind. Up until this point in my life I had been able to make choices based on what I wanted, not always considering what was best for others. The level of personal accountability I was stepping into was far greater than I had dedicated myself to in the past. Surprisingly, it was the small and insignificant choices I was holding on to, such as being openly grumpy when I was having a bad day, behaving selfishly, or indulging in a second glass of wine. After all, I did take pride and effort in being a good person. But there were the tears, signifying that in some ways my old habits had been enjoyed. I felt like a spoiled brat being asked to grow up. I knew with every cell in my body that I was stepping into a life that required a discipline of awareness greater than anything I had previously done. There were no more excuses.

Beginning the next morning I started a daily practice, spending time in meditation and prayer. I explored ways of moving my body to facilitate the flow of energy, recognizing that blocks and stagnation would limit me in some way, and the nature of that kind of limitation is that I would not be conscious of it. I did yoga and qigong. I sat with the Mountain Spirit Beings. I performed the stillness practice they had taught me. I trained myself to become increasingly aware and sensitive to ever more subtle and elusive forces. This was the way I could show Nature and Spirit that I wasn't just saying I was ready, I was willing to do my part and do it well. Somehow I knew what was involved.

In the months that followed, I felt changes that signified and solidified the transition I was going through. I still didn't know what story the Mountain wanted to tell, but realized that my training with the Mountain and my acceptance of its gifts was already a story in itself. I surmised that writing a book and sharing my adventures with others was one of the ways I could honour the Mountain. Hopefully, through *Heeding the Call: A Personal Journey to the Sacred*, I wouldn't be the only one who never looked at mountains the same way again.

Once I knew the story would be told, weaving through the retracing of my steps and recounting the trials as well as the growth, one thing became clear. I would have to be absolutely true to the Mountain. There was no room for any kind of misrepresentation; no poetic license to be taken. The respect and awe I felt for the Mountain and the Mountain Spirit Beings dictated that my level of integrity in sharing our relationship would have to be the highest I could attain. I reminded myself how easily we are influenced by others, how seldom we stay true to our soul's knowing and experience. And I realized in that moment that I would never be able to read another book that taught about shamanism, First Nations spirituality, or the ways of indigenous people and our ancestors. To remain true to the Mountain as my Teacher, every component of the story, and possible future stories, would need to come from my personal experience, my own library of Mountain teachings. My time in Peru had taught me that I could receive what the Mountain offered without distortion. I needed to take that to the next level. This would mean another death.

Reading, particularly nonfiction, had always been enjoyable to me. I loved to learn through the written word. And in that I recognized the irony. I would be writing a story to share with my people while I cut myself off from theirs. Surprisingly, I did not mourn this passing. Over the next days and months I simply accepted what was asked of me. I was able to focus on what the future held rather than what the past had provided. I was embarking on the most amazing adventure I could imagine a person taking. I didn't know what lay ahead, but I knew I would never look back.

Chapter Nine

A Pipe Carrier

The beginning of my medicine bundle.

Fishwoman had been telling me for months that there was a gift coming. She couldn't just wait until the time was right, then surprise me. No, that wasn't her style. She wanted to tease me by reminding me over and over again that she had something special planned. She delighted in that. Originally she had hoped to offer me the gift at our mountain pilgrimage in the spring, but it was not yet ready. This provided more opportunity for me to wait. As the heat of summer faded and the autumn winds started to blow, she began to make arrangements for the ceremony.

She drove for twelve hours to get here, with two grandchildren and one great-grandchild in tow. The night of her arrival we feasted, both to the ancestors and ourselves. After a good night's sleep, she was ready.

There were none of the advance preparations or attention to detail that had been required for my Naming Ceremony two years before. In that case, invitations and responses were shared, food prepared, gifts given and received, and ceremonial instructions outlined for all present. Friends and family were an integral and important part. This ceremony was private—the passing along of a gift from Elder to student. Witnesses from both within the tradition (her family) and outside (my husband) completed the casual circle, held in the living room. Sitting on the floor, she slid a red cloth bundle toward me. Unwrapping it revealed two smaller bundles, one containing a black stone pipe bowl and the other, a wooden stem.

Fishwoman explained that while some pipe bowls were carved from red stone, tradition held that they could be either red or black. The red was more closely aligned with nations south of us, sourced from the red rock canyons and quarries. The black pipe stone represented the more northerly areas. Knowing my strong connection to the land, the mountains, and the local plants, she felt that black was more suitable for me. In a matter-of-fact manner she instructed me on loading the pipe, placing the prayers into it, how it should be held, passed, carried, and cared for. A few hours later she gathered the family into the car and they left.

She was here and then she was gone. I would have thought it a dream except that I was left with something very real. The trust she had extended to me and the responsibility it held were not diminished by the brief time frame. I understood what was involved.

Over the years I had participated in many pipe ceremonies with Fishwoman. She often began by sharing the story of how she came to receive her pipe, its use as a personal pipe, then later as a peoples' pipe. Many times she had shared the legend of how the pipe came to her people:

> The story I was told, of how this was given to our aboriginal people, was at one time, when the people of all nations were here on earth, the higher spirits came down to work with them. High in the mountains the four races met, the four colours; the yellow, red, black, and white. All were gathered together, wondering why they were sitting on a mountain. But they had an idea that they were going to hear from a spirit above, one that would tell them how to walk this world, the spiritual world. They were sitting together in a circle and out from the spiritual realm of the higher power of earth and sky came a voice, and also, down came an object, into the center of the four sacred beings, because we are sacred beings as well. And the spirit above them said, "I give you this object to reach me. I give to those of you that choose to take it. I will show you how to use it." And it was a pipe.

As the story goes, only the aboriginal person picked up the pipe and the spirit said, "When you lift this pipe, and when you speak, I will listen with all my might from the other side. And if need be, you will get many miracles of prayer answered through this way. Though the other three races have chosen not to take this sacred object, there will be a time, after many lives pass, after many years pass, that if the four races could come together and sit and pray with this pipe, then many changes of goodwill will come to happen on the earth."

This is why, as an aboriginal person who walks a spiritual road, I open the doorway to all nations to come and sit and learn from me. And if they would choose to lift the pipe with me, or have a pipe with me, I will help them get a pipe so they can work with Creator. But I don't give it to them readily, they have to spend time, it has to be earned. The gifting of a pipe is a process of knowing the person who is going to hold this sacred object, and that they are going to be honest to Creator. They must have a generous heart in regards to working with people and being with people, with no aspect of their lives being harmful to others. A person must earn the position of holding this pipe. There was a point in my life that I never thought I would be a Pipe Carrier because it is such a high acknowledgment of spiritual life. So a pipe is viewed by our aboriginal people as very powerful, it manifests itself so close to Creator. And so in our lives as we walk and we lift the pipe, there is nothing that we hide from the people we work with. The Creator knows us, so in order to hold this pipe we must be honest to ourselves, to the people, and to Creator above all.

So esteemed is the pipe as the sacred vehicle of prayer that only those of high integrity and fine moral character are entrusted to its use. There is no policing of this protocol. Each individual who holds the honour of receiving a pipe also holds the responsibility for assessing her own character, actions and thoughts, and her relationships with others, to continue being worthy of lifting it. If the carrier falls—through acts of abuse, alcohol or other addictions, or violation to the earth—and no longer deems herself appropriate, the pipe is to be returned to the care of the Elder who had gifted it, for safekeeping. When circumstances have changed, and the person is once again in good relationship with both self and others, the pipe can be returned.

I had never imagined that I would be a Pipe Carrier in a native tradition. Once again I was faced with the enormity of the changes that were happening to me. This wasn't at all the life I had predicted for myself just a few years earlier. I had struggled for so long to accept the implications of this strange calling and now I was comfortable learning how to nurture these spiritual relationships. My heart was full. Nothing could contribute so potently to that development than cultivating a prayer practice with a sacred pipe. I was truly honoured.

Before Fishwoman left that day, we had a few stolen moments in private. She advised me that for a year or two, this would be strictly a personal pipe, and due to my work and relationship with the Mountain, it was likely that with regular practice, the Mountain would eventually speak to me through the pipe. It was therefore very important that if I wanted to share it with others, they needed to be very close friends or family. My sense was that only people who were 'an extension of myself' would be appropriate.

The next day was a Sunday and I had time to linger with my thoughts, go over the teachings in my mind, and prepare for my first solo pipe ceremony. The following is an excerpt from my diary:

> Today I lifted the pipe, the Sacred Chanupa, for the first time. I had envisioned myself moving through the ritual with grace and ease, enraptured by each stage; a gentle, easy flow of smudge,[10] tobacco, smoke and prayer. The reality of the ceremony, it turned out, was quite different. I found myself clumsy. I hadn't laid out all the materials I needed to have on hand. Matches. I forgot the

---

[10] A traditional native practice of using the smoke from ceremonial plants, gently and carefully burned in a special bowl or container, for the purpose of cleansing, purification, and preparation for sacred work.

matches! How much tobacco do I put in each time? Oops, there were two directions to go[11] and the pipe was almost full. Was it okay to take some of it out?

We all have to start somewhere. I tried to release any disappointment I felt at my own shortcomings. I reminded myself of the honour of holding and lifting the pipe. I changed my focus to the prayers themselves and watched the smoke rise upward, into Creator's realm. At the end of the ceremony, I simply sat in silence. I closed my eyes and began to journey. The first thing I noticed when I found myself in Spirit realm was that I was crying. I heard teachings but saw no teacher:

> *You have embarked on a tradition.*
> *We will guide you and support you in this way.*
> *You are surrounded by other spirits now,*
> *in addition to the ones you have come to know.*
> *Another doorway has been opened to you.*
> *See them. Feel them. Know them.*
> *They are all gentle spirits*
> *who teach with love and compassion.*
> *Do not be afraid*
> *to awaken to their presence.*

I gathered up my pipe materials slowly and carefully, wrapping the pipe bowl and stem separately as Fishwoman had shown me. I placed them all in a special bag dedicated to this purpose, so everything would be ready for next time. As I finished, I felt like I was entering a state of limbo. I didn't know what to think. I didn't know how to feel.

The next few hours were, surprisingly, a bit of a struggle. I wasn't able

---

[11] In this tradition a sacred pipe is loaded by first smudging a p be either tobacco leaf or a blend of select plants, then holdi of the seven directions (North, South, East, West, Sky, Ear the prayers specific to that direction are spoken out loud. Tl placed into the pipe.

to focus on the tasks at hand. I felt uneasy and couldn't find my way past it. I became disappointed in myself. The day had started out so beautifully, why couldn't I hold on to it? It finally occurred to me to go outside. Some time in nature and sunshine would set things right.

As soon as I left the front door, I sensed something unusual. I looked around, to 'take stock' and reorient myself. I had stepped into a completely different realm, yet one that looked identical to the one I had always known! There were cars on the street, airplanes in the sky, the sound of busses stopping and starting on the main road nearby. Everything was the same, yet everything was different. I looked closely at the tree in the front yard. As each branch swayed it seemed to be reaching out, communicating. Was it reaching out to me? I surveyed the street a second time. I could sense and know there were invisible nuances of the natural world all around me. They were welcoming me, accepting me. Everything was more alive than it used to be.

Just like that the world had changed. A doorway had indeed been opened and I was beckoned to enter. Lifting the pipe, being invited into a tradition of several thousand years, and carrying it through . . . it changes you and therefore changes the world you live in. I never imagined that entering this lineage, I would notice a physical difference. Yet now I can say that I *felt* it. I marvel at how powerful a simple ceremony can be. This is what ceremony is all about. At an essential level it creates a shift in your being. That's what it's designed to do.

Chapter Ten

Beyond Limits

I turn to the Mountain for guidance.

The sacred Mountain is my Teacher and Guide in the realm of Spirit. When I need help, have questions, or want to spend time developing and nurturing our relationship, I go to the Mountain, usually in a journey. I state my intention first, which lets the Mountain know why I have come. The journey unfolds in my inner vision. The Mountain's teachings often feel more spoken than visual, so I have taught myself how to take notes and journey at the same time. It feels important to honour the teachings in that way. The feelings and knowings I receive are so special I want to ensure that no piece is forgotten, or noted inappropriately. One morning I asked a question of the Mountain regarding the stillness practice it had instructed me to do. This was the answer I received:

> *Wizard rises from his seated position in the East and comes toward me. He kneels down in front of me, then takes my hands and speaks.*
> *"My child, we are always with you. Being with us has now become a part of who you are. This was our intention for daily practice—the being together, not necessarily doing together, which as you know is the next step. But we cannot move into doing without first establishing being. So you see, it was a necessary prerequisite.*

"You have come to know us as part of you. This is correct. We are all in service, together. You no longer have doubts and your fears are being brought to the surface, so they too can be released.

"But know that all aspects of the process we are embarking upon, unfold together. There is no separate time for healing, time for learning, time for developing relationships, except in your own mind, your own intention.

"Limiting your intention in your work with us limits our scope. This is one of the barriers to your expansion. Be ready now to embrace it all—all at once. There are no dividing lines, all flows as one. Limiting possibilities is such a human trait. It does not exist here. Let go of that one barrier and you will go further than you ever imagined. Instead, explore, always explore. Let this be your usual mode of being. Always be on the lookout for what is really happening. Don't define it, observe and be part of it. Be in it and pay attention. This is the basic foundation for all God's work, all work of a divine nature. Your 'presence' is the catalyst which creates opportunity. So, creation can be an ongoing part of your way of being. It can be and is available to you from moment to moment, at any moment. Try it. Trust it. We are ready."

Chapter Eleven

An Unusual Eating Disorder

A patient story: The Mountain's gifts reveal the effects of prayer . . .

W hen Simone came to see me for this particular treatment session we had known each other for a while. We began by catching up on recent events and sharing insights into current life experiences. We were easily flowing from one topic to the next when Simone mentioned, for the first time, her resistance to feeding herself well. She was not anorexic or bulimic, and was quite happy to prepare and serve food to others, but when she was alone her tendency was to ignore the need to eat in favour of other activities. As we talked further, she described that when she thought about eating, and had plenty of time to prepare something, she would actually resist it. Simone was in her early 30s at the time, and quite thin, so weight was not one of her concerns. As we talked, I tried to leave some open spaces, so I wasn't directing the conversation, and she could choose what she wanted to talk about. The next thing I knew she was sharing an experience of her mother's while pregnant with her.

At the regular seven month medical checkup, her Mom received a disturbing piece of news. Her physician expressed concern with the low weight of the fetus and wanted to re-categorize the pregnancy to high risk. Her mother was a woman of strong faith and so naturally reached out to her church for support and solace. A prayer group was arranged and regular sessions planned. Weeks later, at the time of the birth, there were some mild complications and the use of forceps was necessary, but otherwise Simone was a healthy baby.

Simone and I decided to explore that critical time in her fetal development from Simone's perspective. Lying comfortably on the massage table, wrapped in a blanket so she could feel safe and warm, I sat by her side and called on one of the Mountain's gifts. I began by stating inwardly a pure and sincere intention to be in service to Simone's healing needs. Touching her shoulder established the necessary physical connection, which then allowed me to shift my awareness, from me to her. Once the bridge was formed, the Mountain took me deep within Simone's being to access the memories stored there.

Very quickly I saw an image of Simone in her mother's womb. She was about seven month's gestation. I was also able to feel what she was experiencing at the time. She was a delightfully happy and content fetus. She floated in the warmth of her liquid home, comfortable and carefree. I could see that she was quite small for her age yet there were no indications of anything less than perfect health and development. It was a very pleasant time and easy for me to linger there, not seeking to explore further. Then in an instant, I felt her world change. She was now bombarded with intense emotions, seemingly from an outside source. It felt like she was metaphorically tossed one way, then another, then another. I could hear muted voices, strong with intent and relentless. From inside this secluded and immensely vulnerable environment, they felt invasive. I couldn't make out the words but I could register the effect they had on baby Simone. Each one of them conveyed essentially the same message: that Simone wasn't good enough the way she was. *They* wanted her to be different, to be bigger and fatter, and for the first time in her fetal awareness, the unconditional love and acceptance she had always known had been overshadowed by something entirely different.

It's hard to describe in words the shifts of feeling this created in Simone, but they were registered by her being and my sense of the result was that she 'changed her mind'. All of a sudden her world wasn't the blissful place it had once been. And if this was the type of world she was going to be born

into, she didn't want any part of it. Yet she was trapped. She couldn't go back and didn't want to go forward. Thinking back to our earlier conversation, I now understood the need for forceps in her delivery. It all made sense.

Somewhere inside Simone the memory of this was still present and as a grown-up, it was affecting her choices and comfort level in feeding herself. She had come to see me to ask for help, so while still intimately connected with her spirit nature, I asked to be shown what she needed to recover from this wounding and move forward.

The stories we hold inside are like memories, yet no longer available to our conscious recall. They are derived from an experience that affects our being, whether physical, mental, emotional, or spiritual, and they leave an imprint which becomes part of who we are, even though it is not our original nature. I couldn't possibly know what Simone needed to heal, but by still being connected to her, I could ask her spirit. The spirit, the most permanent part of us, wants to be well, it wants to be vibrant. I have never experienced a time when the spirit did not present a solution, although it does require considerable patience, and the resolve not to interfere or make something up.

As an adult, Simone had the ability to receive the deeper message of what the bold, intentful prayers represented, and put them it into a different context than her innocent, fetal-self had been able to. She could now understand that her mother, and the supporting community, wanted only the best for her. But knowing that in her mind was quite different from experiencing it inwardly. The wound was being held in her soul and therefore the 'medicine', the balm that would finally allow it to heal, had to be delivered there.

In the same way that I had been able to access the hidden memory, I was now shown a slightly different story, revealed by Simone's spirit. It was one of being loved and cared for, not only by the mother she was so intimately connected to, but an extended family also.

As the new story unfolded and I narrated it to Simone, we experienced the feelings of it together, moment by moment, as it was happening in present time. It was beautiful. It also honoured Simone at every stage, and as I spoke the words a part of Simone was able to relax inside and finally accept herself.

Her being, now conscious of both the old story and the new one, could make the choice of which to carry forward. In my experience, the newer one is easily accepted. Being more recent in chronological time it is more available to hold on to, and secondly, it has the appeal of serving her continuing good health and wellness.

/ / / / / /

Simone moved away from Calgary shortly after that session, to pursue a career opportunity. We lost touch with each other[12] until three years later, when I was surprised to see her attending a Community Fire Circle I was hosting; an informal evening of prayer, stories, and song, around a consecrated fire. Being in a sacred circle is not the time to catch up but at one point during the evening Simone took the opportunity to ask if I would offer special prayers for a young infant child she knew who was struggling with serious health issues. She asked if we could pray for him to be well and strong. I waited a few moments to respond. Special prayer requests were not unusual at a Community Fire Circle, but given what Simone and I had been through together, I was surprised to hear her asking for the same type of help and support that her mother had asked for all those years ago, and in a surprisingly similar setting. Her own experience had shown the other side of prayer, when a plea for a specific outcome, one decided by other humans with no acknowledgement of the will of Creator, had unfortunate consequences. I literally got up from my chair and went around the circle to where she was sitting, whispered a gentle reminder in her ear, and asked that she think more seriously about her request. She reacted in a way I hadn't anticipated. She didn't know what I was talking about. She was confused and uncertain how to respond. I didn't want to create any discomfort by singling her out so I tried a different approach. I asked her permission to share the story of a particular healing session we had together several years before. Without hesitation she agreed. My hope was that it would be an important teaching about prayer for everyone in attendance.

After the Fire Circle was complete and we were all saying our goodbyes,

---

[12] Some patients stay in touch for years and others I don't hear from again once they feel well. I am comfortable with both. The best possible outcome is that people begin to create meaningful lives for themselves and leave their illness, and sometimes me, behind.

Simone approached me to say that until I shared the story and reminded her, she had completely forgotten about that healing session and the work we had done. She found this quite amazing; it was not the kind of experience she would expect to forget! But our conversation led to an even more remarkable discovery. Not only had she forgotten our session, she had also forgotten that she ever had trouble feeding herself. The awareness of that time had left her being and she had never given it another thought.

Chapter Twelve

Pilgrims

Growing pains . . .

Once a year, every year, Fishwoman and I make a special trip to the Mountain to do ceremony. I call it a pilgrimage. I can go to the Mountain at other times, perhaps even a dozen times each year, but it's not the same. When the Mountain knows you are coming, when it knows you have fasted and prepared, when the date has been planned and the spirits have gathered, it is a different experience. It is a time to acknowledge the gifts the Mountain has given, renew our commitment and friendship, and reconnect with the sacred and potent energies it shares.

Our first pilgrimage was the day after we met. And surprisingly, we did not go alone. The first year there was one other and it grew from there. We were not the only ones who needed a sacred mountain in our lives and somehow others found their way to us. Some were complete strangers until the night before our gathering. There were also friends and acquaintances who knew my story and were drawn to participate. I always understood that part of my role in being the voice of the Mountain was to help others see mountains in a different light. Opening our ceremonial time was one way of accomplishing that.

We learned from experience that late May or early June was best, as the snow was likely to have melted and being close to the summer solstice, the sun would be warm. Always eager to get started I would begin on New Year's Day by phoning Pauline to set the date. I liked to have it marked in my calendar as early as possible so I could look forward to it and begin to prepare inwardly.

After the date was set, I would wait to receive a dream from the Mountain with the theme for our gathering and ceremony. Then, if there was anything asked of me, I had plenty of time to plan and get ready. The Mountain was always generous with everyone and I was happy to do my part. It was hard to imagine a greater joy than what we felt in our hearts when the ceremony was complete and we were heading back down the trail, to home. It was tangible, as if it hung in the very air around us, and we often commented on it. Not that any words were needed to heighten the awareness. The frequent peals of laughter bursting forth were reminder enough.

The Mountain played an active role in the ceremony. Sometimes what it offered were the teachings that it shared through me as its voice. Other times it would instruct everyone to stand and face it, to receive a healing. One year it advised me that I needed to receive the teaching gift for each person long before our gathering date. I was to go there physically, to hear its voice as I had when we first met. I was to take the teachings home and write out a card that would be given to each pilgrim during the ceremony. I was so nervous! If this was to be everyone's gift, what if I couldn't hear the Mountain? What if I couldn't find the way of being inside myself that allowed me to receive it?

Of course I didn't have to worry. I was not doing this alone. The Mountain was offering something to the people. All that was required of me was my willingness and commitment. And that was without question.

The pilgrimages were not without their challenges however. During the early years it was easy for me to set those aside. The excitement of our gathering and the ceremony together with the Mountain nourished me so fully that I couldn't hold on to any of the annoyances or disruptions. But as my relationship to the Mountain deepened, it began to share with me how the others were doing with following through from cycle to cycle, and whether they were holding the Mountain in their hearts and lives in an appropriate, honouring way.

The Mountain asked so little of us, particularly the others. As long as they returned to be with the Mountain in the physical world once each year for as long as they had promised, and took the time and thought to give their small monthly offering on an evening during the crescent moon, all was well. This was the way the Mountain chose to stay present in people's lives throughout the seasons.

As the years passed, we all had equal opportunity to build upon and strengthen our relationship with the Mountain, but this wasn't always what took place. When the Mountain shared its sadness and disappointment with me, it became my sadness and disappointment. I naturally grew protective and that was not well received by the others. It appeared they did not want me to stand out in any way. I was a student, as they were. I was there to receive Fishwoman's teachings, as they were. We learned the songs, the ceremonies, the protocols, together. She was our Elder and Teacher. I was one of the group.

This had worked for a while but when the Mountain came to me in a dream and showed me that the offerings it had requested were not being given, it was time to acknowledge that I had an important role, and it was no longer appropriate to undervalue it. I had been trying to be low-key. I had been trying to ensure that my ego did not get in the way. I wanted to stay humble and quiet. But in many ways it was also clear that I was the leader. I organized the group each year. I helped the people who were coming, some from other countries, to be sure they had everything they needed when they got here. I planned additional activities to maximize the value of our short time together. I arranged Pauline's flight, food, and hosted her each time. I arranged hotel accommodations for the others from out of town, as well as campsites, cabins, tipis, food, extra clothing, and supplies. I divided up the shared tasks so we could each contribute to the ceremony and the preparations. I tallied and collected the financial contributions. And more important, each time we did ceremony at the top of the Mountain, I offered myself as its voice. I shared with the people the gifts it was willing to give. The ceremony wouldn't be the same without that. Each person always took something home with them from the Mountain. I was the bridge that allowed that to be possible.

The Medicine Path

Through my studies with Eliot Cowan and my travels, I had the opportunity to meet a few people in the U.S. and Mexico who worked closely with mountains. I knew from their stories that not all mountains were as congenial, understanding, and patient as ours. I couldn't help but wonder if the group would pay more attention to a loud, angry mountain that instilled fear. Would they be more attentive to the requested offerings? Would they commit themselves more fully? Seemingly there were no repercussions or consequences to not following through.

I suppose it was just a matter of time, then, before the subtle nuances of their inward relationship with the Mountain started to show in the physical world. One such incident occurred during a rest stop on our way up the trail to the viewpoint. Pauline had instructed us at the base, as we were loading our packs and sorting our supplies, that from the time we started out until we arrived at the top, we would be fasting in preparation for the ceremony. We could drink water, but not take in any food. We were about halfway up when one of the group casually took an orange out of her pack and started eating it. Hadn't she heard the instructions from the Elder? As this was a direct violation of the protocol we'd been asked to follow, I felt I had to say something. In the way of a gentle reminder I spoke up, "Pauline asked that we give our hunger to the Mountain as part of our offering." Without hesitation she replied, "Well you can give your hunger to the Mountain if you want to, but I'm going to eat this orange."

It's hard to describe in words the impact of the invisible arrow that pierced my heart. As I looked up, directly into her eyes, she held no malice, and at the same time, no shame. She simply wanted to eat the orange. To her, the protocol was just a suggestion. What did it really matter if she ate an orange? Would the ceremony be different? Was lightning going to strike her down? She was a grown woman, a mother of three; surely she could eat an orange if she wanted to. As my outrage subsided it was replaced with a deep sadness. No, she wouldn't notice any difference to our ceremony for having eaten the orange. But yes, there would be a difference. That's the nature of relationship.

The pilgrimage was a time of gratitude, of sacrifice, of making offerings to the Mountain in the physical world, on her surface, not merely in the

66

comfort of our own backyard. Some of our group had travelled thousands of miles to do so. The Mountain was a sacred place, not because I said so, or because of what happened to me, but because we had all experienced it. In an act of love, compassion, and generosity, it had given of itself to us, befriended us, held us in its circle. For those on a spiritual path who recognized the natural world's ever-present connection to the Divine, this was a privilege. To give of our hunger was so little to give. We were all well fed, lived in comfortable warm homes, and were blessed with the richness of loved ones in our lives. A few hours without food—honestly, we had all eaten breakfast!

The year following turned out to be one of the most difficult. One of the group asked to withdraw from contributing to the hard costs of the pilgrimage: Pauline's flight, her celebration dinner afterwards, and the donation for her teachings. She advised that she was not a willing volunteer to help purchase and organize supplies—she was only interested in getting her own. She asked that she be allowed to separate from the group, right after the ceremony, and spend time with the Mountain alone, then descend later than the rest of us. I recognized that she wanted to further her personal relationship with the Mountain and that she felt a need which she understood to be different from the rest of us. She was trying to honour herself by acknowledging and filling that need. Yet at the same time it was not my role to accommodate personal requests. I had the group to look after. I tried to remind her that what we receive from the Mountain is already so much greater than what we give, and that we need to question ourselves if our inclination is to want to give less instead of more. This path of relationship with Spirit is one of reciprocity.

This woman felt her relationship with the Mountain was important and valuable, yet she wanted it strictly on her own terms. What she was asking from me was not within my power to give. I was there to dream the dream revealing the theme for our time together, to gather the group with consideration for all the practical details, and to be the voice of the Mountain when we arrived at the top. To my mind, what she was needing was some one-on-one time with the Elder and the Mountain, yet this would have required far more of her, both personally and financially, than going with the group. No matter what I said, she did not see it my way. I was upset. She was hurt. I didn't know what to do. So I turned to the Mountain.

Grandfather Mountain stood and responded:
My child, we can see you are hurting, that you are struggling with this. There is no cause for your pain or anguish. The choice was hers alone. It was not supported or encouraged by you. We sense you would like it otherwise, but what of the journey that she needs to pursue? Your distress at her decision dis-empowers her, and you have no right to do that. We understand it comes from your commitment to us and your path, but trust her decision, please. Together we are trying to create and nurture community, a shared gathering to honour the gifts I have given and the traditions which support you in holding those gifts. A community will always flow and change. It is supposed to. When a community is perceived as having something to offer, it will be engaged and received. When it is perceived that the community is more of an obligation than the value it holds, it will be released.

I hadn't previously thought that she was withdrawing from the community, but of course she was. She wanted the Mountain, she wanted the ceremony, she wanted the connection and the time together in a meaningful and sacred way. What she didn't want was what she perceived as all the trappings that went along with that. I guess I couldn't see it for myself because it hurt me that she didn't want what I took great pains and effort to provide.

Everyone was there for their own reasons, including me. I could allow anger and spite to get the better of me and conclude that my reasons were more noble than theirs, because I was there for the Mountain and they were apparently there for themselves, but that would dishonour the beauty that the experience had held for each of them over the years, and it wouldn't be fair. It was alright for their reasons to be different from mine. Acceptance was the path of wisdom.

Despite the struggles beforehand, the pilgrimage that year was beautiful. Pauline and I managed to come to somewhat of an agreement with the woman, and we did what we could to accommodate her without compromising the integrity of the group. In the final moments we all set our challenges aside and allowed ourselves to experience our time on the Mountain wholeheartedly.

It was satisfying to know that we were able to handle the matter maturely, with each contributing what we could to make it work. But in the aftermath I felt strongly there must be a better way. It should be a joy to prepare for our time together, not a conflict. As I sat with this awareness one thing became clear. There needed to be a shift in my approach. I decided to make one small change to the way the mountain pilgrimage was arranged. I had always been proactive in communicating with the group. From now on, I would hold off on that part and wait for the others to inquire when they felt ready. When the stirrings of the Mountain ceremony rose up in their minds and heart, they would get in touch and learn what was being offered, and when. It was similar to the way patients would approach me in my healing practice. My motto had always been—you can only help those who ask. I would wait for the others to reach out to learn the dates and details of our mountain trek. That's all. When they thought about the Mountain, they would get in touch and I would happily follow through with all of my usual planning. This felt right and seemed more appropriate to what was being offered. After all, Pauline wasn't contacting each one of them ahead of time. It wasn't until she arrived at the site each year that she knew who was joining us. I liked the idea. In all other ways, I would offer my support and help, and I would continue to be the voice of the Mountain.

I wish I could tell you that the idea worked well, and that the reaching forward of the others helped to support their receiving through this sacred pilgrimage, and strengthened their relationship with the Mountain. Instead, the inconceivable happened. No one got in touch. No one inquired. No one wrote, emailed, telephoned, or followed through. Not one of them. If there wasn't an email in their inbox alerting them that the mountain pilgrimage was an important part of their year, they didn't pursue it. It wasn't even important enough for them to contact me and inquire why they hadn't heard anything. I could have understood if perhaps one person, or two, didn't respond. In a way it was a test to see if their hearts were truly in it. But all of them?

It was then I remembered the words of Grandfather Mountain, "When a community is perceived as having something to offer, it will be engaged and received. When it is perceived that the community is more of an obligation than the value it holds, it will be released." There was my answer. While it didn't seem much effort to take responsibility for learning about and attending each year's pilgrimage, it was more than had been asked of them in the past. Given the choice, they decided to let it go.

What I couldn't see clearly at the time, and didn't until several years later, was how much that change was needed. When Pauline and I first started taking people to the Mountain, it was the only way I knew to reach out and share with others the gifts that mountains could give. While the mountain pilgrimages were beautiful and enjoyable, they could only reach a handful of people in any given year. Now there was a book that told of the Mountain's gifts and abilities—I had written the story down. Now there was another vehicle to share the true nature of mountains and the possibilities of relationship with the natural world with anyone who was drawn to read it. The book could reach out to more people than was possible for Pauline and I to take to the top of the Mountain. The Mountain's voice was still being heard, it was simply being heard in a different way!

More than that, I needed the freedom to grow and change. During the years of the first pilgrimages I was still struggling with accepting the gifts and moving forward. As I came to stand strong in what the Mountain had asked of me, and willing to offer its gifts to the people, not just to other pilgrims, I entered a new phase of my life and service. At the same time, a different community was gathering and forming, but the momentum hadn't reached the stage where I could know that yet. But I suspect the Mountain did!

Pauline and I still participate in a pilgrimage each year. It is a real joy to share with the Mountain the intimacy of our friendship and our teacher/student relationship. It is wonderful to sit with Grandmother Mountain while she listens in on our conversations and my telling of the teachings and growing I have been blessed with over the previous year. It feels right.

Chapter Thirteen

The Voices in His Head

The Mountain reveals the inner workings of the psyche . . .

I can't tell you the name of the young man in this story. I met him only one time, for about an hour, before the session came to an abrupt halt. He never became a patient, never had a file, and so his name was never written down. But something happened during that encounter that I will never forget, and I suspect he won't either. I had just finished a presentation as a guest speaker for a Sunday morning church service in Ontario when I was approached by his father. The man had read my book and eagerly hoped I might be able to help his son, whom he described as struggling with several life challenges. Normally I like patients to book their own appointments, so I can be sure it's their choice, but I made an exception in this case as I was in a far-away city and only offering sessions if specifically asked. I didn't have much background information to go on, other than the young man was in his 20s and having troubles moving forward in life. These troubles had significantly affected the relationship between him and his father, so they were both looking for a resolution.

It turned out to be an awkward meeting. The son hadn't been advised of the type of work I did and didn't know what to expect. He was a little on the defensive when we met in the lobby of my hotel and I brought him up to my room. He naturally wanted to know what I was going to do, and I couldn't really answer that, as we hadn't even begun. We talked for a while though and I did my best to offer him plenty of background information and a few examples of patients I had worked with. He seemed comfortable with that, so I asked permission to touch him on the shoulder, to connect with him and find out what I could about the source of his troubles. He agreed and made himself comfortable lying on the couch in the little sitting area of my suite. I sat on the floor beside him, called on the Mountain and its healing gifts, and soon began narrating everything I was learning through our connection.

It started with me hearing voices, many voices, loud and insistent but at the same time muffled. I knew by the tone they were telling him what to do but there were so many it was hard to make out what each individually was saying. They felt demanding and very confusing. As I continued to hear them, and share moment by moment what was happening, an internal image appeared. It was strange and somewhat distorted but revealed a hallway that had dozens of little windows in it, all at eye level. Each window could slide open horizontally using a handle that was moulded on one side. The windows appeared worn and scratched so I described them as plastic. Each time a voice would shout out, it was preceded by the opening of one of these windows, then afterwards, it slammed shut. This happened over and over in a chaotic pattern, the sound of the voices now accompanied by the sound of the windows continually opening, sliding, and shutting. To my mind, it was crazy making.

When I got to this part of the inner vision the young man literally sprung himself upward, retreated to the corner of the couch and perched hesitantly on the cushion like a bird. He was clearly distressed. By the time I stood up to see what was happening, he had already started yelling at me from his perch. He screamed out, "They are not plastic, they are glass! The windows are made of glass!"

It was only a few minutes later that he was heading down the elevator, wanting to get as far away from me as he could. I knew his father would be waiting so I wasn't concerned. When the phone rang, and before I had a chance to explain fully what had happened, his father interrupted, stating

there was something I should know—his son was presently hospitalized for schizophrenia, but was home on a weekend pass.

Now I understood how frightening our session must have been. I had literally been taken into this man's internal world and experienced it as he did. I'm quite certain he never imagined that the inner workings of his psyche could be viewed by a complete stranger.

⸺ ⸺ ⸺ ⸺

I can't say what might have happened if I had been able to call upon the Mountain's healing gifts, but I hope that a seed of possibility was planted—that it is possible for someone else to *know* what he is going through—and that the seed may serve in some way to guide him to a skilled and compassionate therapist.

Chapter Fourteen

A Family Reunion

The Mountain must have sensed that the missing pieces of me were affecting my ability to be in service . . .

It was just after Christmas. I had taken some time off and given myself some holidays to be with the Mountain and the Mountain's teachings. As I was doing my practice one morning it came to me that one of my critical blocks and barriers was my fear of the expansion that had been asked of me. When I tried to meditate I would feel tight and bound, in my chest and in my head. I couldn't let go. What was I holding on to? I felt I needed some guidance so I called Eagle and we went to the Mountain. We were immediately seated in the circle of Mountain Spirit Beings and I spoke to them of my intention. I wanted to know if they could help me 'let go and expand'.

Grandmother Mountain goes around to Wizard and places her hands on his shoulders as he sits in the East. I feel like she is imparting some key knowing to him through her hands, something about me. Wizard then rises, comes toward me, and places his hands on my shoulders. Something starts to blur. How do I describe it? I can't feel it really, yet some part of me is aware. I realize I need to stop feeling 'me' in this body and start feeling 'me' as I sit in the circle with the Mountain. Then a light, a whitish mist, descends from my shoulders going deep down inside. I can feel both my resistance and Wizard's infinite patience. I begin to notice how I am locked into my body in a way that creates an inner struggle, an inner tightness. I ask, "What am I fighting? What am I holding on to?" Then I see myself in a stark, empty room, sitting cross-legged on the floor. There is a small window nearby but I am clearly not interested in looking outward. I appear fine—not harmed in any way—yet the sense is that I am confined, that this is a prison of sorts. Even more disconcerting is that the room feels strangely familiar . . .

"There is a place in your heart that is closed and cold. It's related to the tightness you feel in your chest when you breathe. You only breathe a limited amount because you only want to live and experience a limited amount. You want to experience what you know, not what you have forgotten. It's really a fear to be all that you are. Denying one critical part contains you, holds you in."

I paused the journey to prepare myself for what might happen next. I was afraid the Mountain had taken my request too seriously. I was looking for advice and guidance, or better yet, some simple instructions. After seeing myself in that room a flood of realization came to the forefront of my mind. The answers I was looking for were not simple. The reasons were not easy to address. There was a deep wound within me that had not yet healed, a wound I had sensed since my teenage years but had no idea of its origin, its timelines, or ultimately, the effect it had on me. I have no memories before the age of twelve. The first quarter of my life is missing and I'm well aware that this is a classic sign of soul loss. I have been the grateful recipient of many soul retrievals but none has touched upon the 'stark, empty room' inside me.

There were a few things I knew about my childhood—my parents had told me stories. But I could count what I remember about those early years on the fingers of one hand. It was the scope of what I didn't know that was the cause for distress. I couldn't remember any of the homes I

had lived in, where I went to school, how I got there, who my teachers or friends had been. I didn't know if I had a favourite movie or story book, if my hair had been long or short, curly or straight. I couldn't remember even one child whom I had ever played with, or what games we might have played. It was as if I arrived on the scene at age twelve and began living from that time forward.

There was also evidence of a childhood trauma, revealed by the phenomenon of the family photographs. Those that showed me as a young infant and toddler revealed a bright shining face, light blond hair, and a huge smile. Those a few years later, and carrying forward to my teen years, revealed a decidedly unhappy girl. I literally had a frown on my face in every one. I had grown up with some of these photographs on display, so was quite used to it. Yet decades later, when my sister took her first trip back home to our birthplace in England, and reunited with our extended family there, one question was asked of her repeatedly, "Does our Jaki smile yet?" And while I had several nicknames in the household during my growing years, one that my parents gave me stands out. They would call me "Misery." It always seemed that they were as much at a loss as I was—to know why there was no spark, no play, and no joy.

Getting back to the journey, I knew I had the right to choose. I could stop there and not return to the Mountain. But part of me knew that the time had come and I was ready. My fears were not around the scope of healing that might be needed. It was uncovering the mystery that I was afraid of.

I returned to the Mountain Spirit Beings and asked, "Will you help me?"

Without any warning I am lifted up by a cloaked figure I do not recognize. He clutches me to his body and starts to fly. I can tell when we cross over into a completely different realm, as there are mist and sparkles all around us. We gently begin our descent, gliding down into what appears to be a magical, mystical landscape. I feel entranced by it. There is a strong sense of comfort, of being 'home'. My mind starts to run through all the questions I need answered. Where am I? Have

I been here before? What happened to me? And I come to know one more piece. This place was a part of my childhood imaginings, my fantasy life. This was where I retreated when the real world felt cold and harsh. I couldn't remember it in my mind, but being here now, I remembered it in my soul. This place was my sanctuary. And then I died. I died to them. Something happened and I wasn't able to come back. This was the land of the fairies, a land loved by so many children of English ancestry.

The Mountain speaks, "As a child you were separated from your spiritual family and your true nature. The loss was great and affected you significantly. To heal we must return you to the soul-state that is your birthright and free you from the stark and empty room. There is a way—the story can come alive in you once more. Are you willing to accept these beings back into your life? You have lived with the others (humans), and been ignorant of them (the fairies), for a very long time. This will not be easy."

I had never felt so clearly that a part of me had been missing. In my physical life, the void I experienced was emotionless. Here, there was a deep longing that was almost more than I could bear. The answer to the question was, "Yes! Please guide me. Help me find a way."

I allow my focus to return to the fairy landscape. And then I see them. They are all watching me descend. I have a sense they have been waiting. Amidst the mist and sparkles I land on the soft, grassy ground and the fairies come running toward me. As they get closer, they appear larger and larger, until they are half my size. There is one in particular who stands out, not that he is any bigger than the rest. Somehow I know he is my father. He has a large, soft, troll-like nose, long greyish hair, and he exudes a kind and gentle manner. Everything about him speaks of love and tenderness. He approaches and gives me a hug. It is a hug like no other. It is so different I know instinctively that I am to slow down and allow myself to receive it completely. It isn't clingy or bold. It is gentle but firm. It isn't the intensity or the strength of his arms around me that is so meaningful, so significant. It is what I feel inside when he holds me—complete acceptance. There isn't any aspect of his being that does not *and this is transmitted through our embrace.*

And then I see my mother. She is queen of the fairies. She enters on a chariot, her role and her reign very obvious. She carries a wand with a star on the top, a star of pure light. She comes down from her coach, walks toward me and embraces me. This is not the same hug as my father had given me. I can tell she is happy to see me but there is much on her mind, and as if able to read it, I know this is a very difficult time for the fairies, and she is personally responsible to all her clan. She has the weight of the world on her shoulders. She quickly gets back on her chariot and leaves.

Then I notice the rest of them! So many little fairy people, perhaps hundreds, all wanting to greet me. With my mind I wonder if these are my brothers and sisters, as I had just met my parents. But immediately I know they are just family—the concept of brothers and sisters doesn't apply in the fairy kingdom. They come and crawl all over me, laughing and playing, so happy to see me again. It is a blissful moment.

The realities start to blur. As I try to express my gratitude to the Mountain Spirit Beings for bringing me here, for enlivening a part of my soul, I again become aware of my physical body, here in the room of my house. I realize the shift and want to resist, but in the same instant, I know I have been given all that I can manage, for now. I need some time to let the journey experience sink in, to let it become part of my knowing, so I can honour it appropriately. I let the journey fade while a single tear rolls down my face. My final question to the Mountain is, "What should I do now?" They respond, "Spend more time with us. It is really the only way. Then you will feel again. And your fear to expand will no longer exist."

I sat with the experience of this journey, this healing story, for many days. I still didn't know what happened to me as a child, but I now understood the effect that it had. A significant part of me had shut down, the little girl who delighted in the retreat to the fantasy realms. This made infinite sense to me. If there was one quality I was sorely lacking *love me*

...lness. I was a serious person. I appreciated ...ad very little of my own. It also explained why ...learning to journey. I had closed myself off from the ...ur with my spirit. The part about the fairies was surprising ...er. I would never have imagined that a story of fairies could touch ...me so profoundly. I can honestly say that fairies were not something I ever thought about or paid attention to. Yet the feeling I experienced as I entered their realm . . . was unforgettable.

As the days turned into weeks, another layer of understanding surfaced. My story was also a metaphor for a much larger one. In the past few hundred years, as a race and as a culture, we too have become serious—one more consequence of our singular focus on the physically created world. By remembering how to look through the innocent eyes of a child we can better accept the varied and wondrous ways that the realm of Spirit presents itself. What we need is to lighten up, have some fun, and remember how to play, for its own sake. Reconnecting with Spirit has more to offer us than personal development and informed service.

The shift that has grown to encompass most of humankind is also influencing Spirit. The world of the nature spirits, the fairies, is becoming serious too. The easy flow back and forth that has been ongoing for millennia has been interrupted. The realm of Spirit is reaching out to us, reminding us of how it used to be, creating the opportunity to restore balance. And it is to our benefit to do so.

When we accept both realities, when we experience the broader states of being we are capable of, we become happier. Life has more meaning. Joy rises up in our hearts. We are more whole.

⁄ ⁄ ⁄ ⁄ ⁄ ⁄ ⁄

There is a story that Fishwoman tells. It is a story about the existence of spirits. She begins by stating how few people can see spirits nowadays. But it was not always that way. The legends say that many years ago, not only could spirits be seen with the physical eyes of humans, but they were very large and able to exist in our realm. We lived together. If the spirit of the mermaid was playing at the shore of the ocean, splashing in the water

and lapping up the sun and wind, she would appear, if only temporarily, as solid and dense as the rest of us. She would also have the ability to disappear and become invisible, but no one denied her existence.

Chapter Fifteen

The Sweat Lodge

The gifts and blessings continue. What could I have possibly done to deserve these?

hat started out as a typical private student session ended up on a very different note, with Miriam casually commenting as she was packing up to leave, "You know, one of my dreams is to have a sweat lodge on our property outside the city."

Miriam had been to one of the annual Vision Quests that Pauline and I hosted, so we had participated in ceremony together. She had also been a student for a couple of years and I considered her a friend. We knew each other well enough that when she made this comment, I didn't think it an offhand remark. I took it seriously and responded, "Were you thinking of pursuing this on your own, without a traditional Elder? I wouldn't feel comfortable being involved in anything like that unless it was under the guidance of Fishwoman."

Miriam was not a woman to be discouraged by small details. "Well, if you think she'd be willing, we could always bring her out, have her offer prayers on the site, and let us know whether the ancestors and the land would support my vision." After that, it was simply a matter of logistics. I arranged for Pauline to extend her stay in Alberta after Vision Quest that summer, and she and Miriam, along with Miriam's husband and myself, gathered on the land. It was a beautiful location—one hundred and ninety acres that had never been developed. If Spirit was in agreement, the sweat lodge would be the first structure ever built there.

Pauline began by offering tobacco and saying prayers. It wasn't long before she was smiling and laughing and sharing with us how abundant the nature spirits and ancestors were. And they welcomed us with open arms! This was an exciting moment. I had participated in Sweat Lodges with Pauline before, many times, but I had never thought about what it would be like to have a permanent lodge close by. It seemed to me there were a lot of details to be sorted out, particularly, who would run the Lodge? It would be very expensive to bring Pauline out each time, yet neither of us knew of other Elders in the area who might be available and willing.

Afterward, as we were heading back to the city, Pauline said, "OK, one of the first and most important steps is that we need to find a Fire Keeper. Do you know anyone who might be interested? There was only one person I knew—my friend Scott, whom Pauline had met. He had participated in Vision Quest with us and I knew that he looked forward to opportunities that allowed him greater exposure to the native traditions he felt were so closely aligned with his personal spiritual path. He was also a man who knew how to be in service. He often volunteered in a shelter kitchen, helping to feed the hungry and homeless. Once I had thought of him, he seemed perfect and I couldn't wait to ask him. I called as soon as we were home. He didn't hesitate. Right there on the phone he accepted the role, acknowledging that he would need teachings. Pauline remembered Scott and felt comfortable with his acceptance.

Now we just had to figure out a way to bring Pauline out for the Lodges. It was a twelve hour drive from her home and she hesitated to fly more than a couple of times each year. We were already using one of those to bring her out for Vision Quest. I marvelled at how easy it had been to find a Fire Keeper, but recognized that this might be the stumbling block. She must have been thinking the very same thing because her next words were, "Can't run a Lodge without a Lodge Keeper." My heart sank. I really couldn't think my way through to a viable solution. No matter how I spun it, it would either be difficult (if not impossible), or expensive beyond what we

could realistically support on a regular basis. "Well I guess it was inevitable," she continued. I turned to face her, not sure what she was referring to. She looked me right in the eyes and repeated herself, "I guess it was inevitable." I wasn't following her train of thought, so I had to ask, "What was?" "That after all these years together I would be training you to be a Lodge Keeper." "Me? You would be willing to teach me how to run the Lodge? You would be comfortable with me hosting Sweat Lodges here for the people?" She replied, "Well, you've been a Pipe Carrier for a few years now. It's really not so surprising. I always knew I would pass along these teachings to you one day. I just never had any idea when. Until a few days ago there wasn't any opportunity—or need. Now there is. This is one more ceremony you can offer to your community here."

That was the beginning. I could not have conceived at the time all the nuances that were involved. Even if someone had laid out the possibilities, they wouldn't have sunk in. I had to experience it to understand.

Scott, Miriam, and I became the Sweat Lodge team at that site for a period of four years, with Miriam being the Land Keeper, Scott being Fire Keeper, and myself as Lodge Keeper. We also had the support and friendship of a woman named Laurie, whom we fondly dubbed the Circle Keeper. She maintained the list of folks who were interested in joining us, and kept them all up-to-date with the activities and ceremonies. At almost every Lodge, particularly in the early years, we were all in attendance.

The building of the lodge and the first sweat was a glorious celebration. We sent out invitations to those who regularly attended our community fires and to the alumni of our annual Vision Quests. Many were not only eager to help, but also interested in participating on a regular basis. Pauline, Scott, and I prepared the site with offerings and prayers. When appropriate, the others joined in to help build, tie, and cover the lodge. Scott tended the fire.

It was during our second Lodge on the site, and the first where Pauline was not present to guide us, that we truly began our initiation into understanding what was involved. It happened during the first round. I was sitting at the back of the lodge facing the doorway. Everyone else had entered. Seven red-hot stones, referred to as Grandfathers, had been taken out of the fire and brought into the lodge. Scott, having placed the final Grandfather in the center pit, was taking a few moments to complete his tasks outside before he came into the lodge himself. As I was watching and waiting for him to enter, before the door was even closed to begin that round, I had a vision. I saw the entire land area in front of us engulfed in flames, reaching all the way to the door of the lodge. Now, if you have ever been in a sweat lodge you will know that the fire built to heat the Grandfather stones is necessarily large and blazing, but this isn't what I saw in the vision. This was FIRE, in the way the word is used to call the alarm and alert everyone to danger. Because just a moment before all had been normal, I blinked several times, trying to focus. Whatever I did to adjust my vision, the fire was still there. I was confused. My eyes were telling me one thing but my brain was registering another. Scott was just outside. If there was indeed a fire he would be standing right in the middle of it. Seconds later he entered the lodge and closed the door. I had to convince myself that the fire wasn't real. Looking around me, I could tell that to everyone else, all was proceeding normally.

It wasn't until hours later when the Lodge was complete, people had returned to the city, and Scott, Laurie and I were still sitting by the dying flames of the fire, that I shared my vision. To my amazement, both of them had something similar happen. In the first round of the Lodge Laurie found herself remembering a fire that had broken out in the home of her childhood and how frightening it had been. This was a memory that had not surfaced in several decades.

Looking back on it now, Spirit was being very kind. One of us could be ignored, but three? Even novices had to take that seriously. We arranged with Miriam to return to the site the following week, when all was quiet. We held an impromptu ceremony, culminating in each of us sitting with Grandfather Fire and silently asking why we had received the warning. Then we waited for the answer. One by one, we heard the same message, but in different ways. The spirits of the land were not pleased with the set-up of the fire pit area. While we had followed the protocol of the traditional ways, this particular piece of land wanted more. We were shown an area surrounding the fire pit that was a circle of coloured gravel edged with large stones. The land wanted more than to be functional, it wanted to be

beautiful. Beyond that, taking the extra steps would also ensure our safety, the land's safety, and the safety of all who attended. This was FIRE. There would be no argument or hesitation. We now knew what needed to be done and put the steps into place to follow our guidance. It took many months to bring it to completion, but we did our best, accepting that changes in the physical world take time. We received no further signs. The Lodges we held for the people were wonderful. We were growing together as a community and there was such a feeling of joy as we gathered together in the womb of Mother Earth (the lodge) and offered our prayers to Creator.

✶ ✶ ✶ ✶ ✶ ✶ ✶

Many times over the ensuing years I would have the opportunity to build sweat lodges, host Sweat Lodge ceremonies, and take lodges down. It was an incredible learning experience and Scott and I grew much closer in the process, as he continued to offer his skills and gifts as Fire Keeper. Not only did we have some crazy adventures along the way, we really began to understand the factors, both physical and spiritual, that were needed to support a lodge on a given tract of land.

To host a Sweat Lodge, which is a sacred ceremony, is a team effort. It is a result of relationship between the land, all the creatures that inhabit it, the weather beings who can literally caress or destroy it, the property owners, and the people who run the Lodge. If the relationship fails in any one of these areas, the Lodge will not be successful. This will become evident on a physical level, and is not limited to the obvious, such as the lodge blowing over in gale force winds, or snow crushing and destroying the frame. It could be animals or insects deciding to nest inside, people getting ill or disoriented while on the site, or strange visions or sensations received by the people attending. These, and more, could appear to reveal the disruption.

During the years we were involved with our original community lodge, I was also invited to build and maintain a lodge on another piece of private land, located a few miles closer to the mountains. I had been introduced to the area when I was asked to offer some restorative healing work there. The nature of the land's wounding was such that I felt it would benefit from traditional ceremony, and the gathering of the spirits would support the improvements that had already begun. I approached Scott and asked if he would be willing to be Fire Keeper. He agreed. Working at a different location with different natural features, animals and nature spirits, we continued to grow and learn. And once our four years at the community site were complete, Scott and I were invited to consider other areas, including ranches and private farms, as possible new locations. We established a protocol that worked well for these visits, both with the landowners and the land itself.

First, there was the initial visit to the site, spending time with the owners explaining what was involved in hosting a Lodge on the physical level. There was also an assessment of the land for wind, sufficient space for both the fire and the lodge, and a certain amount of shelter from trees; not so much that it created a fire hazard and not so open that there was no natural protection. The second visit was for Scott and I to do ceremony on the land. We would bring a portable fire pit and all the accompanying supplies. We would lift the pipe and offer prayers to the land, letting the spirits know why we had come, and then we would sit with them for hours, waiting to hear their response. It was not a matter of whether the land would respond, Nature always responded. It was more a matter of holding the presence of awareness to acknowledge and hear it. This could easily take hours. On the outside it looked very much like Scott and I were simply sitting by an outdoor fire on a beautiful piece of land, while we held our tobacco prayer sticks and made continual offerings through their smoke, but on the inside it was necessary to still the mind, to open the heart, and to sense what could otherwise not be seen or heard. This required a level of listening that few people can attain in our fast paced, mind-oriented times. It took me years of ceremony and dedicated time with Spirit to be able to hold that precious place, to be able to sink down into it and sit inside of it for as long as it took, never losing focus, never chancing a distraction.

On several of those occasions we came to know that the land could not hold the lodge in the sacred manner that was being asked of it. The land and the nature spirits had been compromised. In one case we came to understand that while the land and its creatures were willing, it would take a minimum of one year of clearing away the negativity and healing the wounds to bring it back to its full potential. Then it would willingly and joyfully hold the

lodge for us. Unfortunately, that location was over an hour's drive outside the city. Scott and I could not commit to the work required and did not have the support of the land owners. Understandably, it was difficult for them to hear that their land was not healthy enough spiritually to be able to hold the sweat lodge in a sacred way. But knowing in our hearts that if we moved forward anyway it would fail the people in some way, we could not agree to participate. The relationship we were trying to build was just that—a relationship—and without an agreement on both sides, it was best left alone.

Chapter Sixteen

Chronic Nausea

A patient trapped in the pain and shock of a great loss . . .

ennifer did not strike me as the type of person who would normally see
a practitioner like myself. She was very comfortable and grounded in
the 'rational' world, and did not speak of any particular interest in the
extraordinary, the invisible, or the mystical.

Unfortunately, over the past year or so she had developed a slight medical
condition that defied understanding and had no cure—a chronic case of
nausea and vomiting. It was actually a co-worker who suggested she come
to see me, and passed along my contact information. Jennifer was desperate
and her co-worker assured her that while my methods might be unorthodox,
I was not scary to be around. She had nothing to lose.

When she first started recounting her story she was quite certain when
it all started, she even offered a date, but as we continued talking it became
clear that the past year had been a stress-filled one and the beginnings of
the nausea, vomiting, the constant unease and anxiety, and the diarrhea,
had all blurred in her mind. Her main complaint, and the reason she came,
was that every day she felt nauseous. She had felt it day-in and day-out
for at least the past five months. It started about 4:30 a.m. and continued
through to dinner time. It was severe enough that she was rarely able to

eat breakfast or lunch, and was surviving on dinner alone. By bedtime it had usually subsided enough that she could feel almost comfortable, for a couple of hours. The next morning the cycle would return.

Previous to this she had always been healthy, very healthy in fact. She experienced an occasional cold or flu, would visit the doctor once a year for a checkup, and had only taken prescription medications two or three times over the past twenty years. She had consulted her doctor about the problem and been given medication, which helped when she was actively vomiting but did nothing for the nausea itself. And it was the nausea that was driving her crazy. It may sound like a small thing, but it was compromising her ability to lead a normal life. She wanted it to stop.

As we continued to talk, she shared that a year earlier she had been laid off from her job. This was difficult as she had only been able to find part-time work since. Six months later she had a miscarriage. It was her first pregnancy and she was devastated. She was only seven weeks pregnant and did not need to be hospitalized, but described it as, "the hardest thing I have ever gone through."

I had a sense of what the trouble was. Jennifer's body was locked in a state of trauma from the recent stresses, particularly the miscarriage. In a sense, it had 'lost its way' and couldn't regain its composure. I knew if I could remove the residual effects of the trauma, the symptoms would disappear and her body would be able to return to normal functioning.

The treatment I gave her took about twenty minutes to complete. I used a plant spirit medicine as an extraction tool. It was gentle, pain free, non-invasive, and she remained comfortable the entire time. When she left, I suspect she was surprised that the treatment was over, as I hadn't appeared to 'do' anything except place my hands on her body from time to time, alternating with taking her meridian pulses at the wrists.[13] But if that was the case, she was too polite to say. I advised her that it could take up to 72 hours to feel the full effects of the treatment, and that every person responded differently. If the treatment worked, she would not need to return. She would be well again.

---

[13] Meridian Pulse Diagnosis is a feature of Classical Chinese Medicine

I didn't hear from Jennifer for several months and often wondered how
she was doing. Then I received this email:

> It has been over two months since I was there to see you and
> I am so, so sorry it has taken me so long to let you know how I
> am doing! I feel great. I had a couple of days of still feeling slightly
> sick but after that I was 100% again! It feels so good and I am
> forever indebted to you. Thank you for all your help.

— — — — — — —

During my teenage years, when I was being bullied or teased at school,
my parents would often say, "Sticks and stones can break your bones but
names can never hurt you." As if hearing that was going to make it all
better! Besides, they were wrong. It did hurt. Each and every one of us has
been in a situation where we have been scolded, violated, abused, frightened, or traumatized in some form. And we all know that sometimes the
inner feeling—the sting—doesn't go away. This human experience covers
a wide range of situations, everything from an argument with a spouse to
post-traumatic stress syndrome. Most of our invisible bruises mend themselves readily, particularly if we are fortunate enough to live in a situation
where we have an abundance of love and support. The invisible, energetic
residue of the trauma slowly dissolves and is released from the body/being.
However, if the shock is too great or occurs more frequently than we are
able to recover from, it can get trapped inside.

To a medicine person (and shamanic practitioner) this is not at all mys-
terious or surprising. There are many examples of the invisible being just
as real as the visible. Depression is invisible, but no less devastating than
an external injury. A medicine person specializes in the invisible, through
the spirit relationships they hold, and then it's really just a matter of using
different skills than what is required in the physical realm. It makes sense
to me that an invisible wound could be healed by an invisible medicine. It is
able to meet the need for healing on the same level that the problem exists.
How would a physical agent be able to do any better?

To heal the residual effects of a trauma that are locked inside a person, you just have to go inside, find them, and clear them out. It's no different than when your apartment starts to smell because you haven't taken out the garbage. If you continue to let it sit there, the smell will remain. And if you can figure out a way to take it out to the curb, the problem will be solved.

Chapter Seventeen

George the Elder

A significant bump in the road almost threw me off course, but the Mountain saved me.

Heeding the Call had only been out for a short time when I received a phone call from a man who introduced himself as George and said he was a native Elder. He told me that he had been reintroduced to the traditional ways in the northern United States and had been part of that culture for fourteen years now. He explained that as an Elder he did not give out his last name, but went simply by George. Without any prompting on my part he went on to describe some of his background and practices. He was 100% native. He participated in the Sundance ceremony every year. He ran a Sweat Lodge on one of the local reservations every one to two weeks and welcomed people of all races. He had a quiet, soft-spoken voice and sounded gentle. He told me he was reading my book and wanted to talk with me. He asked if we could meet for coffee sometime. I said that yes I would like that, and inquired if I could invite my spiritual brother and Fire Keeper, Scott, to join us. He agreed, confirmed with me that I would need to bring him an offering of tobacco,[14] and asked that I

---

[14] As tobacco is considered a sacred and powerful plant by the native people, it is traditional to present an offering of tobacco when meeting with an Elder as a sign of acknowledgement of their leadership and wisdom.

call him back when I could arrange a time. As I hung up the phone I was intrigued. A native Elder was reading my book and wanted to talk with me! He sounded so nice.

It was only a few weeks later that Scott and I met with George at a small, out of the way coffee shop. I gave him the tobacco, quite unceremonially in those surroundings, and we each got a coffee and sat down. George spoke very quietly, so much so that it was hard to hear him at times. He directed all his attention toward me, barely acknowledging Scott's presence, and asked me question after question about how I ran the Sweat Lodge. He asked about the number of rocks I used, how many buckets of water, did I sing to the four directions. After each answer he didn't hesitate to tell me that I was doing it wrong! When he mentioned that there was a specific way to gather the saplings that were used to brush off the hot stones before they were placed in the lodge, I decided it was time to defend myself a little. I shared with him that I had worked with plants and plant medicines in a spiritual way for many years and was well aware of how to pick them in a sacred manner. He responded coldly by saying, "Women can't gather saplings for a lodge, that's a man's job." Then he asked me if there was a mound in front of the lodge. I said yes and he asked me where the dirt came from. When I told him he smiled and said, "Well you got one thing right."

Throughout the conversation I was careful and consistent in letting him know that I was following the protocols of my own teacher, Fishwoman, which were clearly different from his. He didn't seem much interested in talking about Pauline. He kept referring to her as, "the Johnson woman." It was then he delivered the most disturbing blow. He said, "Women shouldn't run a Sweat Lodge, women don't carry medicines, only men do."

I wasn't entirely sure what the purpose for the meeting had been but I'd had enough. It appeared he only wanted to put me down and make me feel like I knew nothing. It was time to go. As we said our good-byes I was surprised that he asked Scott and I if we would smoke the pipe with him and attend one of his Lodges sometime. Politely we said yes, he gave me a hug and we parted ways. Silently I was grateful that the meeting was over and I could put it behind me.

The next day he phoned and said, "So, how do you think it went yesterday?" I was surprised to hear from him but was honest in my reply. I said that it didn't feel very good to be told that I was doing everything wrong. I reminded him that I was following closely in the footsteps of my own teacher and it was important to respect her ways, and to honour the lineage and ancestry that her teachings had come from. I made a point of thanking him for meeting with me. I wanted to be polite. Then I remembered that at one point yesterday, near the close of the meeting, he had actually offered to teach me, given that I was doing everything incorrectly. At the time, in the midst of all the pummelling I was taking, I hadn't acknowledged it. Now with a little distance I could see more clearly. I recognized that it was an honour to be offered this when he had only just met me, so I tried to convey my appreciation as best I could yet be very careful to let him know that I wasn't interested. Soon after, he abruptly said he had to go but we could talk more later. I asked if he thought there was more we needed to discuss. I knew I was no longer willing to answer his questions or share more of my teachings from Pauline—there didn't seem much point. He responded by saying in a steely voice, "We have barely even started!"

I felt the weight of those words fall all the way from my ears to my toes. In that instant I realized I had inadvertently gotten in over my head. There was something ominous about all this. A vague, uneasy fear started to surface. I wondered if he would let this go, let me go. I considered the possibility that I was in the earliest stages of being stalked. I decided to journey to the Mountain for advice and guidance.

I see Grandmother Mountain gathering wood for the fire. Carrying the logs, she brings them into the circle. The mood is very gentle and quiet at the viewpoint today. She places the logs carefully into the fire. They have not been split in any way. I somehow know they have been selected for their size. The bark has been removed. As the logs are placed the feel of the circle changes. We four Mountain Spirit Beings become one. The fire brings us together. Fire has the ability to do that—to create a circle. Grandmother sits in the North.

In my mind I feel I am so much a student of these wise teachers, these special beings, yet as my spirit joins them in the circle, I sense that I make it complete. I am complete. My spirit feels whole here.

I ask about George the Elder. As I say his name into the circle, in the presence of the fire, the feel of the space around us changes. I come to know that he has doubts, even fears. He has concerns about me and what I am doing, how I am holding within me and for my people what he holds so dearly to his heart. He feels I have the ability to compromise what he believes in. He does not easily accept changes to the ways of his tradition and his culture. He sees me as a threat in that way, a seed that could sprout and grow and create change. He does not want this to happen. There are so many threats to his way of life, in these times and in this cultural milieu.

He is not comfortable with the type of change I represent. This is for me to know and understand. I do not follow his ways. He is not my Teacher. I will be gentle but firm in what I know to be real and true. I will hold strongly inside the circle I am with now. I need to remember that I am not the one who decides upon change. That is for a much greater power than myself. I am not even one to question change and my possible role in it, or the ripple effects of it. I am here to walk the path with truth, humility and integrity. That is all I can do.

I had told George that I would be away from the time of the Winter Solstice to January 14th. He called me on the afternoon of the 14th. I didn't want to talk to him. I even considered ignoring the message but my conscience got the best of me and I returned the call a couple of days later. As I was now on my guard, I took notes while we spoke:

"George, what is the reason for us to meet again?"

"This culture and this tradition, it's different. You got into it and that's why I want to talk. My partner, he comes to the Sweat Lodge all the time. He approached me once as I was chopping wood. He is a very humble guy and we started talking and he asked me about the Sweat Lodge and I explained a little bit to him. He can explain some of these ways to you. I also want to invite that fellow—Scott."

"Do you think that I'm offending you?"

"A little bit. That's why I want my partner to see you and explain about my tradition. He can explain it to you and Scott and have a meeting with you before you come to the Sweat Lodge."

I shared with him that I had spoken with Pauline since our last talk and she had advised me not to meet with him again. (What I didn't tell him was that she suspected he had been raised in a residential school, to have the strong opinions about women that he did. She reassured me that even though I was white, I didn't have anything I needed to apologize for. She suggested I stand strong with him.) I also told him that she felt he didn't follow the correct protocols. He wanted to meet with me and ask all kinds of questions about our sacred ceremony, the Sweat Lodge, but he never offered me tobacco. When George heard this, he responded by mocking me and laughing out loud.

"You have to dance [Sundance] what you want to accomplish. You haven't danced so I won't offer you tobacco." He then shared that at one time he got wind of a fellow outside Calgary who was running a Sweat Lodge. "We asked if anyone taught him about our culture and our traditions. He said no so we had to shut down his lodge."

He continued, "If you have a dream, you go to an Elder and they will teach you. Fish and Wildlife won't give an eagle feather to a white person. You have to be native, or a dancer. In our tradition if you want to be a warrior you have to dance. If you want to be an Elder you have to dance for eight years while your pipe gets stronger. Then, referring to Pauline, "How do I know she's doing the true cultural tradition? I read the Bible. It says Christ is the man of everything. The Bible says a woman has to be silent. I don't believe in a woman taking a man's job. There is no woman that can run anything like a man does. They can teach, a woman can be a school teacher, but she can't run anything."

I had a sinking feeling in the pit of my stomach. I tell him that I notice he doesn't refer to Pauline by her first name, yet he made it clear that is the protocol he follows when referring to Elders. I shared that Pauline was offended by the way he spoke about her to me, and that we considered it disrespectful.

"You tell that Pauline (now he was willing to use her first name) that she can come and see the way we do it. She can come to our sweat and our Sundance."

I couldn't make sense of it. On the one hand he fully acknowledged and stated that "If you have a dream you go to an Elder and they will teach you." That's what I did. I hadn't been running around trying to 'play native' and performing their ceremonies on a whim. I had done what the traditional ways suggest—thanks to the wisdom and guidance I received from Eliot. Yet it was not only me he didn't accept. It was Pauline too! When I think of all the Sweat Lodges she runs, the community work in downtown Vancouver with addicts and the homeless, the presentations and teachings she is asked to give, how could anyone refute her?

I suggested that if he had anything to say to Pauline, he should contact her directly instead of going through me. Then I gave him her phone number. Given how attentive he was to me, I suspected he would follow through right away. Sure enough, a couple of hours later she called to tell me what had transpired. She had been quite abrupt with him, saying things like, "Why should I come to your Sweat Lodge? I don't even know you." When he talked to her about 'the way it works' and how much he had Sundanced she responded that she had Sundanced for 20 years! She shared that she received her pipe through her ancestral lineage, not because she was a dancer. All of her medicines were handed down to her from her parents and grandparents. When he talked about me, she told him that she had adopted me and was my Teacher. She didn't go into the conversation word for word, but did tell me that at one point George said to her, "White people annihilated us and they shouldn't be running Lodges."

The next day I saw on call-display that George was trying to reach me. I called him back a few minutes later and took the opportunity to ask, "So, how did it go last night with Pauline?"

"She didn't give me a chance to talk. Every time I was going to say something she interrupted me. She's a Pow Wow dancer not a Sundancer.[15] The Sundance is for the people, they get together and dance for the people. In

[15] A person can be both a Pow Wow dancer and a Sundancer. There are different styles of Sundance for different Nations. Pauline did not attend the same style of Sundance as George so he refused to acknowledge it.

the ceremonial Sundance they fast for four days and nights. When you do a Sundance you get pierced. In my arms—I danced with a buffalo skull in my arms. They pierced my arms and pulled me up into a tree. It was pretty high. You get your pipe from Tree and Stone, from Mother Earth. You have to respect your pipe. That's the way we learn. It wasn't easy. They tied me up for four days. I passed out. I didn't know but they came and took me down and took me into the lodge and I got better."

I didn't know much about traditional native ceremonies, other than what Pauline had taught me, but a few things were starting to make sense. Now I understood why George was continually going down to the U.S. and why his people didn't acknowledge any other kind of Sundance. He had shared enough for me to confirm that he had been raised in a residential school. He had returned to the traditional ways as an adult fourteen years ago, learning from a Nation that was not his own. He looked down upon Pauline and wouldn't acknowledge her, yet she was raised in these ways. She was never taken from her home or her family. She grew up hunting and trapping and fishing. She learned from an early age to gather the medicines and attend the ceremonies. She was called to sit at the feet of the Elders so they could teach her. It was ironic that she had lived and been raised in a traditional life and was now being judged as inauthentic by someone who was quoting the Bible!

Over the next few months the phone conversations continued. He didn't have a choice I guess, because I was not willing to meet with him again. For me, it was important to try to resolve this in a good way, to find a common ground where we could accept each other, even if we didn't agree. The point I kept trying to make was that while I understood now that I had offended him, and some of the other Elders, it was never my intention to offend. I was simply walking the path that Creator had placed before me. I was learning from a traditional Cree Elder, whether he accepted her as one or not.

It was then that he started to threaten me. He made comments about our community Sweat Lodges with details he could have only known if he or someone else was close by, watching. And it was then I realized a small detail that had eluded me before. When he first called he said he'd been reading my book. At our first meeting, almost all of his questions were about the sweat lodge and my role as Lodge Keeper. During the timeframe of the stories in that book, I had not yet received the gift of being Lodge Keeper. He knew details about the lodge I had never mentioned. That's when I discovered he had someone spying on me right from the very beginning.

Now he was gearing up for a take-down. I wasn't conforming to his ways. I wasn't towing the line. He started shouting at me during our conversations (which I believe was uncharacteristic for him), calling me a witch. He said he would take down the lodge. He told me that he knew how to hurt me spiritually, how to send me dark medicine, so I'd never do this work again. Then finally, he threatened to sue me. By this time I had started recording our conversations. Our community sweat lodge was on private property. He had no right to do what he was doing. He had no right to trespass on the land to destroy the lodge.

All of this had reached a height of conflict and tension that I had never imagined possible, particularly since I was trying so hard to avoid that very thing. I was lost. The situation seemed unresolvable. I didn't know what to do. I also couldn't take the chance of risking the safety of those who attended our Lodge. From a place of distress, tinged with sadness, I reached out to the Mountain again and asked, "Have I done something wrong?"

"My child, you, your work, and your gifts have been brought to the attention of many people. There will be curious people and jealous people at your feet. The ripple effects of those who would psychically interfere with you can be felt far away. To counteract those forces takes time and effort, and calling upon your spirit relationships. What you must do is maintain an aura of tranquility and integrity around you. You must see ahead to avoid conflicts. Do not engage others that you do not trust to know you and respect you as you understand and know yourself.

"Sitting in stillness with us, lifting your pipe with us on a regular basis, will help us to help you.

"People are both drawn to and afraid of power. Those who look up to the powerful will test that power. They will not consider you as a weak human with needs of kindness and compassion. They will see you as someone who can handle it. They will push you, test you, demand

from you, and try to drain you. You are starting to be aware of the eyes that are watching you. You must accept that some will be happy for you to fail. This weakens you and strengthens them. You must compose yourself as you do with your patients. Do not take credit for their healing and do not take it personally if they perceive that you have failed them.

"If you hold on to these struggles they will settle inside you and attract more. You must let them flow through you, as the river flows over and around and underneath the damns and the obstacles, or goes over onto the land. Then you will stay clean and clear. The water that slides over the rocks in the creek bed is cleansed and we are the rock that will cleanse and heal you, if you continue to flow."

It's hard to describe in words the comfort this journey and its teachings gave me. I got it. I understood my part. For the next three days I sat with the Mountain. I allowed it to be the rock that cleansed me. I did my part to work on 'being flow'. On the final day of this practice, George called again.

"I just returned from the U.S. I wanted to talk to the Chief down there about you. I wanted to sit and lift the pipe with him and tell him what was happening, what you were doing to us. I asked for his blessing before I took the final steps. I told him everything. At the end he looked up at me and said only four words, "Leave the woman alone."

I couldn't believe my ears. It was over, finally over. The Mountain had shifted it, transformed it, and now it was gone. The Mountain was the rock that could cleanse and heal. How did I become so lucky? And why had it taken me so long to ask for help?

A few months passed and I agreed to meet George the Elder for coffee one more time. When he told me what his Chief had said about leaving me alone, whatever conflict there had been between us instantly dissolved. A few more times George had called to talk. Increasingly I felt sorry for him. I came to understand that he had been 'charged' with being the liaison between me and his group. At first he was proud to be chosen and he took the task to heart, asking me to meet with him, finding out whatever he could about what I was doing and the way I was doing it. In turn he would report back to them. Over time, as things came to a head and I was not backing down, he started stepping up the threats, with their encouragement. At one point however, without him knowing, they had passed along a lie, which he in turn passed along to me. I recognized it immediately and called him on it. At the time he denied it, venomously, but it served to undermine his honour. He also shared with me the name of the man who had been watching me. Again their relationship had started out strong, but in the end, the man reneged on an agreement they held between them, betraying George. All around him I saw things crumble and fall. He had never been a violent man. He was truly as gentle as he presented himself in our first encounter. But he got caught up in defending his rights and freedoms against the enemy—me.

On our last visit I brought him gifts, which included several pouches of tobacco and a fine blanket. It quickly became clear that we no longer had anything to talk about.

Chapter Eighteen

Thoughts

Relationships take time and effort. I realize I haven't visited with Bear for a while . . .

One of my totem animals and Teachers is Bear, and I often look to him/her for support, particularly when I am feeling down, stressed, or overwhelmed. On this particular morning I feel quite fine, though somewhat thoughtful. I realize how much I would enjoy a visit with Bear—it's been a while since we spent some time together, so I enter into a journey:

> *Eagle arrives and somehow helps me to get there today. As the scene comes into focus, I see Bear ambling around the fire to the left, to meet up with me. There is also a tipi on my right. As Bear gets close, he raises his paw as if to give me a giant swat, then lowers his arm, showing me he was only joking. Then he gives me a big bear hug and somehow I know he is telling me he loves me. I have never felt that before.*
>
> *We sit together by the fire, Bear on my left. Bear has a long stick and is poking around in the coals. I notice he is turning over a fish, cooking it. I look at him. Telepathically I know he is thinking, "Well I prefer mine raw but I'm assuming you want yours cooked!" I smile. He says, "I gotta take care of you."*
>
> *We continue our silent discussion.*

Jaki, "Bear, will you help me be strong?"
Bear, "Yup"
Jaki, (Almost joking) "Will you help me be flexible?"
Bear, "Yup."

Bear notes my surprise, and adds, "Flexibility is a function of strength." I try to imagine Bear doing yoga poses, which is what I want to do. Again, he knows my thoughts and states, "Your body is designed to move in many more ways than mine!"

I ponder this for a while then ask, in a very casual tone, "Why haven't I been taking better care of myself lately?"

I had expected that our easy banter would continue but this last sentence changed Bear's tone entirely and he growled out, "Stop that thought! Stop it right now if you ever want my help again. Otherwise, don't bother coming back!"

I freeze in shock and panic. What had I done? What had I said that warranted such a stern response? I only asked a simple question. After a few minutes, when I had regained my composure, I realized I was judging myself, which revealed that I had been lingering in self-deprecating thoughts. My relationship to Bear meant so much to me. I had inadvertently brought my negative mind-chatter into the journey. It hadn't occurred to me what a terrible thing that was.

*I try to feel my way to a resolution but in the process realize how often I think that way, how critical I am of myself. I remind myself that my intentions are good, that I am only trying to keep myself on track and notice when I lose footing. From now on, I must be much more careful with the thoughts that I think. I had no idea that thoughts were so powerful an influence that I couldn't afford to hold **any** that didn't serve me in some way. I needed to get back to Bear. He was probably waiting.*

Jaki, "O.K. I think I understand. I will try to eliminate that thought, and others like it, from my mind. Any suggestions as to what I can replace it with?"

Bear, "I'm on the merry, happy road to health."
We both laugh and the journey is complete.

- - - - - - -

Thoughts

This short and simple journey has stayed with me and I often share the teaching with my students. We all know, or have heard, how our thoughts can affect us, and how beneficial it is—both for ourselves and others—to stay considerate and positive. What a powerful way to receive that message—to be stopped dead in my tracks and given an ultimatum! It showed me how easily we can overlook the effects of what we are creating for ourselves.

I have observed this type of stern warning as a trend in my teachings from Spirit. As soon as I take a step in the wrong direction, they come forward, alerting me to my actions, warning me of the risks. Their position is to bring these matters to my attention while they are still small and manageable. While their sounding of the alarm can be shocking to experience at times, as I have barely stepped off course, it shows their love and attention toward me. It shows how important it is to stay aware and pay attention to what is actually happening.

Chapter Nineteen

A Healing Gift From the Little People

I am reminded to trust the wisdom of the Mountain.
It knows the story that the patients need to hear.

J oanne first came to see me on September 26, 2008. These are some of
the words she used to describe how she was feeling at the time:

> "I've been off work, on disability, for two and a half years. I
> feel rotten. I have chronic back and hip pain. I've been diagnosed
> with depression. My husband left me this past April. It's not a
> fun time."
>
> "I go to a chronic pain center. The first year off work I spent
> $9,000.00. I've tried pretty much everything. I don't have a
> circle of good friends. I feel lonely and isolated."

While noting her medical history I learned that Joanne was taking more
than 20 different medications, including three narcotics for pain, one muscle
relaxant, one for nausea, one for stomach acid reflux, two for depression,
one sleeping pill, and thyroid medication to counteract the effects of the
other drugs. As an added side effect she had lost most of her ability to taste.
She described her diet as containing only seven items—literally—which
were: liquid meal replacement, yogurt, apples, bananas, mandarin oranges,

chocolate, and the occasional bagel.

I saw before me a very lost and unhappy woman. She was unable to move her body smoothly and was in constant pain. Even sitting did not look comfortable. She was quite distraught at the breakup of her marriage, saying that her husband used to be her best friend. She had no idea what had triggered the illness. She remembered being on holidays three years before and waking up with a sore back. She thought it must have been the bed, but it got progressively worse until she was completely unable to live a normal life.

In the first five sessions, I worked to clear and balance her system. I felt a lot of disruption and chaos within her meridians (based on Classical Chinese Medicine) and I wanted to smooth this out as best I could to lay the foundation for some deeper work. During this time she felt a loosening of the grip of depression, cried a lot more than usual—a much needed emotional release—and began to feel more positive. The pain had abated somewhat and she spoke to her pharmacist about reducing some of her medications. In December she received notification that her disability was being terminated as of February 6th the following year. Now that she was single she had no choice but to return to work.

Joanne was progressing well through the treatments but to resume her career in two months! Feeling the way she did, the thought was terrifying. She couldn't imagine being functional by then and this worry further contributed to her stress.

As she sat in the chair of my treatment room, looking completely dejected, I decided it was time to go deeper, that I needed to feel what was happening at a soul level. I asked permission to connect with her and describe what I noticed. I engaged my inner senses and waited to see or feel the messages that surfaced. It wasn't long after, perhaps a minute or two, when a fairytype being appeared. My immediate reaction was to think, "Oh no! How am I going to explain this?" I had no idea how Joanne would react and I didn't want to scare her off. While I had learned a long time ago to honour and trust the messages that came through, this was so unexpected that Joanne and I hadn't discussed the possibility of anything like this. After a few more minutes, very calmly and with a soft voice, I said, "This may

seem like an odd question, but how do you feel about fairies?" "Fairies! I love fairies," she instantly replied. I said a silent prayer of thanks to Creator and continued.

"Well, as I've been sitting here with you, a vision has come to me. These visions are typically metaphorical, and I've found that in sharing them they can really assist with the healing process. Do you feel comfortable if I share it with you?" "Yeah, sure," she replied.

As I turned my attention back to the vision it continued to unfold and I narrated the details to Joanne. "A very small, very beautiful fairy has appeared. She has delicate blue wings and flits about quickly. In her hands is a blue box, you can imagine how tiny it is, and wrapped around it is a yellow bow. The box is a gift for you. It is important that I ask you, seriously, "Are you willing to receive it? If you are, you must declare it out loud." "Yes, I am willing to receive it." said Joanne. The fairy hovered closer and the way the vision presented itself to me changed. I could still see the fairy but I could also see Joanne as she lay on the treatment table. I knew what that meant— she needed to be more involved in the process to receive the healing fully. I continued, "This gift is very special and I need to ask you to try to see what I am seeing so you can work with the vision directly."[16] I described the fairy and the box in as much detail as possible and asked Joanne to allow her own inner images to come forward and flow as the scene progressed. Once she was able to follow, I guided her through our changing roles; Joanne would continue with her inner vision, now narrating to me, and I would simply watch and be on hand to support and help if need be.

She gently took the box from the fairy's hand and began to untie the ribbon. She did this very slowly and carefully. Once the ribbon was off, she needed to lift the lid. At first she hesitated, but when she peered inside she saw a small object that appeared to be made of gold. I couldn't see the object clearly and wasn't surprised. I had come to understand that some things were for me to see and some weren't. In this case, the true nature of the gift was only for Joanne to know. The fairy instructed her to remove

[16] I have found that even people who have no experience engaging their inner sight are able to in this context. I believe it is the strength of the medicine and the influence of the Mountain that makes this possible.

the gift from the box and place it inside her heart, where it was to stay from now on. This took a little while as initially Joanne did not feel her heart was worthy of such a gift. We talked it over and I helped her to understand that this was part of her healing and it was important for her to be well now. In her own way and in her own time she took the golden object and placed it inside her heart. They instantly merged and became one. She described it as a seed that was needed to grow inside her heart and help her to become whole again. Soon afterward, she let go of the vision and simply experienced the subtle shifts and changes inside her physical body. I knew she felt warm and safe on the table, wrapped in the blanket and with the faint glow of the candle nearby. I gave her all the time she needed to stay with what happened and let her know that whenever she felt ready, she could open her eyes and sit up.

Once she did, she looked very peaceful and calm. We talked for a few minutes about what had happened and I shared with her how it certainly wasn't every day that fairies showed up with gifts for my patients—in fact it had never happened before! This experience was unique to her and it was precious. She was to hold the sensations and the memory with her from this point forward. She asked me what this would change and I answered honestly, "I have no way of knowing. You will tell me when I see you next." She left shortly afterward.

I saw Joanne again fourteen days later. As the previous patient left my office, I greeted her in the waiting room and asked her to come in. As she stood up and walked toward me, I couldn't believe the transition. What struck me most was how beautiful she was, and I wondered how I could have missed that before. It took me a few minutes to realize that her appearance hadn't changed at all, but there was something emanating from her, a smoothness, an inner glow, that changed my experience of her. As she walked into my treatment room her gait was even and sure, her steps were solid yet flowing. She walked and sat with no pain. I was astonished and couldn't wait to hear what had happened since I last saw her.

The following are excerpts from the notes I took as she spoke:

"I'm doing awesome. Life has been very good in the last couple

of weeks, really nice. I feel calm, settled. I feel happy in my house. I'm just happy. If I sleep in, it's not a depression thing where I don't want to face the world, it's because I'm so cozy that I'm just enjoying it. My taste buds are coming back so I'm able to enjoy my food a little bit more which is nice. My memory is even better. My mind is clearer. I went for a 4 km walk in the snow yesterday. My back is feeling good. I can't complain about anything. I can't remember feeling this good for a long, long, time. My ex-husband came over for dinner the other night and it went really well. It's been amazing to feel this good."

Joanne was well! She looked great and sounded great. When she spoke, she had such clarity around her failed relationship with her husband and the part that she played in it. She was not afraid to be alone in her home anymore. She was not resentful and bitter at how her life had turned out. There was no longer any pain in her body.

Sometime near the middle of January she returned to work—three weeks earlier than had been asked of her. She told me that she really loved her job as a nurse and was anxious to get back to it. She had always maintained a good relationship with the patients, they liked her, and she enjoyed taking care of them.

I lost touch with Joanne a few months later. I was not concerned. I suspected she had moved forward with her life and no longer needed treatments. I have not heard from her since.

Chapter Twenty

Leave it to the Grandfathers

Sometimes I still feel like such a beginner . . .

I had looked forward to this trip to Vancouver for several months. It was to be the most highly publicized book promotion to date for the release of *Heeding the Call*, with signing events at book stores, an interview on a television talk show, and the teaching of a workshop. I had made some new friends in the area during the time of the manuscript's completion and they were very supportive of the finished product's release. They welcomed me with open arms, offering me a place to stay, inviting people to the book signing, and chauffeuring me through crazy traffic to help keep my schedule. I was indeed grateful. I don't know how I could have navigated all the commitments of those few days without them.

It was also an opportunity to see Fishwoman and spend some time with her. In addition to all the excitement of the book release, my friend Scott had come along, and we were planning a trip to the country to gather some new Grandfather stones for the sweat lodge. Many of the ones we had been using over the years were now cracked or broken and needed replacing. Pauline knew of a particular area near Whistler that was abundant in lava rock, a type of stone that could be heated to red-hot in the fire without exploding, as the river rocks from Alberta tended to do. It was always a treat to be on an adventure with Pauline and Scott and they were equally delighted to share in the excitement surrounding the book events, so our mood was celebratory and joyful and there was much laughter shared between us.

Finding the Grandfather stones, which we anticipated would take an hour or two, took up most of a day. Along with a Vancouver friend, Denis, we loaded into his van and headed toward the highway. As Scott and I had not travelled the road before, there were several places we enjoyed seeing along the way and a few where we wanted to stop and explore further. One particularly intriguing place was a small roadside store with a disproportionately large sign on the roof displaying a single word—Coffee. By late morning a few of us were ready for a second cup, and as the road was sparsely dotted with anything but wild areas we were pleased at the find. When we entered the shop, however, it turned out they didn't actually serve or sell coffee, which had us shaking our heads as we left.

Then there were the crazy directions Pauline was giving us! Honestly I don't think she was used to sitting in the back seat and having to describe the route to someone else. She usually did the trip alone and had certain landmarks she used as a guide—it was an intuitive process. We ended up going hours out of our way, and finding ourselves on a stretch of road so isolated there were no other vehicles, before we realized we were lost. All in all it probably took us six hours to do that round trip, but it was so much fun! And of course Scott and I appreciated the opportunity to collect material for future stories to be told around the fires once we were back in Alberta.

When the day was complete and a new pile of Grandfather stones was weighing down the back of the van, we returned to the big city to take Pauline out to her favourite restaurant. It was a beautiful evening, which we appreciated because the restaurant turned out to be full and there was a line-up outside.

While lingering there in the early evening breeze Pauline asked what my plans were for the following day. I told her about the journey workshop I was teaching. She was surprisingly excited at the news and declared, "Oh I'd love to come!" This took me completely by surprise. Not only had I never imagined she would want to attend, I realized in that moment that I had reservations about it. This was a workshop for people who wanted to experience first-hand some of the methods I was teaching in my book. As

much as I loved Pauline, she had a very strong presence and I knew how effortlessly she could take the people off in a different direction, without any intention to do so. I couldn't afford any distractions. I wanted to ensure that the participants were focused and attentive during the limited time I had with them.

There was the additional complexity that I would be teaching mostly non-native people how to journey and connect with Spirit. This was something that Pauline did naturally. So naturally in fact it was quite likely she would never be able to teach someone else how. She had no method, no technique, no real understanding of a process involved. In this type of workshop her innate ability could actually hinder the others in finding their way. For myself, I had a great deal of difficulty learning how to journey. In fact I still say to my students that in all the years I've been teaching this work, I have never come across another human being who had as much trouble as I did. The long term advantage of this however, is that the struggles, the confusion and the frustration all led me to being an ideal teacher. I understood what was involved and where people could get misled. While Pauline may have been interested to see how I worked with the people, her ease of connection could disarm some of the students, particularly those with a tendency to anxiety when asked to speak in the sharing circle.

I already considered it quite a feat to take a group of 15 people and be able to lead them, in the course of a few hours, from not knowing how to journey to the experience of meeting their totem spirit animals for the first time. With Fishwoman there it would be hard to stay on track and more likely that we wouldn't be able to complete all the required steps.

The truth is, I didn't want her to come. I knew it could change the entire experience for me and possibly hinder what I was trying to accomplish. Without time to consider my thoughts carefully I didn't know how to handle it. How could I pass along those sentiments to Pauline, my Teacher? How could I explain it in a way that didn't sound completely selfish? Pauline enjoyed every opportunity to work with the people, to share teachings and stories. It was during those times that she was really in her element and shining brightly. The more I thought about it the more worried I became. I really couldn't see any way past it. If she came, I knew the workshop would end up being entirely different from what I had planned. But there she was, standing beside me, still smiling to hear that I was teaching a journey workshop the next day, for once in the same city as she was, and she wanted to come along. I should have been honoured.

This was the only moment in time where I would have an opportunity to handle this in person and in relative privacy. In a few minutes Scott and Denis would return; they had only left the line-up to check on how much longer the wait would be. It was either say something now or events would take on their own initiative and mine would be lost in the mix. So I spoke up. I told her that as much as I would personally enjoy her company, I didn't think it would work out well for her to attend.

I backed up my position with reasoning and argument as best I could, but the whole time I was speaking I felt conflicted. My mind had come to believe it was the right thing to do, but once I began, my body told me it wasn't. I was no longer in a relaxed and calm state. Now there was a hint of anxiety in my solar plexus and my voice took on a slightly higher pitch, beyond my conscious control. To experience what was created between us, physically and emotionally when those words were spoken . . . well, it was not the kind of feeling either of us wanted in our relationship. I wish there could have been another way.

So there I was, essentially telling her that she wasn't invited and she wasn't welcome, trying to temper the truth with a soft voice and a gentle tone. She was quiet for a while and then she turned and said one thing, just one sentence that hung in the air and kept repeating itself over and over again between us, like an echo. She said, "You should have let the Grandfathers take care of that."

- - - - - - -

On that evening and in that moment I only partially understood. Over the years since I have come to understand it well and consider it one of her most beautiful teachings.

What it spoke to was how differently we lived in the world. I had found myself in a situation that wasn't going *my* way. I felt I needed to take control, to turn it around, even if there was a cost involved. Pauline saw it completely

differently. If she had found herself in a delicate situation that could possibly harm a relationship, then she would leave it to the Grandfathers, leave it to Spirit. She would pray and advise the Grandfathers that they needed to take care of this one, that there wasn't a way for her to manage it gracefully, and then she would let it go, completely trusting that it would be taken care of. That's what she was telling me. That's what she was teaching me. We didn't have to have that difficult conversation. She didn't need to return home that night feeling like she'd been evaluated and deemed unworthy of attending the workshop. I just needed to give it to the Grandfathers and trust they would take care of it. Whatever happened after that, it was in their hands.

Pauline might wake up the next morning and not feel like attending. Maybe she would decide that after our long day together she just wanted to stay home and spend time with the great-grandkids. Really, anything could happen. If she ended up attending and the workshop went differently than planned, I would simply accept. It was entirely possible that something beautiful and unexpected could happen, that indeed an opening had been created by the very fact that it wasn't following my plan.

A series of events had led to the possibility that Pauline might attend. If I had a problem with that it was better to take it to the Grandfathers and ask for their help than it was to create an uncomfortable situation that could potentially place a wedge in our relationship. I realized in that moment that I didn't trust Spirit the way she did. I wanted to be in control of my life. She was clear that the control was never hers. It was in the hands of Creator.

- - - - - - -

There are times when Pauline and I are together that I record her teachings. After all these years, she still surprises me with stories I have never heard, and as a writer, it feels important that I take the opportunity to document them. The following is an excerpt from one of those sessions, where I recorded her speaking about the Grandmothers and Grandfathers, the way she uses those terms, and how she teaches others to do so:

> In our spiritual way of life, we can't give enough acknowledgement to all the things that give us help. When a tree is cut down

and we use it for wood, we use it for a fire, or for furniture, we always give thanks to that tree, for giving up its spirit for us to have our material things here on earth. Many Elders will say that we are related to everything on earth. Some people think that when we ask them to pray to the Grandmothers and Grandfathers that it is their biological ancestors we are talking about. We do acknowledge our Grandmothers and Grandfathers in our lineage, we put them in a place of respect and love. But the Grandmothers and Grandfathers are also everything here on earth. As I was growing up, I was always told that all of these things that were here before me, that they are all Grandmothers and Grandfathers to me: Grandfather sun, Grandmother moon, Grandfather stars, the mountains. They are the old, old ones. They are in essence my Elders, my Teachers.

We recognize all things in life and that all things have life, and so that is why we call them beings. We are human beings, so they are plant beings, rooted beings, sky beings and thunder beings. We are human beings on this planet and we are the two-legged, but everything out there—we acknowledge that they are part of us, part of our life, part of who we are, and we are part of them.

As you become closer to yourself and understanding all the beings that are here and acknowledging them, you will find that your life is quite a powerful road to walk. That you acknowledge all things on earth, and that they, through time, in dream state or through vision state, will come to you and acknowledge you in a spiritual way. That's unknown to most people, but to the aboriginal people, that's what happens when we go out on a Vision Quest, all of these beings come forth and acknowledge how we respect them, the Grandmothers and the Grandfathers.

I was told that, part of when we say Grandmothers and Grandfathers, is to acknowledge that there is a hierarchy in our system. First we have the Creator that sits above us all, but the Creator can't be everywhere all the time, so he sends his helpers, all of

the Grandmothers and Grandfathers that sit below him. It is
like a lineage from his arm. He gives each one a gift, one dealing
with happiness, one with pain, one dealing with great mysteries. Think of all of the prayers that you have, that is how many
Grandmothers and Grandfathers we have that help us here on
earth. Then we have us. Each human being has a different spirit
keeper, a spirit guide. These spirit guides are sent to you that
way. It is the Creator giving the gifts to the ancestors that sit
below him, and they send the gifts down to you.

Chapter Twenty-One

Talk to the Animals

The Mountain reveals the stories of the four-leggeds too . . .

One of the joys of being able to communicate spirit-to-spirit lies in working with animals. There can be much misunderstanding between domesticated animals and their owners, sometimes leading to years of behavioural problems and conflicts, if not illness. In my experience most animals welcome the opportunity to communicate one-on-one; it's a great relief for them to find someone who 'speaks their language'. The animals I have worked with the most: cats, dogs, and horses, do well with images as the basic form of communication, as they experience their normal day-to-day world in a similar way. Animals are a pleasure to work with, they are typically straightforward, willing to accept help, and afterward, never look back. By comparison, humans are far more complex. We have such strong ideas and belief systems, often resist what's good for us—at least for a while—and can be downright stubborn when it comes to asking for help. The rich dialogue that can be held between humans and animals is beyond the scope of this book[17] but sometimes the patients that show up

---

[17] For those interested in learning more of the rich and varied stories that animals have shared, I recommend Marilyn Geddes' book, *Ask the Very Beasts: Words of Wisdom and Comfort from Unexpected Sources*. Marilyn is a personal friend of mine and can be reached at: marilyngeddes@gmail.com

in the waiting room, or arrange for a house call, have four legs, and I have no intention of turning them away. One of those animals was Hera the dog.

- - - - - - -

Hera and the New House

The following is an email excerpt I received from a student of mine, Claire:

> I was wondering if you could advise us. When we moved into our new home, Hera was very calm and took up a spot near the front window. She seemed contented in the yard too, less stressed and less barking than our old place. We thought maybe she was doing well enough to be left loose while we are away from the house, with all the room doors closed, as this place doesn't have a basement door. She was fine for the first two weeks. However, in the last week she started having diarrhea in the basement on the carpet. Today I put her in the laundry room with a waist high gate at the entrance and when I got home found that she had jumped out, messed on the floor, and then jumped back into the laundry room. Would you be able to ask her what is going on? I seem to remember you saying you can do it from a distance. Your wisdom would be much appreciated!

I had worked with Hera before so I was quite comfortable checking in with her from a distance. Reading the notes below, much of it sounds like a 'conversation' but the communication was initially conveyed to me through images, feelings, and thoughts. I translated them into common language as best I could, so I could share our intimate encounter with Claire.

> Hera advises: "I like the new window in the main room. There is more space for me here. I'm not so close to the furniture all the time. That's nice. But the stairs and the basement give me the creeps! You can feel it before you even land at the bottom. There is an old woman there, a ghost. She talks weird—like

she's from the old country. She's not mean but she gets her face real close to me and just stares and stares. I *really* don't like having her around.

Most of the rest is good. I feel unsettled through. I don't feel like it's MY home, just theirs. Most of the time everything is OK but sometimes I feel really uncomfortable inside."

I ask Hera if there's anything we can do to help her feel better.

"If you could fix things in the basement so the old lady doesn't bother me! Also, I get restless in the winter. I want more smells to expand my world a little bit. Outside it smells like cars and not much else. Maybe leave a few things that smell like me around the house—so I get the message I belong."

Then I see Hera looking at windows, entrances and exits, evaluating the 'flow' through the house, the flow of light and the ways to walk through from one entrance to another. She doesn't like the set-up. I get the impression she'd like at least one window in each direction, so there are no 'blind' spots to the outside. I also sense a hint of edginess, which is part of her inherent nature. She has a low threshold for disturbance and change.

The new home that Hera had moved into with her pet-parents, Claire and Evan, was actually an older home, probably about 50-60 years, in a well-established neighbourhood. One of the reasons Claire was so confused about Hera was that she seemed to enjoy the larger home, and defecating indoors was very unusual behaviour for her. It was fascinating to me that Hera wasted no time in showing me what had been going on. Every day after Claire and Evan left for work, and Hera was in the home alone, the ghost would appear. Registering Hera's repulsion to this strange sight was akin to hearing her say, "That ghost scares the s _ _ _ out of me!" And essentially that's what happened. Hera showed me the face of the ghost. It was an elderly woman who did not appear threatening but definitely made a daily habit of getting extremely close to Hera and staring intently into her eyes. Hera found it so unnerving that she would release control of her bowels each time.

So it was actually Hera that informed Claire, Evan, and I that their new home was haunted! Claire mentioned later that she had sensed a heaviness in that part of the house but had not suspected a ghost. Once this fact had come to the surface, Claire expressed an interest in giving some 'ghost-busting' a try, and asked if I would guide her through it. I agreed—but that's another story. As of the next day Hera was back to normal, and no more messy basement for Claire and Evan to return home to.

Hera and the Couch

It was about a year later that I received a phone call from Claire, advising me that Hera had started urinating on the couch in the living room. As this was quite distressing she asked if I could stop by in the near future to find out why. I went to their home and spent the first few minutes chatting and giving Hera the chance to get used to my presence. When she had settled down from receiving me as a visitor I reached out to create a physical connection with her. I knew that Hera would be 'happy to talk' so I went for the heart of the matter right away. After a few shared images, back and forth, in the way of question and answer, I showed Hera an internally created image of the couch and she immediately showed me an image in return.

Before I share her response, let me provide a little bit more background. Hera was still a young dog and everyone who knew her was aware of her sensitive nature. She had been adopted by Claire and Evan as a puppy, so had never known a home with anyone else. She was quite protective of them and didn't handle visitors well. She preferred her world to be solid and predictable and didn't adjust easily to changes in routine.

The image Hera showed me was one of her 'parents', sitting together on the couch, having a heated argument. As I often do, I had my eyes closed while narrating the session. After receiving this image I opened my eyes to look at Claire. I could see it in her face immediately—she was so embarrassed!

After Claire had a minute to recover she shared that she and Evan had indeed become embroiled in an argument while sitting on the couch, and that Hera had been present in the room. When she reviewed the timeline

in her head, the argument had taken place just before Hera had started urinating there.

It was clear that Hera was so disturbed by the two most important people in her world being openly angry with each other that she took matters into her own hands. She *really* didn't want that to ever happen again. In her mind it was an easy solution—make the couch off limits and problem solved.

To have your dog share with your spiritual teacher an experience you would prefer to be kept private is quite a thing to take in! But it made complete sense of the situation and was the explanation Claire and Evan needed to take the necessary steps to resolve it.

Chapter Twenty-Two

Where Did the Time Go?

Being with a mountain—I didn't yet know the scope of adventures that still lay in store . . .

Nearing the end of each journey to the Mountain, I am always careful to ask what I can do for the Mountain Spirit Beings in return. Most often they reply with, "Be with us." Initially I thought that meant I should journey regularly and spend time with them. But as the years passed and I came to understand the importance of being, as opposed to doing, that small request took on new meaning.

Even with that newfound understanding I was still uncertain *how* to go about it. I was already spending time with them in my morning practice and my journeys. I tried to be creative and ran through some different ideas in my mind but nothing satisfied. Then one day when I was out on a long walk, roaming the hills on a sunny afternoon, a possibility occurred to me. Here I was in a beautiful outdoor environment, on a hilltop where I could see the mountains on the horizon. I had the entire afternoon free. I was in no hurry to return home and no one was expecting me. It appeared an opportune time to 'practice'.

Not really knowing what I was doing, I found what felt like an ideal place and planted my feet firmly on the earth. I raised my arms out to the side, then reaching up to the sky, declared out loud, "Mountain, I am here to 'be' with you."

At this stage of my apprenticeship with the Mountain I knew a few of its gifts, so I was very careful to pay attention and not lose focus. After a few minutes I looked around to see if anything had changed. Everything appeared normal. After a few minutes more I resumed my walk, always on the lookout for something happening. I tried to stay as alert as possible, knowing full well that I didn't know what I was on the alert for!

I continued my walk, scanning the horizon often to make sure I was where I expected to be. I watched for landmarks in the park area that I knew well, and that confirmed my orientation. I can't tell you how long I did this for—I can only say that I did it until the moment I realized I had no idea of where I was, any memory of how I got there, or any sense of how far away I was from where I lost track. And all that appeared to happen in a split second!

I couldn't believe it. There had been no warning, no transition of any kind. It was like my awareness had been completely removed for a period of time and when it returned, I wasn't where I thought I was. This was a large park, spanning several hundred hectares, and there were many areas I had never gone far enough to explore. Looking around, I really didn't know where I was, or even what direction to turn, to head toward home.

I scanned the horizon again. The area I now found myself in was a lower elevation than before and I couldn't see the roadways surrounding the park to get my bearings. But I could faintly see the downtown skyscrapers and I used them as a general guideline. After about 15 minutes I was able to further refine my route. Now facing what I hoped was the path back to where I started, I walked at a fast pace, not knowing how long I'd been gone. In the end it took about an hour to find myself back at the place where I had lost my awareness. And it would take me another thirty minutes or so to get out of the park and back to my own neighbourhood.

I continued on my way in disbelief. It wasn't until I was almost at my front door that I realized what happened. This may sound strange, but the theory that made the most sense to me was that the Mountain had stopped time! I had no idea what to do with a gift like that, or even if it was appropriate for me to call upon it. So I tucked it away as another wonderful, mystical experience, courtesy of the Mountain.

⁄ ⁄ ⁄ ⁄ ⁄ ⁄ ⁄

A couple of years later, while in dire need, my opportunity arose. I had an incident where I hurt my back, resulting in a seized sacroiliac joint on my left side. I knew just what was needed—a one-time chiropractic adjustment to release the lock and I would be fine. I called and arranged for an appointment. My usual chiropractor was out of town and there was someone else taking his place, but I didn't see any cause for concern.

When I arrived at the clinic I was given some information about the stand-in chiropractor. He worked a lot with athletes, particularly hockey players, and appeared to be highly regarded. When it came time for my adjustment, he assessed the problem just as I imagined he would, and placed my body in the same position as my regular chiropractor. When he attempted to do the adjustment however, the locked joint did not release. In the past if that happened I would return the next day and try again. This chiropractor was quite certain that if we gave it a second attempt it would probably do the trick. He tried and it didn't work. I was ready to leave and beginning to feel that this was more than my aching body could handle. He wanted to give it a final try. I politely declined but he was insistent that the third time would do it and would avoid the need for me to return. Reluctantly I agreed and with the third attempt he used a force that I could only imagine he normally reserved for the large, solid, muscle-bound athletes. It released the joint but sent an ominous shudder through the rest of my body.

The next morning when I woke up I literally couldn't move. Chris had an early morning commitment and had already left the house. I had to use the bathroom and didn't know what to do. I forced myself out of bed, which took great care, and surprisingly managed to make it. I didn't do so well on the return trip however. A few minutes later I discovered I had passed out, falling face first onto the dog bed on the floor of the bedroom. The severity of the situation started to sink in. After resting there for about ten minutes, because I didn't have any other choice, I managed to make it back into bed. My whole body was in pain and frighteningly unresponsive to my commands. I was a mess. I reached for the phone and called Terri, a friend and acupuncturist whom I knew well and considered one of my health care team. Luckily she answered, and while making it quite clear that this was an emergency, I asked if she could come to the house and fix me. She replied that she was already with clients but could be here in an hour and a half. I was immensely grateful and knew that she was doing her best but an hour and a half sounded like forever!

It was then I remembered that the Mountain could stop time. I felt this was a valid and sincere request. I checked the time on the digital clock beside the bed, just in case. I got as quiet inside as I could under the circumstances and politely, desperately, asked the Mountain to stop time for me. When I checked the clock again, which I thought was a mere moment or two later, one hour and ten minutes had elapsed. From that point it was less than ten minutes before Terri arrived. It had worked! And it had worked in entirely the same way as before. I lost awareness of time itself and then caught up with it again afterward. I was thrilled.

The acupuncture treatment had me up and moving around in another hour or so, and once I was back to my regular routine, I again set aside the marvel of stopping time. It would be several more years before I would stumble on an entirely new realm of possibilities.

Chapter Twenty-Three

Changing the Flow

I learn more about the nature of my role as a helper.

It was one of the longest, darkest, nights of the year, near Winter Solstice. I was on holidays and enjoying the leisure and pleasure of lingering with my thoughts. I decided to journey to the Mountain and ask if there were any teachings it would like to share.

Soon after I enter the journey I am given instructions to follow. To begin I need to walk over to a tree that is on my right. Near the tree I see a box. I go over and open it. It contains a piece of paper. I open up the folds to discover a map with a specific location marked. I can see the precise spot from where I am standing, so I go there. It is in the center of a stream and I can get within a few feet by standing at the water's edge. As I gaze upon it, I am told to notice how the water's course changes there. The flow is interrupted by large rocks and tree branches and the water adjusts accordingly.

I hear a voice. "This is the work that you do. You change the course of someone's flow, to effect change, and this results in their increased health and well-being. Without you, as the pivotal point, their 'course' would remain unchanged. If they come to you for help then they are not satisfied with their course and are asking for changes. Sometimes your work will take effort and thought and planning. Sometimes it will not—you will simply need to be there, as catalyst, and the flow of their lives will change. Remember, your intention will guide and direct the healing. The nature of its essence and what will serve best will be up to us. You do not need to see/know/or understand all the complexities. You may simply observe them in action."

Chapter Twenty-Four

Rite of Passage

The Mountain tells another kind of story . . .

The young woman who came to see me had been given permission to leave the psychiatric ward at the hospital to spend the weekend with her family. During that time she also arranged for an appointment with me. Upon meeting, I could see some agitation, but also a sadness. She described her career as going well, with new horizons ahead, but her formerly restrained internal dialogue of fear and self-judgement had turned loud and critical. And while there had been no significant outward changes in her life recently, she began having trouble managing the day-to-day stresses and uncertainties. She had become overwhelmed to a point where she feared for her own safety and presented herself at the Emergency Room. They admitted her and arranged for medication and a six-week stay.

By this point in the session I understood that she had become trapped in an internal pattern of thought and feeling that was potentially destructive, and couldn't find her way out. Whatever healing came forward, she needed to feel differently inside. I called upon the Mountain Spirit Beings and asked how we might be able to help. I touched her and established a connection. What was immediately presented to me was a story, but not in the way I expected. Rather than a story from her own experience it was a teaching she needed to hear. The only thing that was asked of the patient was that she listen attentively and try to relax. In turn, I became the storyteller, sharing word for word the tale that was revealed to me.

The first thing I see is feet inside moccasins. They are soft leather, reaching up to the calf, bound and tied with leather string. The feet are dancing and the fire is nearby. Soon, I am able to look up and see the young Indian Brave who wears the moccasins. He looks about 14 or 15 years old, having the firm skin and body tone of an adolescent. He is alone.

As I watch the dance, I come to know the thoughts that precede the placement of every step. I sense two people inside those moccasins, not just one. He dances near the fire and the light of the flames reveal the forest all around him. I sense at a distance a community of watchers but they are too far away to be seen or heard. He continues to dance.

He is a young boy yet he also holds inside the man he is becoming. They coexist but not harmoniously. The dance continues but the grace of the movements ever so slowly changes to reveal the war that is raging inside.

He wants to be one of the hunters, bringing back food for his people. He can see himself returning to the village with the other men, holding a rope that he has made, and hanging from it are eight rabbits. He is proud. His little brothers and sisters, and his mother, will eat well.

Up until now he has been one of the children, running, laughing, charging across the plain to meet the hunters as they return, gleefully checking their kill, assessing the wealth of their bounty. How he loved those times running back to the village alongside. Never again will he be one of those children.

He has been sent to the forest a boy. He is to return a man.

He feels trapped inside that boyish body. He is so ready to be strong. He is ready to give up his childish ways, the games, and the grownups telling him what to do. His body is changing. His desires are changing. He is ready. The dance responds, softening, slowing, until a memory comes flooding forward, a memory of himself a few years before, ill with a terrible congestion and cough. His mother feared for his life and tended to him vigilantly. Through the night she kept him close to the fire, staying at his side so that if he stopped breathing she could revive him. If he coughed she could offer the medicines to soothe his raw throat. Three days and three nights she tended to him. Never had he felt so taken care of, so loved. And as a man, never again would he experience the ministrations of his mother in that way. That was the way for children.

The dance becomes strained once more, his body tightening. He starts to lower his head as his shoulders bend forward ever so slightly. His steps are more forced. The battle of the boy and the man rages on.

He continues to bend forward until he folds at the waist, his head looking down at the earth. He imagines this contraction will continue, both inside and outside, until he is literally a ball of a human being, no longer dancing, but rolling around the fire. It feels inevitable.

And then a sound interrupts the silence—the haunting call of a lone wolf howling. The dancer, even while knowing that the sound is far away, cannot help but look up, as if expecting to see the wolf on the horizon. Of course he doesn't, but as his eyes gaze upward he sees the moon, just beginning its nightly ascent.

He has seen the moon many times before, thousands of times, but now, in this moment, something is different. So full and bright, the moon literally draws his attention toward it. He cannot resist and without realizing the shift that has occurred he changes his focus from the turmoil inside and reaches his attention outward. He had never thought much of the moon before, recognizing it as the women's moon. But here, tonight, it offers companionship and for the first time since arriving, he no longer feels alone.

And in that moment he realizes that every other brave, every single boy in the history of life on this planet has gone through the same rite of passage that he is going through. No exceptions. He is part of the lineage of Man. He is one of them.

He looks again at the moon, seeing this Grandmother now as a member of his extended family. No longer would his mother treat him as a child. It was time for him to leave the comfort of her hearth and *the fire. But Grandmother Moon will always watch over him and every night one of her faces will be there for him to behold.*

*He had transitioned. His body relaxes and straightens. He stands tall in his dance now. He has left his small family and entered into a larger one, the family of earth and sky, the family of Creation. He feels the support of those who have come before him—all those who know what he now knows. And for a moment he questions, he searches. Why had they not told him? Why had this story not been shared at the gatherings and the celebrations? So many stories of life he had heard, knew by heart, but not even a hint of this one. He pauses—and then he knows. This is not a story that can be told. It can only be experienced. It **has** to be experienced. His feet connect with the earth. The fire brings him warmth. The moon brightens the night. He stands as a man and is at peace.*

The session was over. The young woman thanked me and said that she wanted to hold on to the feeling that was lingering inside her as long as she could. To do that, she felt it was best not to talk more than necessary. There was a park nearby she had noticed on her arrival and she wanted to go there in silence and be alone. She left shortly afterward. I never had the opportunity to ask what effect the story had on her, or what openings for healing it may have presented. She moved away from Calgary soon after completing her hospital stay and we did not stay in touch.

What I can tell you is what the story meant to me and the shifts in feeling and tone that were created as I shared it. The story teaches that we all need to transition from child to adult. We all need to leave the safety and comfort of the family home. When we enter the bigger, outer world, complete with responsibilities and expectations, we can either feel alone, daunted by the enormity of what lies ahead, or we can feel held within the greater 'family' of all who have come before, those who were able to accomplish what is being asked of us. We can continue to feel watched over, taken care of, but now from our extended family, Mother Earth who feeds us and Father Sky who watches over us. Feelings of safety, trust, and being capable are internal ones, more often influenced by our thoughts than any possible risk or danger. It is my understanding that this story presented a way for her to feel safe, for her to let go of the tension and the burdens that were contracting her, limiting her, and instead find a different way.

I was struck, during the telling, that this was a story about a man, but it was a woman to whom it was being offered. I don't know why. Perhaps we can all connect with the archetype of the Indian Brave and his Rite of Passage. I had to trust that this story served her well. As with all patients, the outcome of our time together and the effect of the healing work, was in the hands of Creator. She was in good hands—that was all I needed to know.

⁄ ⁄ ⁄ ⁄ ⁄ ⁄ ⁄

When the Mountain first spoke to me in 1999 it said "I have a story to tell" and I continue to marvel at *all* the ways that one short statement manifests in my life. It began with the stories of patients that would be revealed once I made a physical connection with them. Over the years additional types of stories have appeared, of which the one above is an example. This was only the second time a story had come to me in that way—to be spoken out loud to the patient, and the story itself became the vehicle for their healing.

Once I become the bridge for the Mountain to reach in and offer its healing gifts there is an opening that happens within the patient. She doesn't have to create it. The Mountain creates it. She simply needs to be willing to immerse herself in whatever physical sensations arise, whatever images I share, whatever words are spoken, and take them deep into her being. I believe that the combination of sound and images creates a shift in the vibration of the patient and they begin to experience themselves in a different way. This is one feature of the healing. There are others.

The meaning of the story holds another layer. With the intimacy and trust created in such a safe and protected environment, the story can open the patient to a new way of thinking and perceiving. It can be the doorway to a new outlook or perspective. And finally, once received, the story is held within the soul and becomes part of their knowing. In a sense, the story becomes something that *happened* to them.

I have also discovered that when I am out in nature and I sit in the quiet, extending my awareness to make a spiritual connection, stories can come to me. In this case they emerge from the earth, work their way through my body/mind until our skills combine and they are able to be spoken word for word, with no stumbling or pauses, no corrections. In any given moment as storyteller, I have no idea where the story is going, not even what the following sentence will be. I often marvel when they are complete. Each story offers a nugget of insight into life, weaves its way through us to reveal a truth we can now hold inside and draw upon, to help us grow in the wisdom of how to live well.

Chapter Twenty-Five

Canine Calamity

I thought I was just spending some time with the plants!

It was late Friday afternoon and I was just finishing up with patients for the day when the phone rang. The person on the other end wasted no time, "Oh Jaki, I'm so glad I caught you. It's Eva. She's in acute kidney failure!" It wasn't long before the tears and sobs started to flow, filling the space between us.

Eva was a three-year-old Boxer, a rescue dog that a student, Mica, had adopted one year before. Eva had a propensity for getting into trouble and this wasn't the first time I had been called to the rescue, but never before was it a matter of life or death.

Over the previous few weeks Eva had been up to her old tricks. She had opened the bathroom cabinet and eaten several bars of soap, then about ten days later downed a box of ibuprofen tablets. The veterinarian diagnosed that the drugs had poisoned her system and led to the kidney failure. The options looked bleak—drugs and dialysis, with virtually no hope of an actual recovery.

The soonest I was able to see Eva was the next morning when she was brought to my healing practice. She lay on the floor and I sat beside her, reaching out my hand to gently touch her while she rested. It didn't take long before the connection was made and a flood of information became available. With my inner sight I could see the inside of her kidneys and that they had been exposed to some kind of caustic substance. The tissue was weakened, red and raw, and in some places looked almost shredded. The tubules that connected to the ureter were not in good shape either and I began to understand why the kidneys were not able to function. What I was seeing was essentially burned tissue, so I suspected it was the soap that had actually precipitated the crisis. Because Eva was young and other-wise healthy, her system was initially able to manage the kidney damage, but the increased stress of the drug poisoning had created an almost fatal combination.

I continued the internal viewing through the rest of her organs then changed my focus to her meridian system. By tuning in to the function of each one I was able to receive another layer of vital diagnostic information.

Eva was not in good shape. I didn't know how much I might be able to help her, but one thing I was clear about—I was going to try. I removed the residual shock and trauma from her system to help her organs shift toward recovery. I balanced the meridians and went very carefully through her body looking for places where the internal life force was blocked or not flowing smoothly, and did what I could to re-establish proper function. Then I stayed in the connection with her until I knew the medicines she needed. In this case there were two physical remedies that would serve to cleanse the poisons from her blood, and soothe and heal the damaged areas. One was red clover blossoms and the other was flax seed. As soon as I received the vision I knew this was an unusual application for these plants. The medicine gifts they offered and the situation that Eva was in created a unique combination, and opportunity, for them to come together. As it happened, I had a supply of recently harvested and dried red clover blossoms in my office, waiting to be used.

Mica and her husband felt they had nothing to lose and were willing to give the protocol 100% of their efforts. If at any time there were additional danger signs they had a prescription from the vet which they could get filled immediately. One thing we didn't have to worry about was whether Eva would be a compliant patient. If she would eat soap still inside the wrapping

she was not going to turn her nose up at the mixtures I was recommending. She was also fortunate to have two caregivers who were extremely devoted and would follow the instructions for the plant medicines exactly as given. As we suspected, she gobbled them up without hesitation.

For the first two weeks Eva came in for treatments twice a week, and after that, one treatment per week in my office with an additional long distance one in between. She appeared to be managing well on the therapy. She was certainly in a weakened state and required a high level of home care but otherwise appeared to be holding her own. After the first few weeks she started to get stronger and more active during the day. We were hopeful at her progress but still cautious. We maintained this protocol until her return visit with the vet.

At Eva's six-week follow-up all tests came back negative! She was going to be fine. As her kidneys were still healing, her fluid intake was carefully controlled for another six weeks and then gradually returned to normal. Long before then she was back to her old self.

A few months before the crisis with Eva I had spent some time with Chris at his family's cabin in the woods. The season was ripe for red clover blossoms and there were some densely populated areas near an old service road where they would not have been exposed to heavy car exhaust. Red clover blossoms prefer to grow in disturbed areas so it is common to find them along road sides. But the busier the road, the more likely the contamination of the plants. I was excited at the pristine find but at the same time hesitant about harvesting the medicine. At the time I didn't have a purpose for them. I knew the value of the plant but I also understood our all-too-human tendency to want things 'just in case'. To gather the plant parts to sit on a shelf in a cupboard was no way to honour such an incredible gift from the natural world. The only reason to harvest was because there was a need. I had to be certain. So one day I stopped in the area and sat down in the middle of the patch. I simply sat there and closed my eyes. I knew immediately there was no way I could leave without collecting some, and furthermore, I needed an abundant supply. I invited Chris to help me gather them. I taught him how to know which flowers were ready and which should be left in the field. We offered them tobacco, I said a prayer, and explained my reasons, as best I knew, for taking them. After bringing them back to the cabin I carefully dried them in the sun, placed them into airtight bags for safe keeping, and then stored them in a cool, dark corner.

When I began the healing work with Eva, I gave a silent prayer of thanks, both to Creator and to the plants, for gently nudging me to be prepared. I was both humbled and immensely grateful that I had paid attention.

Chapter Twenty-Six

Time in Nature

As always, Bear keeps me on track.

I see Bear ambling along, approaching from the left. She circles around a tipi that is slightly off to my right and comes behind me, continuing on to her place by the fire, at my left. She pokes at the fire with a stick, repeatedly, getting it just the way she wants. The fire has a lot of red-hot coals today. The reason for my journey is that I have been very busy, didn't sleep well last night, and woke up feeling weak and vulnerable. Now, as I sit with Bear, I start to cry.

"Bear, will you help me?"

Bear gets up and walks around the fire, opposite to where I am sitting. She rises up on her hind legs and roars. I see her belly and her shaggy fur. She is a huge and imposing figure yet all I feel as I gaze at her, is love. Continuing in the same direction she walks around the fire back to me and starts to lick my face and neck. She is so playful and warm, a stark contrast to a few moments ago. Then with no warning, and one huge and determined swat of her paw, she pushes me down on the ground. She continues to push me as I start to roll, having no time to get up in between. I don't know what to do. Fear and panic start to rise within me. I am naked and vulnerable. I know this is a journey and she won't truly hurt me, yet I can't help but respond to the situation I find myself in. As she continues to push and force my body the disorientation affects my awareness. Then the scene I find myself in changes . . .

The fire and hearth seem far away now. I am in the forest. Bear is gone. I am all alone. A deciduous tree offers one of its branches to cover me and I scramble to lean up against its trunk, a kind offer I won't pass up. Once settled I almost instantly fall asleep.

I am awoken by a little bird, chirping and hovering in mid-air in front of my face. In that instant I can't imagine a more beautiful way to be awoken. I stir in my spot but find it quite comfortable so I'm in no hurry to get up. The bird however, has other plans, so I rise and follow her. She takes me to a stream where I wash with the enticing cold, clear water. Then I allow the sun to warm my skin. The bird says "See, this is what you need."

／／／／／／／

One of the wonderful things about journeys is that they offer you an experience of 'being'. In the journey above it didn't matter that my physical body wasn't participating. 'I', in all my awareness, woke up in the forest to the sound of the chirping bird and it completely changed my experience of myself and how I would prepare for the day ahead. I stayed with that simple teaching for quite a while. "This," as the bird said, "is what you need." Not only did I have a new start to my day, it was a gentle reminder that in order to stay in balance, I needed to spend time outside, with my plant and animal friends. I recognized the call.

A simple journey can do wonders for the spirit. It doesn't have to be long, involved, or complex. This particular one took less than ten minutes. What is important is that we allow ourselves to be moved by these experiences. Once I opened my eyes I didn't return to my old way of being. I carried forward the teaching, the healing gift I was given. That part was my choice.

Occasionally in a class or workshop I encounter a student who has taken many workshops with different teachers and yet still hasn't found what he's looking for. I remember well a young man who described in his introduction his quest to experience this other reality. He kept looking

where other people said he would find it but, it continued to elude him. During our afternoon together exploring journeying, totem animals, and a few other ventures into the non-ordinary realms, he received a teaching from one of the animals that appeared to him. It was a very clear teaching, one sentence actually, yet quite profound. I don't remember the words but I remember being struck by his tone of voice as he shared it with the group. It was clear he felt no sense of wonder, awe, or gratitude. He relayed the experience in a dull, matter-of-fact manner, as if he was passing along the details of a telephone call.

I was determined not to let it go and move on. I asked how he felt about receiving the message. Again he surprised me by answering that he had heard it many times before and that every time he did this kind of work he received something similar.

It was then that I understood. It wasn't the case that nothing was happening for him. It was that he had put up a wall between his experience and his heart. He didn't want to open himself up to *feel* what was happening, to let it envelope and change him. He literally received it like words on a page or words coming from a television set. They held no meaning because he didn't allow them to. Yet at the same time, this was what he was desperately searching for. A part of him knew there was something missing and compelled him to keep looking.

For this to change, for him to change, would require a shift in his relationship to his soul. He needed to give himself permission to feel. I know that because the Mountain helped me to feel. It broke through my armour and encouraged the soft and tender side of me to show through. As long as this young man was willing, that kind of healing could come in a variety of forms. But in addition, his life experiences could nudge him to awaken to his feelings. I sensed that if he found someone to love, someone to share his life with who would love him in return, he would slowly start to open. Sometimes we just need to find ourselves in an environment where we are well liked, well regarded, and treated with consideration and care—the gentle medicines. Then we start to feel safe enough to express ourselves, to let our personalities and characters come out. After that, it doesn't take long for the heart to follow.

Chapter Twenty-Seven

Personal Vision Quest

One way to find the balance between the physical and the spiritual.

Pauline and I were preparing for a Vision Quest, just the two of us. I was particularly excited as Pauline was willing to come to my neck of the woods and I had selected what I thought to be the perfect spot—the backwoods camp at the other side of the Mountain where I had spent a critically important three days and nights, many years ago. Before we could leave the city, however, there was much to be done. With no helpers to support us or attend to our needs, we set about completing each stage ourselves. The fasting began after dinner the evening before. In the morning we had a cup of hot tea to warm us and prepare for what lay ahead. It was traditional to enter the Sweat Lodge before heading into the forest, so Pauline had brought five Grandfather stones with her from the West Coast. I prepared a fire in the backyard. A few hours later the stones were red hot. It was time.

We created a makeshift lodge using the patio chairs in the yard, turning them backward so we could drape tarps and blankets over them and still have room to sit in between. We took the stones out of the fire with a pitchfork, brushed off the ashes with a small branch cut from a spruce tree overhanging the yard, then placed the Grandfather stones in between some large, hollow concrete bricks left over from a construction project. They served as a container so the stones would not slip or roll. We gathered water in a bucket, grabbed a ladle from the kitchen, and two sitting mats. Pauline had her plant medicines on hand: sage, sweetgrass, diamond willow fungus, and cedar, to burn on the stones. We crawled inside and Pauline conducted the ceremony, completing two of the usual four rounds. It was hot!

After the sweat I sat by the fire and made the prayer ties I would need to hang inside my Vision Quest circle: seven large squares of coloured cloth, each with a prayer carefully placed into a handful of tobacco, secured into the corner, and tied. We packed our bags and loaded the car, carefully reviewing everything we would need for the next three days and nights, both camping and ceremony supplies. Then we headed out to the mountains. Once there, I stopped in at the Visitor Centre to make sure I knew where to park and locate the trail head. It had been a few years since I'd been to that spot—we didn't want to end up in the wrong place. The park warden remembered speaking to me on the phone a few weeks before and said, "Well, it looks like everything worked out just the way you wanted it. You'll have the place all to yourselves." I said a silent prayer of thanks to Creator. This meant that we would have complete privacy in a mountain forest, be able to drum and sing to our heart's content, and have the sacred fire going day and night without any hesitation. "Oh, there is one thing you should know," he continued. "There's been a family of cougars spotted several times on the ridge not far from where you'll be camping. Make sure that the two of you stay close to each other, for safety reasons."

Hearing those parting words should have been cause for concern. After all, it's quite something to be told that your Vision Quest circle could be shared by a family of cougars! But I was with Pauline and she had a very different relationship to animals, and the natural world, than most people I knew. How many times had we done Bear Ceremony together, welcoming Bear Spirit into our gatherings? How many wonderful stories had she told of bear encounters? I assured myself that cougars were simply another one of God's creatures. I was with someone who was well versed in the ways of man and nature. There was no cause for alarm.

The warden then went on to advise that the designated parking area for the campsite was under construction and we would have to park off the

road on the side of the highway, near the entrance to the trail. He assured us this was to our benefit as it represented a short cut, shaving 3 km off the hike. Three kilometres! I hadn't remembered the trail being that long, and here were Pauline and I carrying everything uphill, including an axe. This was indeed good news—a little touch of grace—one kilometer instead of four. I said another little prayer of thanks.

Getting back to the car I told Pauline about the shortcut. She didn't know the trail but was appreciative of any small adjustment that would make our hike in easier. And on that happy note, I casually added the part about the cougar family. "Cougars!" she screamed out in response. "Cougars! I'm terrified of cougars!" So much for my ill-conceived and naïve theory of native Elders. My Indian companion had some fears after all.

The thought of turning back was inconceivable. We had made the commitment, prepared ourselves physically and psychologically, completed the first half of the Sweat Lodge ceremony and were already in the mountains. Besides, we had made a promise to the spirits and we couldn't let them down.

It seemed to take forever to navigate our way up one kilometre of trail. Once at the campsite, we collapsed onto the ground in an open meadow, grateful to be able to put our packs down and rest. Later we settled on a couple of spots for our circles, deciding to build the fire between them; that way each of us could leave our circle and there would still be someone to stay with, and tend to, Grandfather Fire.

Pauline defined the edges of our Vision Quest circles, approximately eight feet in diameter, with a mixture of tobacco and buffalo sage. We hung our prayer ties as high on the trees as we could reach. We gathered spruce branches to use as the 'door'– the protocol for leaving the circles temporarily—if we needed to pee, tend the fire, or move out of the shade to warm up in the sun.

It rained the first evening and throughout the night. We had set up our sleeping area very simply. A tarp was placed on the ground with our sleeping bags on one side. The other side could easily be folded over top in case of rain or cold, creating a sandwich effect. This worked to hold off the direct rain but we found our sleeping bags were damp all the way through by morning. The second night we decided to change our strategy and hung part of the tarp above us, providing more of a roof covering. While it helped us stay drier, it was also much colder without the extra layer of protection against the mountain frost.

So far, so good. The wet and cold were our only challenges. In the early morning hours Pauline and I smoked our pipes together, then filled them again with prayers of support and protection and let them sit out, as they had previously, creating the sacred circle of Spirit that was holding us during our quest. After that, I spent a few hours either sitting or lying in my circle. When the sun came out for a while I left my shady spot to lie down on a small patch of grass nearby and warm up.

I was enjoying the luxury of the sun's rays when I received a vision. A male spirit appeared to me and asked, "You don't want to be so afraid do you?" I thought this an odd question, as fear wasn't an emotion I was experiencing at the time. I was cautious about being in the forest and the cougar warning, but otherwise felt amazingly safe nestled so close to the Mountain and under the protection of our pipes and the spirits. So I didn't answer right away but did sit up to pay more attention to what was happening. The spirit man then came and sat across from me, carefully placing three objects between us, side by side. They all looked the same, very much like pine cones, about the size of a chocolate Easter egg. Without any accompanying words he pushed one of them toward me, offering it to me. Somehow I knew it represented a healing gift. I looked at it carefully, then adjusted my gaze to take in the other two. These three objects, and the gifts they held, were everything I had ever wanted. If I had three wishes, they were these, and now I could reach out and touch them. But something wasn't right. I had helped Pauline host Vision Quests many times and knew the teachings around receiving a vision. If one came, it was always best to ensure that it was indeed from Creator, and in support of my well-being and wholeness. I remembered her words and the teachings we offer to others, "We don't ask for anything of indulgence, we only ask for what will help us sustain our human lives, to understand what it means to be a human being, and to try to be compassionate to all beings that are here." I looked up, stared at the spirit man and asked firmly and strongly, "Are these from Creator?" He seemed to fade slightly so I asked again. He faded even more. I had my answer. This was a

trick. This was a game that was being played with my ego, luring me with the promise of fulfilling my dreams. Once the vision had cleared, the more I thought about it with my rational mind the more absurd it became. Pauline had warned me about such tricksters. I was pleased I had the presence of mind to reveal it for what it was. I went back to my circle, completely solid in my desire to stay true to my commitment and not be swayed or tempted. By the time I had put away the door I had left it all behind.

On the second day, early in the afternoon, as I ventured out of my circle to the outhouse, I was surprised to discover that my back was quite sore. I hadn't done anything I could think of to have caused it and I certainly wasn't exerting myself. I returned to my spot deciding to ignore it, but it wouldn't go away. Within a matter of minutes the pain had escalated to the point where I was on my knees, rocking my body back and forth, moaning. In those few minutes everything changed. I was no longer able to sit or stand, and the harsh reality of the situation came flooding into my awareness. I was in the middle of a medical emergency and if it didn't subside, the only way I could be helped was to be helicoptered off the mountain. How on earth was that going to happen? How would Pauline get back to the car, find her way to the Visitor Centre and get the help that I needed? I was the one who had planned our stay at a remote site, beyond the reach of other campers and hikers. What had I done?

Pauline was at my side in an instant, doctoring me. She rubbed my back and sang healing songs asking the ancestors to come and help. She found a piece of leather and smeared tree sap on it, then warmed it over the fire and placed the soothing poultice over my right kidney, which was the source of the pain. I hadn't taken a drop of liquid since our cup of tea the first morning, and so far had found the fasting remarkably easy to manage. But I did have a history of kidney stones from a decade before, where a stone had become lodged on its way out of my body and required surgery to remove it. The thought that my kidney might be weak as a result had never occurred to me. I seemed to recover extremely well from the procedure and had almost forgotten about it. Now here I was, not only afraid, but embarrassed. Pauline got some water and placed a little orange juice in it, which we had brought along, just in case. I drank a few ounces, feeling incredibly weak. I slowly lowered myself to a reclining position and covered up with my sleeping bag. I was sure that if I moved even one muscle unnecessarily, I could trigger a stronger reaction. I had to stay still for as long as possible.

It was then that I had my vision. I saw a man with an eagle feather head-dress and eagle feathers all the way down his arms. I knew he was Eagle Man. He spoke to me, saying, "You need to dance and you need to move." I understood that he was offering general advice, what I needed in my life, not that I was to dance on this particular day! Then he brushed my whole body down with his eagle feathers. I knew he was cleansing me and offering a healing. He continued to talk, "You do not need to push yourself to the limits. You need to take care of yourself." There was so much I understood from those few sentences. He was giving me permission to leave the Vision Quest if I needed to, and to drink the water that my body was so desperately asking for, without feeling like a failure. He was also offering important teachings for my life and my work ahead.

That was it. I have to confess that, in the wake of it, I was disappointed. I had hoped that my vision, if I was privileged to receive one, would carry something profound, or provide a deep insight into my path or my future. To have a vision that basically said, "Take care of yourself," well, it wasn't as flashy as I'd hoped. At the same time, I was beginning to feel quite a bit better and decided to stay resting in the same spot, now feeling safe enough to move around a little.

A short time later, when I was able to be up and about, I shared the vision with Pauline. She was so pleased to hear that Eagle Man had come and that the ancestors had responded to her plea! She confessed that she had been silently regretting she hadn't brought her eagle fan to brush me down. So when she heard that Eagle Man himself had appeared, she was delighted. She could stop being concerned for me. She knew that the spirits were taking care of the situation.

I woke up on the third morning with no pain whatsoever, even though the night had been very cold. When any part of my body had become exposed to the air, it was only a matter of minutes before it woke me. As a result I tossed and turned all night. In the pale morning light I could see a layer of frost on our tarps.

It was the sound of Pauline's eagle whistle that had roused me. The sun hadn't even peeked its head over the horizon. I estimated it to be about 4:30 a.m. Pauline played her drum and sang her songs, and in the comfort of my healed body I lay there for a while, basking in the listening and the developing twilight. When I got up, I smoked my pipe for the final time, blowing the smoke into the mists of the forest.

We packed up and headed out with my back feeling strong. We managed to get to the Jeep with only one or two brief stops, a feat in itself. When we hit the highway I was alert and focused. Having no food and only a few ounces of water and juice, I marvelled at what the human body was capable of. We arrived home and prepared the closing sweat, starting with lighting the fire to heat the Grandfather stones. It would be several hours before they were hot and we were both exhausted. Pauline went inside to have a nap and I dozed while tending the fire. A couple of hours later we completed our closing two rounds, then afterward, burned our prayer ties. The Vision Quest was officially over. We could now eat and drink again.

Later that day, after Pauline had returned home and the house was quiet, I decided to journey to Eagle Man, the one who came to me in my vision. I wanted to thank him for tending to me and the offering of his medicine. I also had some questions about the different roles of Eagle in my life from this point forward, as my totem animal was also an eagle. I felt I needed clarification. Eagle Man returned without hesitation and spoke directly to my concerns, "In this form I bring you different medicines." I inquired further, "May I ask the nature of those medicines?" He replied, "When I brushed you down with my feathers I was offering you a healing. Eagle feathers have the ability, the power, to change a situation. As the feathers move across the body they can restore the natural state, the state of balance. This cannot be done with physical feathers alone. You must have been offered the medicine to do this work. Now that I have come to you, you may call on me to assist you in your work with others. I am an able and willing helper."

"What can I offer you in return?" I asked. "Stay in service. Take care of yourself. You are strong but you have limitations. This does not have to be a difficult road for you. As your heart continues to open, you will enjoy your work even more. When you call on me your hands will be my wings.

Learn the eagle dance. It will help you stay strong and well. Call me in and we can dance together. I have been with you for so long but now was the time to come forward." And with that he flew away, leaving me with an exquisite feeling of being safe, held, and cared for.

⁄ ⁄ ⁄ ⁄ ⁄ ⁄ ⁄

A few weeks later, while going through some of the working notes I had compiled for writing *Heeding the Call*, I came across an entry of one of the very first 'spiritual' experiences I had ever noted in my journal, dated 1998. It described a vision a reiki practitioner had received while working on me. I was so struck by it I wrote it down as soon as I got home.

Soon after the treatment began she saw a mountain, which she described in great detail. (At the time this held no relevance for me but I now recognize it as the Mountain.) She then asked if I had felt anything at the back of my head and pointed to a place just above my neck on the left side. She went on to say that a spirit had appeared and described him as a large man with the mask of an eagle and many feathers reaching down his arms. This Eagle Man performed a psychic surgery on my brain, at the location she described. He removed something that had apparently been held there then turned to her as he was leaving and said, "It is time for her to remember."

Chapter Twenty-Eight

Carlotta's Curse

It is important to remember, when dealing with those who would cause harm to others, that they need the medicines too.

arlotta originally came to see me to address some physical health concerns. She had recovered from a serious illness that she described as having "taken a few years of her life away," and while she was now functional again, she believed it was possible to feel even better. The medical profession had helped her this far, and she was very grateful, but she wanted to feel the energy and vitality she had experienced before she became ill. She had been an active woman and enjoyed many sports, particularly mountain climbing.

We worked through a short series of meridian balancing treatments and she improved rapidly. She had a strong physical constitution but her illness had shifted the natural symmetry between the left and right sides of her body and the underlying life force. A little fine tuning was all she needed. During those treatments Carlotta began to share a little of her life story. It was a study in contrasts. She was a very beautiful woman, one whom I would describe as 'well put together'. She was stylish, articulate, talented, with a strong career focus and a passion for travel. Yet for every blessing she had received there seemed to be an accompanying curse. She had been sexually abused as a child and I could tell that the wounds, while more than 40 years old, still felt fresh. She had never married and reluctantly shared that she had no desire for a sexual relationship. In fact, men in general did not hold much appeal. Her recent illness was not the only one she had experienced in her life. She had been dealt several devastating blows, more than any one person would normally be exposed to. The word 'curse' literally came up over and over. It seemed an odd word for this woman to use, yet as I got to know her I began to understand why. Many of the events of her life did not make sense, and the nature of some experiences were so bizarre, they literally defied explanation. The result was that she never felt safe in the world—ever.

Once her physical well-being was taken care of she asked if I could be of any help with this deeper issue. Previous to meeting me, she had never known such a thing might be possible. I agreed to do a journey for her, an exploration into the invisible forces that influenced her life. Carlotta was not physically present for this journey. I waited until a time when I felt I could move easily into the state of being required. Then I began:

> Almost immediately upon entering a trance-like state, I meet Raven, one of my helpers. I let him know that I must enter into the mystery so that I may find what is otherwise unseen and unknown.
>
> The first image is both shocking and nauseating. My physical body wants to recoil, to stop the scene from unfolding. I try to balance the repulsion with the knowledge that if this is insight into Carlotta's life events, then it is much more difficult for her to experience than it is for me to bear witness. I need to be strong.
>
> I see Carlotta, looking very much as she did the last time I saw her, except that she is hoisted into the air, impaled on a long stick. She looks like a tortured puppet, her arms and legs dangling and her body controlled. My eyes follow the stick down to its base, hesitating all the while to find what is at the source. I see a dark figure, cloaked and hooded, with the stick in his hands. There is a frightening, negative energy around this being. He controls the stick and is, in some ways, able to control what happens to Carlotta.

I know I must approach him. As I do, he is completely oblivious to my presence, so delighted is he with his toy. I clear my throat to get his attention. He is startled and looks up. There is a black snake with a forked tongue inside the cloak. He looks at me and hisses.

Snake, "What do you want little girl?"

Jaki, "I'd like to know what you are doing."

Snake, "Go away. It's none of your business." He then turns back to his game.

Jaki, "It is my business. I have been asked." He immediately gets angry as he knows what that means.

Snake, "You can still choose to stay out of it. Now go away."

Jaki, "I don't want to. I am committed to fulfilling my promise."

Snake, "Agh!"

He puts the stick down. I'm not sure why. Is he going to speak with me, try to harm me, or get rid of me? He starts to 'pace', slithering back and forth in an agitated manner.

Snake, "You do not understand. I have an agreement, an arrangement. This one was given to me many years ago when she was still young."

Jaki, "Who gave her to you?"

Snake, "I'm not telling." As the snake thinks back, I see a flash image of an older man wearing a plaid shirt and pants that look too big for him.

Jaki, "Why do you want to keep her?"

Snake, "Well, to tell you the truth she is sometimes quite boring, especially lately, but in the past she's been quite a bit of fun."

Jaki, "You are harming her."

Snake, "I don't care."

There is often a point in journeys like these, where it is clear that my own knowledge and wisdom are limited and I cannot possibly know how to navigate gracefully toward the desired outcome. I pray and wait.

Jaki, "I'd like to strike a bargain with you, so you will give her to me and I will free her."

Snake, "You don't have anything I want." He is hissing and getting very angry now.

Jaki, "Yes I do." I telepathically show him an image of a beautiful female snake, one that he could potentially mate with.

Snake, "Where is she? Give her to me. Now!"

Jaki, "First, a few matters we need to discuss. You must give Carlotta to me, knowing that I will remove the stick and free her. Next, you must remove yourself from this galaxy, so she can feel no further threat from you. And finally, the female snake I showed you is a free being. I do not own or control her. You need to negotiate with her directly and offer her a reason to be with you. I can only pass along the invitation."

Snake continues to pace. I can see/feel that his goal is to manipulate me, to outsmart me, to keep everything for himself and leave me with nothing—not even a resolution. He comes to realize that I have no battle with him, no personal agenda, other than my request. Because I am acting out of service for another and not for myself, he has no ability or power to persuade or coerce me. It takes a few minutes for this realization to sink in. I hold the image of the female snake in my mind so he continues to see it. He starts to get angry and frustrated again.

Snake, "You don't understand. She is mine. Why would I want to give her to you? I am not done with her yet."

As I continue to wait patiently, I see more clearly the connection between the snake and the man in the plaid shirt. My heart starts to race. It is not the snake who holds the mal-intent toward Carlotta (although he has enjoyed tormenting her for decades). He has been operating as the servant of this man, a man who is no longer in the physical world. The focus continues to shift toward the man. I see him in a woodworking shop, sawdust everywhere, tools and benches all around. When he stands up straight he has a slight hunch in his upper back. I come to understand him on the inside as well as view him from the outside. In many ways he is a normal man but he is trapped in what he wants, a trap so strong that he cannot acknowledge any wrongdoing, in fact he must not. He follows the same urges in death as he did in life, but they manifest differently when there is no physical

connection. *This is the man who forced himself on Carlotta when she was still a child. Even in death he is still clutching her, controlling her, to relieve his own distorted needs.*

I find his presence extremely distasteful. If I believed in evil I would say that I had just encountered it in this man. It was much easier to deal with the snake—although vile, I could sense he was a follower. I know what I have to do. The man is trapped in a mental perspective, an illness, that has driven his desires so strongly he cannot extend his awareness beyond his own psyche. He never cared what he was doing to Carlotta. I call out to get his attention. He looks at me and my feelings toward him are amplified. Yet I now know that I am here to offer him healing.

Jaki, "I am here to help you."

Man, "I don't need any help."

Jaki, "Listen very carefully—I am here to forgive you for your sins."

Those last words could not have been more shocking, even if they had been spoken in the physical world. They came through me effortlessly in the moment yet they were not born of 'me'. I had no idea I was going to say such a thing. But now they were real—they had been placed into the space between us. And after a few more moments there was also a comfort, knowing that I was not alone. I was being guided. I was there as a helper, to do my part.

I offer him the most powerful medicine I know—the medicine of the Mountain. I am not privy to how the Mountain heals in this way, I simply ask and wait. After a time, I know that it is done.

The man is now barely able to acknowledge me. He has found his heart, and I see the irony—it was always about what he wanted. The place he now finds himself is infinitely better than any place he has been before, in life or in death. I barely interest him and he has difficulty paying attention. As I feel this, I let him go, watching quietly. He has a golden thread connected to his heart and he will follow wherever it takes him.

I return to Carlotta. The snake is gone and the empty cloak is abandoned, like the sloughing off of old skin. She is lying there, still attached to the stick, weak and helpless. I remove the stick and take her in my arms. I ask the Mountain to offer her too, the gifts, so she may begin her life anew.

A few hours later I called Carlotta and told her that the curse had been lifted. I was careful not to share any details of the journey. The only way she could be truly free was to have nothing to hold on to, no thoughts or images, no memories of what had transpired and of what had been holding her down all those years. She trusted me so she agreed.

A few months later she called again. Everything was fine. Nothing strange or unusual had happened and her health was good. But she was having trouble moving forward. This was new territory for her. I knew what she was talking about and it was not an uncommon response to this type of work. There had been such a dramatic shift and no accompanying understanding of what had actually changed, how or why. There were no details of the resolution to hold on to. Carlotta felt like she was in limbo. She didn't know what to let go of. She was stuck.

I was pleased that she had called and that we were able to work through this final step together. This was the moment when a decision needed to be made on whether to share the details of the healing journey. We arranged for a session to discuss it further and for me to be on hand to offer support if she decided to go through with it. In this instance, the need for resolution and the interim freedom and relief were such that we both felt she could receive the information in a healthy way. I handed her a typewritten copy and left the room so she was free to privately express any emotions that surfaced.

In the meantime, I created an aromatherapy blend that would offer both emotional and psychological support in moving forward. I trusted the plants would be able to support Carlotta now, in all the ways that she needed. In addition, I felt that she understood the nature of the medicine being offered and would be able to receive it, and allow it to help her.

When she returned from reading the journey she was unusually quiet but I was not concerned. It was a lot to take in. Her parting hug gave me the confirmation that we had indeed done the right thing. The curse had been lifted and she was free. More than four decades of turmoil now made

sense, not in terms of her understanding, but in terms of her deep knowing. She walked out the door with an air of confidence. I never saw or heard from her again. I trust there was no need.

Chapter Twenty-Nine

The Healing Light of Plants

I am shown yet another way; I had no idea the plants had still more to give . . .

As I completed my morning practice, I wanted to linger in the silence for a few more minutes. A recent journey to the Mountain was still with me, one where I had been asked to "Feel yourself as *us*." Today the urge to follow through was insistent. I smudged with copal and closed my eyes. I tried to picture myself as one of the Mountain Spirit Beings, seated with the others in the circle. That felt nice but wasn't enough somehow. I played with the feeling. Without the idea occurring to me, I found myself clothed in my white buckskin tunic.[18] *That* felt better. Then without noticing a transition, I found myself inside the Mountain, and my awareness of myself was very large, solid, and strong. In there, it was easy to feel like a mountain!

I was enjoying the meditation when something shifted. I saw myself sauntering along the mountainside in a meadow with Bear beside me. I sensed that we were together as spirit beings. It felt extremely comfortable to amble along with Bear at my side, like old dear friends. I started noticing the plant people that were prominent in the forest meadow. I thought about

---

[18] A ceremonial dress the Mountain had given me.

Bear and all the plant wisdom she held. I approached one of the plants. As soon as I held my hand near its flower, it offered up a small ball of light to me. It was beautiful beyond words. My mind became more active, struggling to understand. I had never heard of, or imagined, a plant offering its gifts in that way. It struck me as being powerful medicine. I was mesmerized and wanted to stay with the experience, to explore the possibilities, but I could feel the connection beginning to fade, even though I was hesitant to let it go. As I took one last look around, I noticed that all of Creation held a ball of light inside, that it could bring to the surface to offer me—the stones, the raindrops, the leaves of the trees, all of it.

／ ／ ／ ／ ／ ／

It was spring and the wildflowers were blossoming. Over the winter, and through many winters now, they had been with me every day, helping to heal the patients that came to see me in my healing practice. While their roots had been suspended in the frozen earth and their leaves and stems buried in the snow, their spirits had been strong and viable.

In gratitude for their medicines and in humility for their depth of service to my people, I wanted to give something back. What I could offer in return was a mere token compared to what they provided but was no less important an exchange. My heart longed to celebrate their blessings. I decided to lift the pipe in honour of the plant spirits and their gifts.

It was also time to respond to a specific request. The plant people had asked me to 'see' them in a different way. As the last of the winter blanket melted, the ground was now ready. I thought about how to do this. The plants asked so little of me and were so patient. I wanted to be sure to take the time and dedication required. I committed to three days. I gathered my supplies for a trip to the mountains. I decided to work with juniper, one of the Mountain's plant allies.

I packed my medicine bundle, which had grown since its early days of holding the pipe alone. It now held the small stones that formed the basis of my medicine wheel, along with carvings representative of my totems and animal helpers. I made sure I had plenty of pipe tobacco (this time a special blend of dried plants from the mountainside), and smudging plants (juniper,

copal, and sage). I also brought offerings to my teachers: tobacco, berries (for Bear), raw fish (for Eagle), and rosehips (for Raven).

When I arrived, while still close to the parking lot, I stood at the base and presented myself to the sacred Mountain with a prayer in my heart, then sprinkled tobacco across the ground. I scrambled down to the lake's edge to offer Grandmother Water the same. I began to walk, not really knowing where my feet were leading, but trusting they would take me where I needed to go.

The path changed from roadway to walkway, the feel changed from city to forest. I looked up at the trees that flanked each side of the trail and they appeared to create a portal, inviting me to enter. I sensed that when I passed through I would have arrived in sacred territory. As I approached, I held a pouch of tobacco in my hands and in the same instant that my toes touched the threshold I decided it should be marked. I took a large hand-ful and made a line across the path, continuous from one side to the other. It was now a doorway and I prepared to step across, humbly, consciously.

Once on the other side I looked around, startled by the change. Every-thing was vibrant. I could see nuances of the rock face of the Mountain I couldn't discern before. I was physically slowed; it was the only way I could gather and receive all that was being shown to me. Each step was careful, considered, and I realized I could not travel far. I found myself smiling, in awe of the unexpected transition.

I noticed a small grassy hill just ahead and thought, "If I settle myself on the other side I will be out of sight to passers-by who might take the same trail." Once there, I laid a small blanket on the ground and placed my pipe bundle in the center. I opened my pack and lit some juniper and copal. After smudging myself I unwrapped the pipe bowl first, then the stem. Holding them over the smoke I joined them together. I reached for the tobacco blend and loaded the pipe, calling out to the spirits: the Grandmothers and Grandfathers of each direction, the earth and sky. My prayers were for the plant people and our deepening friendship. Once the pipe was loaded, I lit it and began to puff, first coaxing the fire to spread equally through the bowl, then allowing the smoke to rise. This pattern was repeated as we worked together—plant, fire, stone, and air—to send my prayers to Creator.

During the final round, I mused: "As human, I provide the prayers. I am willing to declare my request. These are transformed, with the help of the tobacco and the elements, into smoke. No longer invisible, I can watch them rise and play in the breeze." As if in confirmation, I heard the wing-ed ones above me calling out their willingness to take them even higher. As I released the last wisps from my mouth, I was struck by the completeness of the ceremony. I carefully set the pipe down, closed my eyes, and revelled in the perfection of the moment.

A few minutes later I remembered why I was there. The plant people had asked me to see them in a different way, to see and notice all aspects of their being, each and every time I encountered them. Now I was ready. As I sat with them all around me, I tried to adjust my focus, my way of seeing, so that I could catch glimpses of their subtle nature. Unlike my teacher Fishwoman, I have never been one to see spirits, other than in a journey. And while the pipe ceremony had allowed me to notice the vibrance of the natural world around me, I found I still could not see the plants in the way they desired. I took a deep breath and told myself it was a growing and learning process. It may not come right away. I continued, holding both the goal and the enjoyment of reaching toward it, within my being. I reminded myself it was not possible to fail. Every attempt would bring me closer.

Then I got it! Why didn't I see it before? I was to bridge the worlds. I was to recognize that I was experiencing both the physical world and the world of Spirit, and had been since I entered the portal. I needed to engage both my outer and inner forms of seeing simultaneously. My physical eyes were to note and enjoy the beauty and my spirit eyes to see the light, the vibrations, and the subtle layers of energy. The worlds had merged before me and my form of seeing needed to follow!

I did what I could to engage myself fully. I played with ways of seeing, different types of focus. I tried to transcend what I believed to be possible. I was entering into entirely different territory than I had been in before. All those times the Mountain had asked me to expand, to go beyond anything I could imagine. I understood what was needed. I wove my way between the worlds of sight, vision, and appearances. And I found it.

To touch on that ability, to get a glimpse into that skill, was surprisingly

exhausting. Within a few minutes I had to let it go. Holding myself in that state of being would take some practice—but I knew how to do it! Now, I just wanted to close my eyes and rest, so I decided to journey. That way, I could maintain my connection with the plant people:

I call Eagle and we quickly and easily descend to the Lower World. Bellarina, my plant guide, appears on my left. I offer words of appreciation and fill her in on the gathering activities. The scene changes somewhat and I am surprised to feel her behind me, brushing my hair. As she does this I notice that in the journey my hair is thick and long, and the gentle but thorough brushing feels exquisite. I linger in the pleasure of it. I think of raising two boys and never being able to brush and braid their hair. I find myself nostalgic about the rewards and comfort of this simple act. The scene changes again. Bellarina is still behind me, grooming me, but my long hair has been replaced by... wings! Slowly and a little awkwardly, as if these wings had been tucked away for many decades, they now respond to Bellarina's delicate fingers and start to expand and spread. She continues to groom me, checking where the wings attach to my back, making sure there is no discomfort or soreness as she guides them to open after all this time. I can't help but wonder if the reunion at the fairy landscape held more than I had already gleaned. As I orient myself and gather the courage to fly, I start out gently, hovering above the plants. Their teachings reach in to me, I do not hear them, they are just there:

"The plants will no longer keep any secrets. All will be yours for the knowing. You are one of us. Come, let's play."

I suspect I would still be frozen in awe if I were not having so much fun flying! Bellarina encourages me to swoop and dive, to stop and start, to practice landing ever so gently on the leaves. I quickly discover that I 'know' the plants through the bottom of my feet. I hear, "We are part of the same ecosystem, the same fertile ground. We know each other as we know ourselves." All too quickly I am a tired little fairy and lay down on a sprig of juniper, tuck my little hands gracefully under my chin and go to sleep. In the physical world the journey has ended.

Later that day I returned from the mountains and prepared the juniper I had gathered. I buried some of it in the earth. I created a small fire in a cast-iron pot and placed a sprig on top, to burn. I set some in a bowl of water and I left the rest to the open air, sheltered, yet exposed to the breeze. I knew it was important for my learning that all the elements contribute. Each specimen received a pinch of tobacco to complete the ceremony. I left them all outside and came in to prepare some food—I was so hungry.

Early the next morning I brewed a cup of juniper tea. The first thing I noticed while drinking it is that I wanted to close my eyes and look inward. I was relaxed, my mind alert and attentive, but not in the usual way of having thoughts, instead being more interested in awareness and what I had the ability to notice. I was drawn to seek out where energy blockages were present in my body.

Then I wanted to move, to shake and wiggle, to release tension and relax further. I began to feel itchy and wanted to scratch all over. I couldn't lie still. I moved onto my yoga mat, hoping to perceive what was happening more accurately. So many itches, I had to move and scratch them all. Yet at the same time a deeper part of me was quite calm. I wished that part would take over!

Within a few minutes the energy started to flow and I felt as if I had been cleansed. My body tingled all over, feeling very alive. I no longer wanted to lie down. I wanted to get up and do something. I started to wonder if moving energy was part of juniper's medicine. Drinking the tea, I became aware of my 'stuck' places. Is that because juniper was bringing them to my attention or was I noticing where the energy was blocked as juniper attempted to move though them? But wait, I am getting ahead of myself . . .

There was something comforting about the tea. I enjoyed it.

I call out to Juniper and journey with Eagle to the Lower World. Bellarina is there, again to my left, yet she seems closed to me somehow. I touch her wings but she is like a statue. I open my wings to fly around to the front of her. She is so much bigger than me. Hovering there, I kiss her forehead. She smiles and slowly comes to life. I feel like I have been tested—more for myself than for anyone else! Was I able to move

into my fairy nature at will? Although I didn't acknowledge it before, the Lower World was dark and dull when I arrived. Now it was full of colour, vibrance, and beauty.

"Bellarina, I have come to meet with Juniper and learn about the medicines. I also want to learn through my feet, as I was shown the possibility yesterday. Do I need instruction from you?"

"Everything you need is available to you. Just remember who you are."

I ask Eagle to come with me, but he chooses to stay with Bellarina. I am on my own. Very quickly I find a huge sprawling juniper plant. Smack dab in the middle I see the plant spirit, an unusual being, showing himself as a short, very rounded man, contentedly eating juniper berries like candy, popping them into his mouth one after the other. "Hi there." he says. "Good of you to come. Call if you need me." And with that he crosses his arms over his chest, closes his eyes and prepares to take a nap. I really will have to do this alone.

Ever so gently I light on one of the branches, being careful not to get poked by the sharp leaves, which are awfully big and pointy to a fairy! The instant my feet land I feel how alive it is. I introduce myself. "I am here to learn more about your medicines, sweet Juniper. Are you willing to teach me?" A round orb of light is immediately released from somewhere in the plant. It is clear-ish white on the inside with a definite blue-ish tinge around the edge. The orb of light moves toward me.

"Healing light of Juniper—what can you teach me?" I sense I am in the presence of the sacred and the powerful. The orb hovers closer. I feel small and humbled, yet not insignificant. I know it is here for me. I sense its willingness to teach, to communicate, but I am not receiving anything. I don't know how to open myself up. I don't know what form of communication is effective here. Then I remember Bellarina's words and I relax and try to trust myself. As a fairy, I am a being of light. This should not be difficult.

As I open myself more I have a sense that the orb has somehow connected with me and is transmitting information directly into my heart, completely bypassing my conscious awareness. I have no idea what the content is. My breathing takes on a strong, even rhythm. As

I breathe, I absorb. I absorb the light of knowledge from this orb. In the physical world I lie down to relax and allow this to continue (I had been sitting up in the journey—to take notes). Then I am drawn into my physical body again, itching, noticing where the energy is blocked. I scratch and try to get comfortable.

As I place my attention back to the Lower World I decide to experiment. I ask a question of myself. "What plant parts are needed for the plant essence I am to make?" I immediately know, "leaves and berry, with leaves still attached to the stem. The heat of the day is vital—full sun. Move the plant parts around if necessary. Full sun for as long in the day as possible. The resulting elixir will enliven, awaken, and push through the system of those who imbibe it."

After I acknowledge that the information is there, inside of me, I also realize I now know the song of the juniper plant. Everything stops for a moment while I take that in. My first plant song! Thoughts start to surface as my mind wants to engage. I can't help it—I am so delighted to have been gifted a song. But in the journey my body is still connected to the Spirit realm and is gently revelling in the bliss of the song and its effects. I feel so calm, so whole.

Then another knowing comes to the surface. The song is a medicine song. It is to be sung over patients as I place my hands a few inches above their bodies. It will cleanse them, as smudge, and open their bodies to healing. This will be helpful for those who are hesitant or resistant, yet they still need to be comfortable enough to have the medicine woman sing them a song.

Wait a minute! What were those words? A medicine woman! Am I a medicine woman?

I hear a response, coming from no place in particular. "If not before, then now."

"Thank you orb of light, thank you Juniper. Thank you Bellarina." I return.

It was not until later that afternoon when I sat at the kitchen table to have a snack that I realized fully what had happened. I had received an initiation.

The plant people shared with me what the depths of our relationship will be. They know what is in my heart and have offered their help and support. I am blessed.

Chapter Thirty

The Sun Never Stops Shining

There are so many ways that the medicines heal, but they all reach into the spirit, and begin their changes there.

The personal account that follows is from a young woman in her early twenties who is an occasional patient of mine. In the work we have done together there has never been anything particularly dramatic or story-worthy that happened, yet she kept coming back. One day I asked her why. She said she would think about it and a month or so later I received this response, via email.

I have thought for days about how to properly answer the question, "How does Jaki help me?" At first I wondered how personal my response should be and then I wondered how detailed it should be. Then, all at once, the answer came to me: Jaki helps me see the sun.

I love when the sun shines in my eyes or when it comes streaming in my windows in the morning. I love when it warms me gently and when it reminds me that spring and summer are just around the corner. But sometimes I fall so deeply into myself and my own sadness I forget to see the sun. I forget to look for it. I walk by the warm, sunny patches on my carpet without even an acknowledgement. Yet every time I walk away from Jaki's office, it is as if the sun is shining on me once again.

Sometimes when I see Jaki, I am relieved just to have someone listen to me, to ask me questions about how I feel and what I think. A few times she has noticed me holding tension in my body that I had ceased being aware of, and she rubs my shoulders or pays attention to certain pressure points. After those sessions I emerge feeling like I have put on a new pair of shoes, only in this case, it is a new body.

There are times when I see Jaki that I have nearly completely lost my grip on who I am and what's important to me; times when I wander the days of my life aimless and confused. Those are the times that Jaki will realign my energies, balance the inner parts of my spirit. Sometimes when that's not as effective as we'd like, she will go one step further, deep inside of me, to correct the real problem. She finds and delivers the message that my soul has been trying to give me, that I had stopped searching for and listening to. After those sessions, I have emerged feeling like I have put on a pair of old comfortable jeans, ones that used to fit, and that I now fit again, thanks to her help.

I go to see Jaki when I feel lost and sad and lonely. I go to see Jaki when I am confused and scared and disenchanted with life. Every session, her treatment varies a little from the time before, but I keep going back because every time I see her, I remember that the sun never stops shining. I just forgot to look for it.

C.L. Calgary, Alberta, December 2009

Chapter Thirty-One

Being

No matter what, keep reminding yourself to Be.

I am immediately at the Mountain. Grandmother slides out on a conveyor belt (she had done this once before), then Grandfather, then Wizard, and me. Very consciously we each step off onto our places on the ground, in the four directions. The tone is light yet careful. It feels like we are getting ready for something, or waiting. A wavy blue light starts to rise up from the ground around us. I feel like we are on a stage and there are lights to illuminate us to the audience. Then I begin to feel the effect of the light. It changes how I perceive mass and density. I feel less connected to the physical world, its weights and burdens. I shift my awareness to my spirit self, into her body. By comparison my physical body feels heavy and dense. My spirit body feels larger and lighter, and its awareness of itself is different. It is 'light'. There is no other way to describe it. It is light (not heavy) and it is light (composed of light). There is a particular sensation to being a 'being of light', a type of tingle, very subtle, but always there and always felt. In the physical body we feel our density with every thought and every movement. In our spirit body we feel the illumination/radiance of our light in the same way.

I realize so strongly the different way I am bringing myself to these *ꜣday. Before, I went to the Mountain to learn, to receive the ꜣtallment of my training. If nothing seemed to be happening, I ꜣd ask for something. At the same time the Mountain was always ꜣcouraging me to 'be' with them, to sit in stillness. I understand that now in an entirely new way. I want to place myself into the experience and simply exist within it. I realize how much this will teach me, even though my cognitive awareness of 'what' is being taught will be less. It is all about 'being'.*

After all these years, more than a decade, I still need to be reminded. The hold of the physical is so strong, so prominent in my awareness and through my five senses. It is as if I need to be reminded every day that there is a spirit inside this body, that the physical body I experience is only one aspect of who I am.

When I do ceremony, when I smudge, when I lift the pipe, when I offer the medicines in my healing practice, then I remember. I do these things every day. Ah, there's the rub. It is how we bring ourselves to our days, to our work, to the others in our lives that is important. It is possible to be participating in a ceremony, even a Sweat Lodge, and not be experiencing your spirit self. We need to allow the ceremony, the medicines, the prayers, the trees, the rivers, to help us change that. The teachings about 'being' are there to remind us that we need to do our part.

This is where a lot of us have trouble. We ask. Then we wait. Which is a good start. But after we ask it is our responsibility, our part of the relationship, to bring forward that aspect of ourselves that can receive what we have asked for. If it is closed off, how can it be open and available for Nature and Spirit to influence it? This is the basis for all spiritual work. There are no exceptions. Spiritual work requires that Spirit is involved in the process. A physical body can help to bring the spirit forward, through our posture, our intentions, the focus of our minds, but there is a point where the spirit needs to awaken, to step forward and take the helm. Ceremony creates a physical environment that supports, even encourages this. So the important question of self-reflection on your spiritual journey is not, "What am I doing?" The question is, "What part of me am I bringing forward?"

Chapter Thirty-Two

How the Day Begins

Growth and change continue. I don't need to ask or strive.

Over the years, slowly and almost imperceptibly at times, I become drawn to participate in day-to-day experiences and life in a different way. I don't decide to change anything. I don't consider the shifts then implement them. I experience the changes and the recognition of them at the same time. It is an intriguing way to live! How my days begin are one such example. I used to rise with the alarm clock at the appointed time and follow the usual pattern of eating, cleansing, and preparing for work. Now the day begins with reverence for the natural cycles, what is happening both outside of me and within me.

I gently awaken before sunrise. I can't tell you how that works, except that it does. With each season the passage of the sun across the sky, its sunrise and sunset, follows a slightly different course, and my body responds. In the winter months I sleep late, long and deep. Sometimes in the season of the longest night I wonder if I will ever rise early again! But as the sun changes its course, so do I, effortlessly. I adore the twilight, so much so that on the rare occasion I sleep in, I feel I have missed a significant part of the day. When my eyes open and I catch the hint of returning light through the window, there is no hesitation, I get up. I want to experience the waking of the earth and the waking of my body/mind at the same time. They seem a natural fit.

I have a morning ritual I like to follow. As it is still dark, I don't turn on any lights. Instead I use a few candles, just enough illumination that I can find my way. I go outside to offer prayers and copal to the spirits, to welcome them into the day with love and acknowledgement. One advantage of performing this small ceremony in the wee hours is that my neighbours can't see me, or the smoke from the copal! I do in fact, live in a very large city. I come back inside and make coffee. I sip and enjoy the warmth and bitterness while the world and I come to full awareness. It's important to me that my mind stays quiet at this time, as thoughts can detract from the experience. I find this quite easy now, although it took me years to master. When the world is dark and quiet my mind follows and becomes more active with the growing light. Once I can see easily, I sink in to my morning practice. Afterward I am ready to begin my day, to speak, to reach out to others, to be in service.

There is a saying I once came across in a greeting card: "How you spend your days, is of course, how you spend your life." I believe this to be true, which is why the beginning of each day, the way in which I bring myself to what will follow, is important, not only because my days tend to be very full but because they are full of mystery. It's not possible to know ahead of time what will be needed, what work will be done. My patients are only names on the calendar until I see them, touch them, and learn what we need to do. I can have a good idea but I must always be willing to set that aside, and listen carefully to what doesn't speak, so I can know the best way to proceed.

This same premise holds true for all of my work, the hosting of ceremonies, the teaching, and the writing. Even when I set my work aside and spend time in nature, I never know what is in store. I may receive a healing from a plant or a story from the land. Everything follows and is held in the wake of what has come before. I like to make sure I am ready.

My husband, Chris, has had to make some adjustments to the way he starts the day, to accommodate me. He would prefer someone to talk to, someone to have coffee with. He would prefer to sit across the table from

me like we were in a little breakfast bistro somewhere. I have to confess that's rarely the way it happens. Yet he is so respectful. He will glance my way to see if I make eye contact in return, or wait for me to speak first, so as not to interrupt my reverie. I usually get up before him and have the dawn to myself, but it is several hours until I have completed my practice and am ready to say, "Good morning."

Yet, as in all relationships, there must be give and take. I may have just set my intention to get out of bed, when Chris is struck by a desire to embrace his more primitive, primal roots, and in what seems to me a very gorilla-like manner, leaps over to my side of the bed, grabs me in his arms and starts making endearing grunting noises in my ear. These are often followed by a series of quick, gentle kisses, planted all over my face and neck. On those days, the spirits will just have to wait.

Chapter Thirty-Three

Dark Medicine

The realization that I am losing friendships through the choices I have made is hard to bear. Yet in the end I have to be true to myself.

For the first few minutes after I awoke I enjoyed the dawn, the soft covers all around me, and the peace and quiet. It took the full return of conscious awareness before I remembered the dream. As soon as I did, I also remembered how disturbing it was. I wanted to forget but I knew I shouldn't. It was about the Sweat Lodge so it had to be important. Reluctantly I got out of bed to grab a pen and paper and crawled back in, remembering as much as I could:

> The sweat lodge I found myself in was not our usual lodge and there were only four of us, a very small number for a sweat. From the beginning the tone and mood were different from normal, with no sense of community or comradery. We completed the first round and then Scott, our Fire Keeper, got up, got dressed, and left. He had not warned me that he would be leaving after the first round and I felt he was abandoning us. Who would now tend the fire and bring in the Grandfather stones? As we prepared for the second round I realized that we had not used

any of the medicines in the first round. Not only that, we had not brought in Grandmother Water! This did not seem possible. I suggested to one of the others that we find a soup ladle so we had something to use for pouring the water over the Grandfather stones. There were only three of us now and the other two were rapidly losing focus.

The scene changed and we were in an open, public park. The sweat lodge still felt like a sweat lodge but really it wasn't. There was no covering, no actual lodge, just a pit next to where I sat with the Grandfather stones. In my heart I was still in the lodge, but not to the outside world. The other two were out of sight now, gathering supplies or doing some other task. The scene felt very wrong. I was overly exposed considering a Sweat Lodge was a spiritual ceremony. Then I noticed people over to my left, far enough away that I couldn't speak to them, but close enough that I could see them fairly clearly. One of them was a woman. As I was looking over in her direction I saw her gather a small object in her hands, light it on fire, and throw it toward me and the stone pit. The object landed on the far side of the pit, just at the edge, and went out. I was becoming increasingly distressed. I turned to look again in the same direction. Now there was a large man, quite imposing, sitting in the same spot where the woman had been a few moments before. He was also gathering something in his hands, which he lit. Looking right at me he threw it hard. It landed in the center and the entire pit burst into flames.

Then the scene changed again and the sweat lodge was in someone's back yard. It was a real lodge. There were still only the three of us but we commented on how much safer we felt there. Then Scott unexpectedly returned. He was still dressed in his city clothes, so was not expecting to participate, but at least he was with us.

It was afternoon before I had a chance to call Fishwoman and tell her about the dream. I knew it was important. Knowing that also made me hesitant to call. Part of me just wanted to forget and pretend it was an ordinary dream. But I knew better. No longer could I get away with thoughts like that.

Luckily Fishwoman was home and answered the phone. She had time to talk, and listen. I told her of the dream, everything I could remember. Afterward her first remark was, "It sounds like someone might be jealous of you." I thought about this. I guess it was possible but it didn't feel right. Then she asked, "Is there someone who doesn't like the work you are doing? Someone who has a problem with it?" I wouldn't have thought it before, but upon hearing her words I knew there was someone—an old friend who was disturbed by the turn my life had taken. She was devout in her religious practice and had openly shared her discomfort at some of what I had disclosed in the first book. The encounter had saddened me at the time, as it showed I could no longer be as open and honest with her as I had been in the past. In addition, her husband had taken the position of not wanting to speak openly about my work. Most recently, she had begun putting her own twist on my sharing of events, going away with her own understanding, and not the one I was trying to portray. I hadn't realized until this moment—she had become righteous about her own beliefs with the result that she felt mine were misguided. At our last encounter she had actually stated that her 'God' would not be pleased with me. As all of this came flooding to the forefront of my mind, I shared some key pieces of the situation with Pauline. She felt it was appropriate.

Fishwoman then offered her advice. I needed to lift my pipe and send the flaming arrows back, but in my heart I was to hold the knowing that I was sending them to a good place, not simply doing what had been asked of me. I was to pray for the two souls who had tried to harm me. She invited me to call upon two of her helpers, the Rainbow Spirit and the Mermaid, to keep harm away from me. She continued, "Perform this ritual each day for four days in a row. Remember that you work with Creator who is loving and kind. You do not work with dangerous spirits. That is not a good thing to do. Because those two have bad intentions toward you, you must ask Creator to protect them and pray that they may come to understand."

I performed the ceremony as instructed. On the first day, it was difficult to send the arrows back without malice. I was angry that I was being judged, that my choices and my path were not being respected. I persevered, repeating the prayers and working through the internal visuals over and over until I felt they were true. My efforts were rewarded with the ease of the ceremony on the following days. By the completion of the fourth day I felt a sense of freedom and a renewed, gentle confidence in myself.

Later, upon reflection, I knew this was not the first time someone had imposed a dark medicine on me. But I was greatly relieved to discover that my soul now had ways of informing me, creating the opportunity for me to turn it around.

~~~~~~~~

One of the unfortunate consequences of the turn my life had taken is that I found myself losing friends I had imagined would be with me for life. It had not previously occurred to me that someone would feel so strongly about my path, a path that brought me wellness, joy, and purpose beyond measure, and still come to the decision that it was best we parted ways.

In my mind I have gone through all the reasonable arguments, all the possible justifications. But I am still left with the emptiness, the hole that is left behind after they are gone.

I wish I could tell you that I had found a solution, and that in the end, all was well. But in this one instance I cannot. I've had to move on, telling myself, though not convincingly, that if this was the wedge that destroyed our friendship, then it wasn't really solid to begin with.

I keep moving forward however. I can hold the sadness of the loss in my heart but I trust the path that has been laid before me. I trust my Teachers and my knowing. This is who I am. I can no longer be anyone else.

Chapter Thirty-Four

A New Name

When our spirit is suffering and our light is so very dim, we can't help but turn to the Great Spirit, who perhaps has some extra to share.

Natasha first came to see me in the summer of 2005. I remember she cried a lot during that initial session. She described a very complex mental health diagnosis: the multiple conditions she was reported to have filled more than one page single-spaced. What was meaningful to her was that she had been struggling with depression for twelve years, seeing a psychiatrist for ten, had attempted suicide, and been committed to the psychiatric ward against her will. Her professional and personal life, including her marriage, were falling apart. She was taking four different types of medication. On a physical level she had been struggling since her teen years when she was diagnosed with mononucleosis and teen fatigue, had very difficult periods which included pain and mood swings, and had surgery to remove an enlarged lymph node. Into adulthood she was diagnosed and treated for breast cancer while in her twenties. At the time of our meeting she smoked a lot, both cigarettes and drugs, and experienced states of agitation and anxiety. She suffered from seasonal allergies, frequent migraines, breakthrough menstrual bleeding, had issues with food and digestion, and in describing herself said, "I spend a lot of time in my head. I need direction on how to know which impulses are good for me and which ones are not." I noticed in our first few sessions that she had difficulty balancing her awareness between what was going on around her and what was being generated on the inside. The constant chatter of thoughts took priority, resulting in other obvious things being missed. At our third appointment when she told me, "I discovered this past week that I was mis-taking some of my meds. I was actually double dosing on a very dangerous drug. I could have had seizures!" I was not surprised.

Natasha was very committed to her healing and was not concerned that it took almost six months for the first signs of improvement to be more than fleeting. By winter that first year she was starting to have good weeks as opposed to days or hours, better energy levels, less anxiety, and less physical tension. She described her holidays as "the most stress-free Christmas I can remember. And I am not depressed." More important, she summed up her progress as, "I no longer carry around the belief that it's just a matter of time until the 'big bad one' (a depression so profound she would not survive it) comes and gets me. This is the biggest improvement and it's huge."

One year into her treatment she was well enough that her physician began to reduce her medication. Her outward life appeared much more functional; she was more aware of what was going on around her and could discern more readily what were other people's issues and problems from her own. Up until then the treatments were focused on balancing the meridian pathways, identifying hidden food sensitivities and adjusting the diet accordingly.

As we worked together to clear away the more superficial symptoms, and help the body and mind function normally, the deeper issues began to surface. Natasha did not know how to experience life from the inside out. She had always allowed others' influence to dictate her choices. She had grown up taking on the beliefs and desires of others so strongly that she had lost touch with her own. When it came right down to it she didn't know what made for a good marriage and what didn't, what type of career she might enjoy working in, or what she was actually good at! There was a deep anger and sadness inside from living an inauthentic life that had led to her depression. Her spirit had been wounded and her vitality compromised from the relentless focus on pleasing others.

I knew we could continue to work together on her wellness and she would improve, but I sensed a readiness for a significant shift. I sat in prayer and contemplation to determine what that should be. It actually didn't take very long. She needed a powerful medicine to begin living a life that was truly hers and I knew what that medicine was. She needed a new name!

A new name would provide a profound catalyst for change. As excited as I was to know what she needed, I was also clear that it was not within my rights to impose something so potent on another person. The request needed to be taken to a higher authority.

I met with the Mountain Spirit Beings and advised them of my plea. I had prepared well for the ceremony, so when nothing happened I was not concerned. I knew that waiting was sometimes necessary. In a strange way it felt like the universe itself was gathering its focus and directing its energies to determining, and presenting, the new name. Minutes passed. I continued to vision myself at the Mountain viewpoint with the others. And then it was spoken, at first sounding like a whisper on the wind, then repeating, getting louder and clearer each time. The new name was to be Anya. The following is how she received it, in her own words:

> "I had been seeing Jaki for some time when at one of our sessions she told me she had a gift for me. Even with her preface that it was a somewhat unusual and special gift, I was still rather surprised at what she offered. The gift was a new name: Anya.
>
> At first I didn't know how to feel about it. A name is a powerful thing! There were many expectations placed on me by my family to be a certain person, and that person's name was Natasha. My immediate reaction was to be concerned over the implications of moving away from that name. What would my family think? If I wasn't Natasha, who was I? But, my trust in Jaki was implicit. She had never let me down or steered me wrong. Following her recommendations was not always easy, and the effects were not always instantaneous, but every support she had offered had

improved my well-being. And while I didn't know it yet, "Who was I?" was precisely the question I needed to start asking myself.

So, not yet knowing what a perfect gift it was, I embraced and accepted it. I started out very slowly, using it as a new nickname with special, close friends. I didn't use it at work and never mentioned it to my parents. Over time I began to realize that I had never liked hearing the sound of my given name, particularly when my mother used it. It always seemed like she chose it more for her than for me, and that "I" was not the person attached to that name. I felt like it made me the possession of the person using it, that the name was used to create a certain impression for others rather than to create a connection between me and them. And so it summoned in me feelings of resentment and distance—which is a hard thing to acknowledge about your given name.

I did not know enough of Jaki's methods at the time to ask how she knew that this was the medicine I needed, or how the name itself came to her. And I have never asked. I know all I need to know; which is when someone calls me Anya, it makes me smile, and it draws me to them. Because it is who I am."

Anya continued to come for regular treatments for another four to five years. Her psychiatrist was amazed at her progress. She was able to discontinue all medication. She not only became a more functional person, she was able to discern what worked for her and what didn't. She ended up leaving her marriage and her former administrative position, and went back to school to pursue a career she had secretly wanted for years but never allowed herself to consider seriously. She found a spiritual path that brought joy and delight and committed to it. She was a pleasure to be around: smart, funny, thoughtful, kind, and cheeky in just the right amounts. Everyone she met enjoyed her company and sought out more time with her. At a ceremonial fire that we held together in 2011 I declared out loud "You are now well."

⁄ ⁄ ⁄ ⁄ ⁄ ⁄

To some, a six-year healing journey may sound like an incredibly long time. In this particular case, it is helpful to remember where Anya was when we first began. She appeared destined to failed relationships, anxiety and depression, ongoing physical symptoms, and perhaps a lifetime of medication. Of that six-year investment, the first year yielded results that many would have been satisfied with. But Anya wanted to be truly well. She had felt sick and tired and depressed for as long as she could remember, and that was on her good days. She stayed with the treatment until she felt like a new person. And that person was her!

Many months afterward, at a gathering of six apprentice practitioners who were studying with me, we held a sacred fire circle and I asked Anya if she would share her story. I thought it would be an inspirational yet realistic view of what these budding practitioners had signed up for, and how healing can sometimes take time. As Anya shared, she spoke about a pivotal event that happened just before we met. I had never heard her speak of it before. When we talked after the fire she found it hard to believe she had never told me . . . but then . . . we always had other things to discuss in our sessions together. I later asked if she would write it down for me:

Approaching the summer of 2005, I was at the end of my tether. A series of mental and physical health challenges had come to a crisis point at the end of 2002 and I had suffered a complete breakdown, being hospitalized against my will. For the two and a half years since then, I had been trying desperately to get well, gathering myself, clawing my way up from rock bottom, and sliding back down, finding a new low each time.

In desperation, I went to visit my parents in the hopes that we could mend some of the rifts between us and that I might find a safe haven and some compassion. The visit did not go well. The second day I was there, I tried to tell them what I was struggling with, but they didn't understand. There was a huge scene and I ran from the dinner table. I found myself outside, at the end of their property, which is on a cliff top overlooking the ocean. I had not attended church since I was a little girl and had no relationship with God. I did not acknowledge a higher power and did not pray. Yet I stood there, at the top of the cliff smoking a cigarette, sobbing hysterically and yelling at the stars.

"What do you want from me? I have done everything I could. I have tried everything! And I have nothing left. Nothing! I am totally alone! I don't know who I'm doing this for anymore. You need to throw me a bone because I am done, you hear me? Done!" I calmed down slightly, enough to be aware of myself. "Look," I continued, in a more reasonable tone, "I don't actually know who I'm talking to, or how these things work, but you need to send me a sign, right away. I need a sign to know that it's going to be OK, that I am not alone, or I'm done—this time for good! I'm not sure how these things work, I understand in the past you may have sent a star. I just need something, or . . . I am giving up the fight. Right now!"

At that precise moment, someone below me must have walked to the water's edge in the complete darkness and turned on a powerful flashlight. And that flashlight must have been pointing up and back toward land, because a bright beam of light hit me right in the face. More striking was an extraordinary sense of calm that flooded my entire body and being. I remember feeling actual calmness in my arms, which, to someone who has been living with intense anxiety, is a miraculous gift. At the same time, I knew, I just knew, that it was all going to be OK and that I was not alone. I heard the words, "The source of light is man."

I laughed out loud. I cannot do justice to how profound, how uplifting and at the same time grounding, the experience was. It was enough to fill me with a sense of my own worth and a renewed sense of purpose. I returned to the house and calmly told my parents that the visit was not working out and that I was going to leave the next day. My mother sneered at me in response, "Are you sure that's wise? I really don't think you're stable enough to be alone right now." "I can stay with friends if I need to Mum," I said. To which she followed with, "Really! Do you think any of your friends are going to want you like this?"

As soon as I returned to Calgary, I received a phone call and was invited out for the evening. When I arrived at the restaurant, one of those present was someone I had met before and not particularly liked. Yet on this occasion she seemed taller, lighter, and brighter than anyone else in the room. And she spent the entire evening sharing with me some of the remarkable experiences she had received recently while working with a woman named Jaki Daniels. That was the night I found the first step on my path to wellness.

Chapter Thirty-Five

Bear's Presence

Pauline has this way of dropping teachings into my lap . . .

It had been a long winter, as it often is here on the prairies, and as I sat in contemplation and reflection, I marvelled at the depth of relationship that Bear and I had developed. This wasn't something I strived for or planned, it seemed to evolve all on its own. I thought about Pauline and her connection with Bear and the Bear people, and the next time I saw her, remarked about the closeness Bear and I had achieved. Pauline was well aware that Bear is not my personal spirit animal, but one of my medicine wheel totems. As I described to her the turn our relationship had taken, she slowly started to smile.

I looked at her, puzzled, then said "What? What are you looking at me like that for?"

"I know why your relationship with Bear has changed, why it has deepened and she has become such an important teacher in your life."

"You do?"

"Of course. It was a few years ago now that I gifted you with the Lodge Keeper teachings. Since then, you have been calling Bear and Bear medicine into the lodge in the third round, the healing round. You have learned the Cree songs and have been singing them out loud with all your heart, so you can lead the people to Bear in a good way, in a strong yet gentle way. Bear has responded. Bear has come to you and offered you many gifts in exchange for this. I am not surprised. That is what happens in this way of life."

Chapter Thirty-Six

A Day Off

Pauline understood what no one else could.

It was the season of early summer and I was in Vancouver with Pauline. It was the last day of a whirlwind visit and I had spent the final morning offering her a treatment. Now we were having lunch together before I caught my flight home. As we ate and talked, I felt myself relax and settle. The hectic pace of the past few months was coming to a close and I was looking forward to finding an easier balance between work and life. This internal shift must have been more obvious than I had hoped because at one point Pauline piped up and asked outright, "What's going on? You're awfully quiet all of a sudden."

"Oh, sorry!" I immediately responded. "I was just enjoying the down time, unwinding a little, and thinking. Things have been busy for quite a while now. You know, the last day I had off was Boxing Day."

Without a moment's hesitation she countered, "Get used to it. You'll never have a day off again."

⁄ ⁄ ⁄ ⁄ ⁄ ⁄ ⁄

That brief encounter happened several years ago, yet Pauline's words stayed with me. I even shared them with a few people I knew and can honestly say they were not well received.

I have few advisors in my life, as there are not many people who fully understand what I do and the ways in which I am called to do it. But there are always those willing to dish out advice, whether requested or not. It is not unusual once someone finds out what kind of schedule I keep, for them to regale me with a greater wisdom of time management than the one I seemingly possess. I am advised to take weekends off, take vacations like everyone else, and simply say 'no' to any request that doesn't fall within the scheduled parameters.

Interestingly, those same people, when they or one of their family is in need, expect my considerations to fall outside of the rules they have just handed down. Of course I'll make myself available when it's 'them'.

This may sound like a frustrating situation, and it may have been in the past, but no longer. Helping others in need is what I do. I am happy to help and willing to commit my time, skills, and resources as best as I am able. For me the solution, and therefore the comfort level, lies not in increasing the rigidity of my work life and leisure time, but reminding myself of my personal limitations as well as the size of the community I serve. If it all gets to be too much, I need to reestablish my priorities by not extending further outward, and instead, keep my world small and manageable. Having had a healing practice for 25 years, it's a wonderful position to be in when your long-standing patients now bring their children, and those children are teenagers! I don't want to give that up. Still, it is difficult to close the door once the waiting room is full, metaphorically speaking. But I'd rather do that than to ask those already present to leave. The role of the traditional medicine person was to serve the community that served them in return. It's not helpful to extend myself beyond that, though there were times when the temptation got the better of me and it was quite a boost to my ego.

After *Heeding the Call* was published and I did some travelling for book signing and promotion, I would often stay a few extra days and offer my services. This seemed a reasonable response to the increasing number of emails I was receiving from folks I didn't know, asking for my help. While some of these sessions were indeed helpful, and others were the beginning of long-term friendships, I learned early on that it's all too easy to feel important, to feel like I have 'arrived,' and get carried away. I discovered that pushing myself to the limits ultimately takes me away from the people who need me back home. And it doesn't go just one way. I need them too. In a sense they are the butcher, the baker, and candlestick maker. They are valuable members of my community. We don't all have the same skills—why should we? I dedicate myself to my work and I appreciate it so much when they do the same. Then we can really be in service to each other.

As a medicine person you come to realize that as your helping role becomes acknowledged by others, in a sense you *are* the medicine. While you always need to keep in mind that you are simply a vessel, and your spiritual work is to become as clear and pure a vessel as possible, what you have the capacity to call forth, through your dedication to the path and the relationships you hold with your partners in Spirit, shapes you into a particular kind of vessel.

Different types of containers are most suited to the contents they will hold and that they will ultimately deliver. Olive oil is best held in a pouring style vessel, with a spout that easily controls the amount released. A butter dish needs to be open at the top, to allow access for a knife. A salt shaker is crowned with small holes to facilitate its even distribution on the surface of food. In all applications, the form and function of the container itself enhances the delivery of what is held inside. In walking a medicine path, this is the part that is our work in the world. This is where discipline is required. Every day you must strive to be a more effective vessel, to see more clearly, to become aware of the blocks and filters that could taint the purity of the medicine. Every day you must be willing to shed what is no longer useful. This is the human part of the work. It is not easy. Many of us are attached to our perspectives. We like the way we think. We enjoy our particular take on things. It is part of what makes up our character and personality. So it's a fine line to see where you are limiting your possible spiritual growth and ability to be in service, and where you are being true to who you are and how you express yourself.

Once you recognize and accept yourself as a vessel of the medicines of Nature and Spirit, you accept the responsibility to hold the knowing of what that means, in a good way. Just as when you become a Pipe Carrier and you accept responsibility to hold the pipe appropriately or return it for safekeeping. A medicine woman is someone who understands the influence of the medicines, their application, timing, and appropriate need. As she walks through her daily life, she is carrying the capacity to offer those medicines with her, literally. That is why she, and people like her, are known as medicine people. As such, at any moment, they may be called into service. As vessels, they should always be prepared to initiate delivery.

So the medicine person walks with a particular type of awareness, always being on the lookout for when a need arises. This is what Pauline meant when she said that I would never have a day off again. It doesn't mean that I'll never have a day to myself, never have leisure time, never be able to go on holiday or to have fun. What it does mean is that I am always carrying with me the tools to be in service, and the timing and the needs that arise are outside of my control.

In many ways, her words were not only potent in their message, but a testament to the trust she places in me to serve with the gifts I have been given. She understood what no one else in my world did, though I admit it probably took several more years to truly understand it myself.

Chapter Thirty-Seven

Contemplating Suicide

Soul retrieval can also help a patient to trust that the cries of their soul have indeed been heard...

I met the following patient purely by chance. As she describes below, she literally found me in the phone book and called to ask if I would participate in an informal survey she was conducting for a university class. I couldn't really answer any of her questions; they didn't apply to me, but as I took the time to explain why, she came to understand a little about the nature of my practice. She called back to book an appointment. I saw her only three times, but she was willing to write down her experience so that I could share it with others.

Before I met Jaki I had been severely depressed for seven years. I had been hospitalized twice for suicide attempts and saw no reason in living. I struggled through each day, never happy, just living for the sake of living and living to appease those around me. I saw no future and no hope. I had tried so many different treatments. I had tried a variety of antidepressants and made sure that I was living healthy by eating right, exercising, and getting enough sleep. I had talked to counsellors and psychiatrists, but still nothing helped. It seemed that everything I did just made things worse. I had given up on ever getting better and just accepted my fate. And then a ray of hope finally shone through—Jaki. I had an assignment in school to call different health professionals and learn more about them, and was flipping through the yellow pages when I came across Jaki's number. I called and talked to her and just talking raised my hopes that maybe, just maybe, this was the one thing that could help me. I booked an appointment with her and that was the best decision of my life. The first appointment she spent getting to know me and balancing my meridians. I didn't feel any different after that first time but I wanted to give it another chance as I didn't want to live like this anymore. The next appointment she went into my awareness and described things about me that nobody else had ever known. Who she was describing was exactly me! She fixed the broken little girl inside and right after that I felt a change. Being a pessimist I thought it was only my imagination and that things would go back to the way they were before. However, that didn't happen. What was really amazing about it was that it wasn't something that I had to think about or consciously fix. It was just something that had happened. I had gotten my will to live back. I now experience joy and happiness and contentment in my life, something I never would have thought could happen to me. I see again a point for living. I wake up each day looking forward to it rather than dreading it. I can't believe how much my life has changed and how it feels to be happy. Everything is so much clearer and brighter and more positive. I can't thank Jaki enough for the wonderful difference that she made in my life.

S.G. Calgary, Alberta, 2009

One of the most significant features of the treatment session for S.G. was when I "fixed the broken little girl inside." This type of healing is known as soul retrieval, and is considered one of the classic indigenous healing methods, having been used in one way or another by indigenous peoples all

around the world for thousands of years. Often taught as a cor̄
shamanic training, it is a remedy, or medicine, for soul loss, whicʰ
when a part of us 'shuts down' in order to cope with a trauma, anᴅ ᴖ
never re-establishes its former place within the context of our character,
personality, and soul. Almost everyone experiences some form of soul
loss, as life often presents challenges that are more than we can handle.
Children are particularly susceptible, as they are naturally innocent and
sensitive, and have very little control over what happens to them and what
circumstances they find themselves in. Depending on the sensitivity of the
person and the degree of soul loss, it's possible to significantly affect how
they feel and function for the rest of their lives. In a traditional setting, the
medicine person would always be on the lookout for signs of soul loss,
particularly in the aftermath of a crisis. When signs were evident, it was a
fairly straightforward matter to restore the isolated soul part and return the
patient to wholeness. It simply required calling upon the skills to transcend
the realm of the physical and enter into the territory of the soul. From there,
a variety of methods and techniques could be used, depending on the culture,
training, and inherent abilities of the practitioner. In our modern society,
we aren't savvy to the signs of soul loss, and even if we were, we seldom
have an understanding that there is a remedy available, or have access to
a trusted resource that can resolve the situation quickly and efficiently. In
S.G.'s case she never understood the 'cause' of her distress. She had no
knowledge that one of her life's wounds had created a tear in the fabric of
her being. But losing the will to live is a sign of deep suffering. Her soul
certainly felt the effects of the loss.

It is a strange sensation to have another person describe your inner
thoughts and feelings, and even stranger when the memory is so vague it is
almost intangible. Yet when the words are spoken and the story is revealed,
a part of you knows that it's true. After all, it's your story.

What's more, when a patient's secret inner world is revealed during a
session, it creates an atmosphere of trust that serves to bond the therapeutic
relationship. It helps the patient to feel that they have made the right choice.
There is a validation and authentication to their inner experience that they
may never have imagined possible.

I remember once when I was working with a woman in her late fifties. During the session a strong image appeared of her as a young girl, about six years old. I could see what she was wearing with amazing detail. She had on a navy blue pleated skirt with a white collared blouse and blue sweater, with only the top button of the sweater done up. Her legs were bare until they reached the top of her white socks, which were neatly tucked into her patent leather shoes. I shared every nuance I could but it turned out it was the feeling that accompanied the visual scene that stirred something within her. I described a strange sensation when I looked at those clothes. It was like something in the scene was frozen and I couldn't even imagine her wearing anything else. This struck me as odd and I told her so. Afterward the woman shared that when she was in the first grade, she had only one outfit to wear to school each day, which matched exactly the one I had just described. Every single day, all year round, rain or shine, winter or spring, she wore those same clothes, was constantly teased by the other students, and eventually grew to hate it. Over time it became one of the most embarrassing memories of her life. She was in awe that another person could find that memory stored deep down inside, particularly when she hadn't thought of it for years. From that moment on, she trusted the stories that arose from her soul and allowed herself to receive them fully.

⁓ ⁓ ⁓ ⁓ ⁓ ⁓ ⁓

Ironically most patients leave my treatment room without ever sharing that I 'struck a chord' with their intimate selves. When I narrate during a session, patients are not usually *just* listening—the words, the tone, the mood, the feel—all conspire to take them into a different experience of being. Usually, they want to stay with the feeling as closely as possible and not risk any disruption by speaking out loud. Once the session is complete, those personal 'aha' moments are often overshadowed by the more dramatic aspects of the work. Almost every soul retrieval patient goes home with some detail that held particularly potent meaning for them. These are the stories they share with friends and family, the ones that clearly portray the intricacies and possibilities of this type of healing work.

Chapter Thirty-Eight

It's Never Too Late

Through our thoughts, actions, and words, we can help to restore 'right relationship' with the natural world.

My assistant arrived carrying a large bag and flashing a distinct twinkle in her eyes. When I greeted her at the door she immediately asked if we could spend a few minutes together before her work in my office began. We sat on the couch and she opened the bag to reveal a beautiful, handmade drum and tom.

Without any prompting on my part she described the process of finding this particular drum. She had been looking for months, shopping at stores, asking others who had purchased drums as well as those who made them. It was on the internet she finally found what she was looking for. She told me the story of the man who made it, the animal skin she had selected, the type of wood frame, and the long wait until she was finally able to hold it in her hands.

Then her tone changed and she became almost apologetic, stating that she needed to be completely honest. As the drum had been commissioned from someone she had never met, and given the brief long-distance and detached relationship the craftsman and herself had shared, she suspected the drum was not made in a way that honoured the death of the animal that had contributed its skin. Likely, it was made like any ordinary drum, with no ceremony involved.

My heart went out to her. She now held in her hands the drum she had always wanted but an important piece was missing and she was looking to me to reconcile it. As it happened, I knew exactly what to say to put her at ease.

I described a hypothetical scenario. What if I was making a drum? I don't hunt so would have no way to ask the animal if it would be willing to sacrifice, or to acknowledge that sacrifice appropriately. I too would be forced to find a hide, likely from a leather supplier, risking that it may have come from a distinctly mistreated source. Then I would have to purchase the frame and sinew, again with the plant and animal at best disregarded, to arrive home to put it all together.

However, when the drum was complete I would take it into ceremony to initiate it, enliven it, and prepare it for our work together. No matter what its origins, the hands that built it or the courier that delivered it, when it became a tool for me to do sacred work, it too would become sacred.

It was now in her hands. She could choose to change the course of what had happened with the drum up until this point. She could begin with ceremony. She could give thanks to the animal that gave its skin, to the tree that provided the frame, and to the man who built it. Then it would no longer matter what had come before. Held within each moment is the possibility for a new beginning. It was never too late to acknowledge, honour, and respect all the elements and stages that had brought this drum into her life. It's never too late to be sacred.

Weeks later, around a ceremonial fire, I shared the story and the teaching with Scott. He embraced it fully and in the years since has often passed this particular teaching along. How many times do we stop ourselves short because we don't like the way others do things? We don't like the way our neighbours apply herbicides to their lawn. We don't like that a relative works at a lumber mill. We get angry that yet another oil rig appears in the forest or farmer's field, or even that the city keeps sprawling outward, requiring more land to be clear-cut and levelled, stripped of all life and natural habitat.

This is the world that we live in. These changes are being made to support the species that we are and the number of occupants of Mother Earth

we have become. We all want food, shelter, light, heat, and roadways to maintain our lifestyles.

We do not have direct control of all the factors that support our lives. We are responsible for acting wisely when we can, but if we can't, then instead of feeling angry, victimized, or let down, we can instead consider the opportunity to turn it around. It's another important step that we can take toward a reciprocal and balanced relationship with Mother Earth and Nature.

A few years ago there was a G8 Summit meeting held here in Kananaskis, the very same wilderness area where the Mountain resides, where Fishwoman and I host Vision Quest each year, and where our community goes to experience nature, and to reconnect. To accommodate the dignitaries, the meetings and other events, parts of the forest were laid bare and buildings erected. Our pristine wilderness was swarmed by politicians, reporters, other invited guests, and of course, protestors. I was incensed. "Couldn't they have picked somewhere already inhabited?"

All I could think about was the Mountain and how close they would be. I mentioned my distress to Fishwoman and she suggested we go there before any of the destruction happened, sit on the mountainside and lift our pipes. We had a chance to inform the land and the creatures, to warn them of what was about to happen. We had the opportunity to let them know that we valued our relationship with them even if others didn't. We went to the Mountain that day and we poured out waves of love and appreciation for the land. We would not forget that it was a sacred place, in fact we would hold that more strongly than ever now, to balance the opposing influence.

As it happened, it turned out to be one of the least violent Summits held in recent years. It was the land itself that suffered the most compromise from the event. But Mother Earth knows how to renew and replenish, given the chance. We were able, at least, to prevent an almost inevitable shock and trauma. We were able to offer support and condolences. We did what we could, knowing where the wounds could cut the deepest, and held our resolve to keep the land, and all that it offered, in the highest regard.

Each year when we arrive to host Vision Quest, the land welcomes us more warmly than the year before. The ancestors join us in our ceremonies, the animals that visit are calm and respectful. The visions of the people get stronger, and the feeling of being held in the arms of Nature and Spirit is unforgettable.

Chapter Thirty-Nine

Origins of Disease

There is a responsibility inherent in working with the gifts received from the realm of Spirit. We must be diligent to do our part.

Taking my understanding of health, healing, and medicines to the deepest level possible is undoubtedly one of the passions of my life. More than thirty years later, I'm still learning, still growing, still pursuing the quest to understand all the nuances of health that I possibly can. The following journey intention exemplifies this tendency:

"Teach me about the origins of disease, with particular attention to the nonphysical aspects of our body and being."

I find myself looking at a type of body, a hologram? It floats above some elusive surface. It has the overall shape of human form, but no features. I see it circling while lying prone, so I can see the head in front of me, then as it turns, the side, then the feet. It appears black with a golden network of light that either covers the surface or is embedded throughout—I can't tell which. I feel there are many beings around me, as if I have found myself in some very large observation chamber.

I realize the golden network moves throughout. It is not a network of energy pathways. It is a grid system that divides the body into units.

In the form I am observing, any piece can be removed and examined more closely. Ahhh, not quite! It is what remains within the hologram that is of importance, not the piece that is removed.

In the figure before me the outer area of the grid, over the right hip, is taken away. I can see disease in the energy field remaining. On the physical level the flesh looks like it has been eaten away: it appears raw, open, and rotting. The light that runs through it is of a colour and density that I know are incorrect.

I ask, "What does this teach me?"

I receive an answer but do not know who is speaking. "The physical hip is eroding slowly. Bone is diminishing in strength and increasing in porousness. The body in this example would need a hip replacement in your medical model. The energy that should be directed to maintaining bone has been redirected into the energy field as the 'rotting flesh' look. That energy is dense, heavy, and dull. It does not have enough light of its own or enough access to Divine light, to sustain it. It is like a growing mass of pain and separation, resulting in the physical hip degeneration."

I ask, "Can it be healed? What do we know about the source/origins of the dense energy mass?"

"This particular mass belongs to a male and is the result of much angst and turmoil. He spent decades of his life being unhappy and dissatisfied with his work, with his family, and the state of the world, yet he did nothing to improve himself or to find solutions. But he did suffer: he had much emotional pain. His mantra throughout his life was 'why does it have to be this way?' yet if we look back, further into his history, we will see him as a child. He was often left alone and had no siblings. His mother was a chain smoker who worked nights and had little time or use for him. His environment was always polluted in one way or another. He cried a lot as an infant and soon lost his trust of the Divine, especially as it exhibited itself through human nature."

"How do we fix it?"

We fix it with Love, yet in this case it has progressed too far. The dark mass has a stronghold, as it exists in his physical body, in his

energy field, in his mind and his memories. His patterns of being are firmly established. He is not willing to receive what he does not know exists. But he can receive some relief. In our male model we are able to temporarily remove the physical component to see the effect on his field of energy. This allows us to work directly with the field, in this case at that precise location, efficiently and effectively. The heavy, dense rotting energy has almost become solid and can be removed. This is easy and difficult. The easy part is to remove the energy mass similar to what you understand as extraction, or even physical surgery. It is how to reestablish the energy field afterward that is difficult. You see, the hip of the physical body has already degenerated, so we cannot restore the field to full light and brilliance. That would be discordant and bring much confusion to the physical bone structure at this stage. Also, each individual person has an energy signature which needs to be maintained at all costs. This is the reason some of your transplant victims access memories and feelings of others. This is not how it should be. The energy signature is critical; it must be maintained and not disturbed. As we know we cannot affect a cure, we do what we can to establish a moderately diseased field which can exist with both the physical body and the greater soul. The nuances of that methodology are not to be revealed now. It was most important for you to understand the complexity of the healing work you have inquired about. There are many of what you call 'energy workers' who are ignorant of these realities and therefore dangerous. They believe that the removal of physical symptoms and pain, even temporarily, is a success. But what of the inner nature of the patient? Has the work and tasks performed 'healed' them, that is, moved them to a greater understanding and acceptance of themselves and Creation? Or has another dis-ease been placed within them? Another disruption to their signature that now needs to be accommodated? You in the physical world should not interfere in realms where you have no true assessment of your influence. We will end here today."

- - - - - - -

s a pivotal journey for me in understanding disease and how, at
st essential core, we are all beings of light and energy. This light
energy moves and flows in predetermined patterns that provide the
roundation for our functioning and are unique to each individual. This
journey opened up a novel opportunity for me to explore the nature and
basis of illness in my patients. What I discovered in practice however, was
that this matrix, as I came to call it, would only show up on occasion, and
not every time I asked. Being so grateful for its presence when it did appear,
I hesitated to ask why. I was quite content with the trust and understanding
that some things were not meant to be. There is a reference in the journey
that to "*restore the field to full light and brilliance would be discordant and bring
much confusion to the physical bone structure.*" That's a potent message that
not all healing is about restoring full health. And more important—that
I cannot know what is truly in the best interest of the patient. When I
have asked for the matrix and it did appear, I have been able to request the
removal of one of the outer parts of the grid to reveal what was happening
underneath. In some patients I have been privileged to watch the healing
light restored, and their pain and distress diminish.

This highlights one of the most beautiful aspects of spirit medicine; its
use is necessarily guided by a higher force, one that is truly intelligent.
This prevents the errors that result from human judgement. I am not the
source of the medicine, I am the means through which it is delivered. I do
not assign the dosage or control the speed in which it is received.

When medicines become separate from their source, dried herbs for
example, they have lost their life force, and therefore their capacity for
intelligence. They still contain physical and chemical components, so they
retain therapeutic potential, but the healing properties are now guided by
the hands and minds of humans. The plant no longer has a spiritual component to give. It is also limited to helping the physical body and has no
ability to support the greater whole. In my experience, this is not where the
root cause of most illness lies. This limitation further dictates that only the
symptoms, the signs of distress, can be treated. While I fully acknowledge
that symptom relief is important, and sometimes necessary, I no longer
consider it a form of healing.

Chapter Forty

A Song for the Earth

Humankind are part of the naturally created world and the web of life.

In the shadow of the Rocky Mountains there are many special places. The raw beauty of the land endures and the more we find ourselves immersed in city and concrete, the more valued these pristine locations become. These areas have a long history of traditional use, some of them being recognized as pathways used by First Nations peoples to travel from prairie, through foothills, to the mountains. When we find such a spot, we naturally want to spend time there, and to stay as long as possible. Nature provides the sanctuaries we need in our modern day lives.

The family that called for my help had built their home on one such property. The house had been artfully designed to fit in with the landscape and to enhance the natural features rather than take away from them. It was a stunning piece of architecture. When the transformation of the land was complete however, the celebration was subdued. It was clear there was something wrong.

Perhaps it was the inherent beauty of the natural setting that highlighted what might otherwise have gone unnoticed. Perhaps it was the contrast between how it felt to be there before and how it felt afterward. It's hard to know all the factors that brought forward the awareness that the land was no longer the same. I was grateful that the owners had paid attention and reached out for help.

When I first arrived at the property I went for a long walk. There were places on the land that took my breath away—literally. A stress response would overtake my body and it became difficult to breathe. In other areas my reaction was more subtle. I just wanted to keep moving and not linger there. Overall, the land around the property was much too quiet. It struck me that the songs of the natural world were not being sung there. The entire area was in a state of shock.

As I continued to walk, I purposely extended the perimeter, in search of a nearby area that felt untouched by all the changes, an area that felt sacred. Remarkably, only a few feet away, there was a stone ridge that attracted me as the ideal place to perform a small ceremony.

I gathered the owners and a group of four participated in smudging, drumming, and singing to the land, acknowledging and honouring its ancestry. Within minutes everyone felt a tangible wave of happiness wash over them, rising up from the ground below and cresting over the ridge. This was significant, as the others had no previous experience or knowledge that such a thing was possible. It was confirmation that the land was longing to return to its natural state.

There was no doubt that we had established a connection. It was now time for a deeper inquiry. Still sitting on the same ridge, I shifted my awareness to deep within the earth beneath me, then waited to see what messages and images the land brought forth.

I go through a cave-like dark tunnel. I feel like I am boring into the earth. There is a sense of violation. I am making a tunnel where none has existed before—metal into stone, cold, hard, determined, void of understanding and acknowledgment. The vibrations reach outward to the rooted ones and create an altered pattern in the messages they receive from the earth. Their spirit becomes numb and they survive in a type of suspended animation, here, yet not fully here. I realize the entire property needs a soul retrieval for the nature spirits to return to their full vibrancy. I come out of the tunnel, backwards, and find myself

on the land. Its voice has been silenced. The void that was created is strongest where the house and outbuildings stand, but there is also anger in some outlying areas. The land beyond the immediate influence is still strong and I note that it is watched over by the mountains. It was the vibration of the massive machines, accompanied by their smell and noise, that compromised this area, not the structure itself. I come to understand that all creatures of the earth are free to build their 'nests' in whatever way they choose, using materials provided by the earth. Yet none, other than humans, violate the sanctity of underground stone. Dig a foundation into the earth—yes, build your structure upon the earth—yes, but do so in respect of the natural outcroppings and formations of the land. I hear the words, "Your people are welcome to live with us, we only ask that you consider our livelihood, as you would any other good neighbour."

I returned to the site the following day with Carol, a student and friend. Just as we were about to begin another round of ceremony, a small red fox with a bushy tail trotted across the grounds. I took this as a sign—a very positive one. As I sat and began to extend my awareness, I knew that I needed to drum. I lit some sage to have it burn gently while we worked. I had learned the day before that this land was responsive to our ceremony and our offerings. Today, if it was to receive any kind of healing, it must begin with a process of opening. There remained a blanket of stillness and quiet that hovered eerily over the place.

A part of this land's soul had retreated deep under the ground. It was clear where I had to begin.

As I entered in, to approach and see what I might find, a cloud-like misty face eased tentatively forward to meet me. I recognized it as a soul part yet it was not trapped in the usual sense. It had separated during the trauma created when the foundation of the home had been excavated and had been waiting ever since to be shown that it could return. "Yes," I tell her (for she appeared female to me), "it is time to come up and out, and step back into the light." Then there was no longer one face, but a cascade of them. These were followed by the faces of many four-legged creatures.

Carol and I offered tobacco, then sat patiently for the next steps to be shown. Slowly and quietly, then louder and clearer with each repetition, a song was given to me by the land. I wasted no time in teaching it to Carol. We sang it out loud three times. Afterward, it felt wonderful to feel the now-silent echoes still hanging in the air around us. I sensed spirits in our midst. I closed my eyes and saw them approaching, tenderly, with bare feet. Their skirts were woven and brightly coloured. I saw no faces. It was the way they walked upon the earth that they wanted me to see. They walked to the rhythm of the song we had sung! This was Nature, alive and responsive. The spirits and the ancestors heard every word and adjusted their footsteps accordingly. I heard, "Keep singing, keeping perching, keep playing. We are with you."

I took my awareness back into the ground below. I found myself in a cold and rigid place. It was hard to move. There was no 'give' in the earth there. I had to push my way through the stiff roots and stone. I saw a small patch of light up ahead and a little to the left. I kept pushing toward it. When I arrived, I knew what had to be done. The song wasn't given as a mere gift. It was given to use as a medicine to sing the soul back into this place, and reach into the depths where the shock and stillness could still be felt. I found a clearing large enough that I could stand and sing. And so I began. I sang the song that had been given and as I did so, it was like lighting a match, offering fire and warmth to the earth and all of its roots, and as each part received it the warmth spread further and further outward. I sang the song a second time and all the subterranean creatures gathered round me, as if I was Snow White calling to them in a Disney movie. They placed themselves in a semi-circle and swayed their bodies to the song. During the third round, the stone people started to revive and reclaim their spirit nature. They were returning to life! Once this happened I found it difficult to keep my awareness below the surface. I was up on top,

then below, then on top, then below again. I was experiencing that there was no longer a separation! They were connected once more because they flowed back and forth and with each other. In my physical body I lay down on the earth. I realized what had just happened and it was very humbling. I wanted to stay still and quiet for a while.

It was a privilege to be part of this land's return to wholeness. It was also a very important teaching—that when we humans took the time and effort to consider the effects of our influence here on the earth, we could heal any wounds that may have been created in the process. The land knew what it needed and that it needed help. We made ourselves available and the land responded by teaching us the song that we could offer back to the earth and the nature spirits.

We can heal the rift that has been created between us. Humans are as much part of the balance of nature as any other creature. We are supposed to be here.

Chapter Forty-One

Wrongly Accused

The effects of a trauma can completely bypass the physical body and enter into the emotions and mind.

Jeff came to see me in the winter of 2003. He was at that stage in life where he was preparing for retirement. He had first started working as a teenager, when the family homestead needed more grown-up contributions, and never since had the opportunity to stop, other than the annual two-week vacation. A life of hard work had worn him down somewhat but his retirement was the light at the end of a long tunnel. He could hardly wait. When it was close enough to be counted in months instead of years, he found himself embroiled in a dilemma that he could never have foreseen, and which directly threatened his future. He was accused of stalking a young girl and the court case was pending.

The young girl was a cashier in a supermarket chain and Jeff worked for the same company as a transportation clerk. In the course of his duties he would occasionally come into the store. To the cashier he was one of those creepy old men who was always flirtatious. Jeff, being the friendly type, and admittedly one with an eye for the pretty girls, would often give her a wink and a smile, saying hello when he saw her. It turned out the two also lived in the same neighbourhood. It was one of Jeff's habits to take an after-dinner walk each night, and it was during one of those walks that she recognized him, became concerned, and assumed he was following her. As the nightly ritual continued, she became convinced.

During the first few months after the official charges were laid, Jeff was not at all concerned. He knew he hadn't done anything wrong, trusted the law, and figured it was just a matter of time until the truth came to light. He felt confident that if he had to go to court and speak his piece the judge would rule fairly. Unfortunately the waters became quite muddied after that when his lawyer advised that the young woman was in possession of a tape recording that clearly portrayed his guilt.

Now Jeff was angry. He couldn't understand what might be on the tape or how she came to have it and he began to fear he was being targeted. If the distorted evidence was considered viable he could be found guilty. His wife, who had always been trusting of him, now began to suspect that perhaps he had deceived her too. After all, the evidence doesn't lie.

In the end, it turned out the young woman didn't have any tape recording. She had made it up to scare him and get the upper hand. Finally, after many months of angst and turmoil, the case was dropped. In the process Jeff discovered that his accused was from a family 'known' to the police for frequent disputes that escalated out of control. Once everything was over and life settled back to normal, Jeff found that he was not able to move past it. He thought about it all the time. When he came to see me, he said "I don't think there will ever be a time in my life from now on when I am not angry. I am angry every single day. I hate what she did to me."

Jeff was a reluctant patient in the sense that he would never have come to see a practitioner like myself unless he was forced to. And in this case, his wife had done just that. She couldn't stand living with him the way he was so he finally agreed to come. As it happened, his workplace was also trying to assist in his recovery and had scheduled him for a psychiatrist appointment the same afternoon. He had never seen a psychiatrist in his life, but this route made sense to him, and besides, it was covered under his health care plan.

To me, this was a textbook case of an emotional trauma that had not been able to dissipate once the crisis was over. He was unable to let it go because the residue was literally trapped inside him, disrupting and interfering with

any possible peace of mind. I used a simple extraction process to remove the residue, a healing method common to indigenous practitioners. Our time together was one hour, after which he went on to his next appointment. I saw him for a twenty-minute follow-up twelve days later. His first words to me were, "I'm feeling much better." He went on to say that he was now moving on with his life and hardly ever spoke of, or thought about, the incident.

I found out months later that he never went to another psychiatrist appointment either, but he sure figured that guy was good—after only one appointment he was all better!

Chapter Forty-Two

Health and Vitality

Bear helps me gain a perspective I didn't have before.

"Bear, what advice do you have for me to be as vibrant and healthy as possible?"

As soon as I see Bear ambling toward me, I feel nervous, I don't know why. Perhaps because I have been sternly warned before about speaking of the negative, or considering myself in a negative light. Could this be influencing me today?

As I breathe, I am aware of how much larger my physical body is than the one in my journeys. I am so lean and fit in the body I have when I visit Bear. Bear comes around and sits on my left. He plops himself down by the fire with a bit of a sigh—I sense he is tired. At first I wonder what he has been doing but then I have a flash—what if he has become tired because I have become tired? I know we are connected. Sometimes I think we are one. Could I possibly be influencing Bear's health and strength? I then sense that his inner organs are not as clean and tuned as they should be. Perhaps he is aging or wearing out. How can that be?

Bear speaks, "You see me and you feel me. You are correct. I am, or more accurately, can be, a direct reflection of you, of your state of being. You really must eat more fish and take your cod liver oil. You need to trim the fat, especially around your middle. Look at you here, lithe, flexible, pale, and beautiful. You are thin yet so strong. You are quick and agile. Your system is not only well tuned but finely tuned."

He starts to cook me a fish in the fire. I sense he is a little perturbed or frustrated with me.

He continues, "You make strange choices that I do not understand. When I eat, I eat to build strength, which I need to protect my life and those of my little ones. You are bombarded with choices that do not serve you and you have no discipline to avoid them."

I look over at Bear with a slight embarrassment. 'He' now feels like a 'she' and I think, "She takes such good care of me." I shift my gaze to the fish crisping in the fire and she telepathically responds—"We both need to eat fish!" I can feel there is more she wishes to teach me. It is clear that the fish needs to be cooked whole. Then I am to peel the skin and eat only the flesh. I try to imagine a 'filet' and it just doesn't work. I look to Bear again. Her silent teachings continue. There is something just under the skin that I need for nourishment. As the fish is heated on the outside and the skin chars, it releases a substance which melts into the flesh. When I remove the skin while still hot, it is there as part of the nutrients of the meal. When a fish is skinned cold, this layer is removed and discarded, leaving the fish less able to nourish. As I eat, the fish is so juicy and tender, so clean tasting. I can feel how its protein is easily accepted and received by my body.

As the journey ends Bear and I are sitting side-by-side at the fire. We each have a poking stick like the one she uses to cook the fish and we gently play with the logs and coals as we share stories and enjoy our time together.

When my full awareness returns I find myself in a slightly altered state. I am aware of the mind/ego/identity/sense-of-self and my body as two different aspects of my being. From that state of dual awareness the thoughts start to flow. The body has no choice but to do the best it can with whatever "I" give it. If I under-eat, it must bear

the burden. If I over-eat, it must find ways to store the excess. If I exercise, it must meet my demands. If I am lazy, it must still respond to my intentions to move. The body can and will inform me, but depending upon my relationship to it, it can be a powerless victim of my mind/ego. I decide what goes into my body and what doesn't. I decide if I want to eat unhealthily, if I have a craving, or a desire for a certain food. I rule with my mind and the body must comply. After all it is MY body. This is not the ideal relationship. This is a victim/perpetrator relationship.

The body is wise to its own needs and has many ways to inform 'me' of them: hunger, thirst, stiffness, pain, restlessness, sleeplessness, bad breath, pimply skin, and the list goes on and on.

What if I listened to my body and responded to its signals? We all talk about listening to our bodies, but I mean eating when hungry and not eating when not hungry, even though it may be dinnertime. How often have you stayed awake when you felt tired? What about noticing thirst and then inquiring how best to quench it—hot tea, cool water, juice? Let the body inform and advise, not the mind/desire/ego.

The more you listen to the body, the more it will communicate with you. This type of relationship will spill over into other aspects of your life. Learn to listen and be aware of the subtle signs around you, releasing the mind's desire to dominate every move, and experience the freedom.

Chapter Forty-Three

Becoming an Elder

I had no idea I was ready.

I knew this was no ordinary dream, that this was a *big* dream, even while I was still in it. It started out innocently enough. There were several people sitting at a large, round, wooden table. The one who immediately captured my attention was Eliot, one of my first teachers in the traditional ways. Eliot meant a lot to me and I knew from past experience that his presence in a dream was not to be taken lightly. In his arms, held close to his chest, was a tiny infant, perhaps a few weeks old. This babe-in-arms had a white gown, white knitted socks and hat. It squirmed and made sounds as it tried to turn its head from side to side, adjusting its body to maintain its comfort. Being so small, one couldn't help but be struck by how helpless and dependent it was.

I recognized a few of the others at the table. They were Eliot's most senior apprentices, now all shamans in their own right, having completed six or more years of their twelve-year commitment. I didn't belong to this group. This was Eliot's world, the shamanic path of the Huichol people of Mexico. I felt like an outsider.

The baby started to squirm and whimper so Eliot adjusted his hold on its body. As he did so, with great care and attention, there was a moment when the baby's face became visible. It was not the face of a baby! It was the face of an Old One, an Elder. Without words being spoken I came to know that Eliot had taken on a huge responsibility. He had agreed to care for the Elder for a period of three years. During that time, the 'baby' would not grow, it would stay completely helpless in body, yet wise in spirit. It would be a teacher for Eliot, inviting him to enter the sacred mysteries. In turn, he was caregiver, 24 hours a day, 7 days a week, 52 weeks a year. In this work, there were no babysitters, no partners, no significant others to help out. Eliot was one of the busiest people I knew and he had accepted this baby as his charge. Perhaps because I'm a mother, I could feel the weight of his decision, and my mind immediately went to many of the practical ramifications.

I was still sitting there at the table, trying to take it all in, when Eliot spoke for the first time. I can't remember the words exactly, but he told me that his time with the Elder was soon drawing to a close. He lifted the baby slightly, to disengage it from the warmth of his body, and held it toward me. He asked if I would be next, if I would commit three years of my life to taking care of the baby Elder.

It was too much. I couldn't do it and I didn't understand why he was asking me, instead of one of his own apprentices who were obviously on hand. What did it mean? Was he inviting me to enter the Huichol tradition? I wasn't interested in that. I had found my tradition. I knew who I was. I forced myself to wake up, to extricate myself from the decision entirely.

/ / / / / /

Pauline and I were hosting our annual Vision Quest in the mountains, which is always a special time. It was Day Three and the second group of people were coming out of their circles in the forest, so grateful for the fresh fruit and hot tea after their time of fasting. Scott, our Fire Keeper, informed us that the Grandfathers were ready. The Sweat Lodge could begin anytime.

I looked around and Pauline was nowhere to be found. I was used to this. While I didn't know where to find her I knew what she was doing. She delighted in being an Elder and whenever anyone needed her, she was there, being so fully present in her attention to them that in those moments, nothing else mattered. As much as I loved Pauline this put me in the awkward

position of always being the one to interrupt, to remind her that everyone was waiting at the lodge, that they had eaten and were ready to enter.

In any other context the Elder would naturally take all the time she needed and no one would dare to intervene. The Elder came first, and in so doing, no one could be ready until the Elder was ready. That's just the way it was. However, Vision Quest was an exception. It takes a particular kind of strength and courage for those raised in a Western culture to be able to go without food, water, comfort, and shelter, while alone in the forest, for up to three days and three nights. In those first minutes and hours after returning to camp and to the group, the world of Spirit can fade quickly, even without conversation or eye contact. Yet everyone is asked to stay with Spirit until after the Sweat Lodge is complete. Then they may return to the physical world.

In the Cree tradition, a Sweat Lodge has four rounds. In each round, red-hot Grandfather stones are added to the centre pit, and with song and prayer, the Lodge Keeper unites the stones with Grandmother Water, creating the steam. During Vision Quest participants initially enter the sweat lodge for only two rounds and are then taken and placed in their circles in the forest. That way, they stay 'in ceremony' for the duration of their time there. Once they have been signalled to return to camp, they enter the lodge again for the final two rounds. This completes the ceremony and prepares them to re-enter the physical realm.

I found Pauline sitting at a picnic table with one of the questers who had returned to camp the day before. They were deeply engaged in conversation. I had no choice. My heart was with those who needed to enter the lodge, which was exactly where it should be. Pauline and I were a team. We balanced each other out. When I was not available for the people, she was, and vice versa. I sat down beside her. They both knew immediately why I was there, no explanation was needed. A few minutes later we were all standing and saying our good-byes. It was time for our guest to return home. Her time with us, for this year anyway, was done.

Quickly changing into our full-length flannel nightgowns, which may surprise you to hear is the ultimate Sweat Lodge attire for us 'life-givers', then scurrying along the path, we met the others, and were ready.

Pauline entered the lodge first, acknowledging 'All Our Relations' before crawling inside on her hands and knees. I followed afterwards, her apprentice, seating myself to her right and preparing myself inwardly to take over as Lodge Keeper at a moment's notice, if need be. Pauline was a decade older than me and recently diagnosed with a heart condition. She never hesitated to 'pass the baton' if she felt weak or tired. The Vision Questers and some of our camp volunteers crawled in after us and took their places around the circle inside the lodge. Scott passed in the medicines and we were ready for the Grandfathers.

"Grandfather coming in" Scott announced as he lifted the red-hot stone out of the fire, brushed off the ash with a cluster of spruce boughs and carefully placed the pitch fork in the center pit, releasing the stone in the appropriate position, representing one of the four directions. "Welcome Grandfather" we all replied in joy and unison, while the medicines were placed carefully upon it to elicit the cleansing and purifying smoke. When seven Grandfathers were inside, the door was closed and the prayers began.

What is spoken inside the lodge is spoken to Creator. While we may all have ears to hear and witness, the prayers of the others are acknowledged as private and are never shared, or spoken of, again. The only stories that can be told are your own. That day in the lodge something was spoken that I can share, something I never imagined or anticipated I would hear, not so soon anyway. Inside the lodge there was a moment in time that separated the past from the present and the future. In that moment, one of the circle called me Elder. A few minutes later it happened again. Then again. Pauline had always been generous in her acknowledgement of me as her number one 'apprenticer', but she had never referred to me as an Elder. At the time we had been working together for about ten years and I was the first to admit I still had plenty to learn.

Strangely, after we came out of the lodge, the title continued to be used in reference to me, strikingly often in fact, even from those who had not been a witness to it inside the lodge! Within the next half hour it was as if a new word had been placed into everyone's vocabulary, in reference to me, and they all wanted to try it out loud to see how it sounded. Over and

over it was used until finally Pauline turned to me and said, "Well, I guess Creator has spoken. You're an Elder now."

⁄ ⁄ ⁄ ⁄ ⁄ ⁄ ⁄

Just like that, my life had changed again. Until then, I hadn't even known the protocol of how or when someone became recognized as an Elder. I later came to learn that it is an expression of respect and honour conferred by a community of supporters. There are no established prerequisites. It is an acknowledgment of the service the Elder provides, the recognition that she is a trustworthy source of teachings and wisdom, that she is the holder of ceremony, and the liaison with Spirit on behalf of the group. While it was certainly an honour to be regarded in that way, I recognized that for all intents and purposes I was really just a baby Elder. I imagined it would take about three years to transition fully into the role.

Chapter Forty-Four

Oh My Aching Back

Another heretofore unimaginable root of illness.

I don't remember exactly how or when it began, but I started to experience back pain on a regular basis. At first I was not concerned, having had back problems off and on since the birth of my first child, but generally the discomfort would resolve with the usual type of dedicated care: stretching, exercise, and a course of chiropractic treatments.

This particular time however, I couldn't shake the pain. I tried a new chiropractor and followed his intensive program diligently. The problem remained. The longer it lasted the more I felt that I was missing something—that there was a contributing factor to the issue I wasn't aware of and that's why it wasn't improving.

I've always found that when it comes to my own healing, or that of my family, where I am emotionally invested in the outcome, I would prefer to ask someone else to engage Spirit on my behalf, rather than approach directly. That way there is no bias. It's also a nice feeling to ask someone else for help. When it comes to journey work my friend Marilyn is always my first choice. So when I approached her about the back problem, she was happy to help.

Marilyn embarked upon a journey with this intention:

"Jaki sees a chiropractor three times a week for back pain. He has been treating the hip area and there has been some improvement. However, within 36 hours of each visit the back tightens, 'locks up', and the pain returns. Jaki asks, "What is triggering the locking up of the back?" "What information, guidance, and support can you offer that will assist her in permanently alleviating the condition?"

I travel with Diamond Back through the forest of the Lower World to White Cloud's clearing. White Cloud and I greet each other warmly, as we have not spent time together for a while. I state the intention, and wonder what he will have to offer. He begins:

"Jaki is a leading edge thinker. This may seem an unusual expression to apply to her and her work at this time, for she is grounded in ancient ways, and aspires to simplify rather than complicate in all she does and in all she offers. But leading edge she is indeed. By this we mean that what she is putting forth, what she is launching and about to launch, are cutting edge and powerful practices that are delivered to her, through her teachers, from the highest of high places. The energy that is channelled through her is immense in its quantity and searing in its quality. The physical system, therefore, must be acutely aware, tuned, and available for this process to occur.

Imagine, if you will, a hollow bamboo reed through which substances can pass, or into which substances can be poured. Begin by imagining water flowing through. This it can do with great ease, even if the volume of the water should increase. What cannot pass through will simply overflow and run along the outside. The same can be imagined for a flow of sand. Much can stream through, perhaps with less ease than with water, yet it would not stop up, it would simply overflow and fall along the outer casing of the reed. Let us now increase both the density and the amount of the substance we are pouring. Let us attempt to pass a stream of golden nuggets through this reed. As the nugget stream begins, those small and rounded easily pass through. But soon a larger, rough-edged one tumbles forth from the source, and it passes through

until it reaches an imperfection, a narrowing, an impediment formed by the growth ring of our bamboo reed, and its passage is stopped. But the flow continues and even those smaller, smoother nuggets that would so easily have passed cannot now move beyond the obstructing gem. The pouring of the nuggets continues and eventually the weight of what comes forth exerts pressure on the blockage and grinds it further into the inner flesh of the reed, perhaps even scarring it as it moves however imperceptibly, before it is once again locked into place. The reed itself can do nothing, but hope the guiding or in this case, the pouring intelligence, realizes what has happened and acts to stem the flow, more carefully choosing what can be passed with ease, or, is prepared to wait until the reed grows and offers up a wider opening. Have you a picture of our somewhat odd analogy? What we are striving to explain to you is that the selection process—what will flow through and what will not—is independent of the containing vessel itself. In other words, it is the guiding hand of Source, Great Spirit, that regulates the flow."

(Now addressing the teaching to Jaki directly, even though she is not present.) "Jaki, long ago you offered yourself up as an instrument, as a channel if you will, through which, like the reed, much could flow freely. We recognize this as the statement of your true Service—to be a transmitting and transmuting vessel. Because you have demonstrated an astonishing capacity for this work, because we have seen that this capacity has continued to expand, no matter what was offered to you, because the flow moved smoothly, and for the most part, in an unrestricted manner, more and more has been offered through you in this way. The teachings of water pass easily, as do the teachings of sand. The realm of golden nuggets is now upon you, and the vessel, your physical system, has not yet the capacity to allow the free flow of these irregular substances through the hollow reed that is your channel. And, we recognize that this has been an oversight on our part! Yes, even we can act with overzealous enthusiasm when we find one so capable, so willing, and so dedicated as you. No wonder you are in such pain. No wonder you are seeking relief from first this one and then that one and then the one over there — all these helpers with the kindest and most

loving of intentions! We hope this brings a smile to your face, for even so it makes us laugh as well. We have so convinced you that Spirit has its own intelligence, one might ask, "How has this come to pass that we have assisted in the 'locking up' of one of our most smoothly flowing beings?" Forgive us! We will attend more closely to our responsibility of honouring and supporting your physicality so that you can live on Planet Earth in true comfort and fluidity."

"And now we turn to practical matters—the alleviation of the pain you are so frequently experiencing. We will send you shortly for a treatment from the Healers' Circle, but first wish to comment on the steps that you have been taking for your own care. We say that you are doing too much and the focus is upon what is amiss in the structure and musculature of your form. Always the emphasis must be upon the areas of the body that are working well, are flexible, and that have no pain. Attention must be focused on these areas of wellness and the invitation offered there, that the well-being from these areas flow into those that are the more afflicted. In this way, attention, that is always the catalyst for growth, will focus on what is working well rather than on what, in your mind, needs fixing. We hope you understand our words here. And you, in your meditations and in those quiet moments when awaiting sleep or returning from it, can turn your attention to the inner vibrations of those areas where all is well—perhaps your arms, your legs, or one side more than the other. Offer the invitation for those vibrations to move into the areas that cause you pain and gently feel their willingness to do so. You will be surprised by what can be offered towards relief in this way.

The stretching benefits offered through yoga are excellent for your physical system, for you are a mountain, and inflexibility is an inborn state with you. So anything you can do to limber up will draw the energy of the earth and the heavens fully and completely through your form. We offer this caution however. Remember that two things are happening. First, we are constantly asking for the expansion of the capabilities of your physical system. Second, you are taking steps, through treatments, to realign your form so that flexibility and pleasure

counteract inflexibility and pain. So the system needs time to respond and it needs space to hold the form of that response. We suggest that you move much more gently into activity, that there is no forcing, that you begin from a place of asking your body what it needs not only in challenge, but also in support. We cannot predict what it will say but we assure you that if you listen it will speak to you. In time, there will be a settling, an easing of both intensity and frequency of locking up in pain, and the awareness of energetic harmony and flow will intensify greatly within you. You will be pleased."

I thank White Cloud on our behalf, the other unseen teachers who spoke here today, and Diamond Back, for leading us to this information. Diamond Back and I take our leave, each returning to our respective homes.

- - - - - - -

My back problems were actually being caused by an enthusiastic oversight of what was being offered to me from the world of Spirit, and as a result, I was becoming limited in my physical function and experiencing pain! How could such a thing happen?

Let me offer some additional context. When I teach students about journeying, I am very careful to take the time necessary to help them understand the role of their intention and the nature of what they are asking for. I like to say that the intention sets the parameters for the journey experience. Generally, the sky is the limit when it comes to possible topics, but I do offer several cautions, for example, never phrase an intention so you are asking about 'success' or 'time'.

If you inquire of the Spirit world whether a venture you are considering will be successful or not, the most common answer will be yes. From the perspective of Spirit, everything you do, everything you learn, is successful. There are no failures, only failed opportunities. In a similar way, how can something that is essentially eternal offer you advice about timing? One thing I have noticed over the years of working with the Mountain is how amazingly patient it is. But when I think about how long mountains exist compared to how long I will live, it only makes sense.

I've also noticed in my work with Spirit that there are times when some of the practical realities of living in the physical world are lost on them. How could they not be? For the most part, physical world struggles are not what we inquire of Spirit anyway! Mostly, they teach us about love, relationships, and healing. They help us transcend the weight of the physical world with a lightness of being that we are also capable of holding. It is this 'light-ness' that is their area of expertise, the realm of their own experience. And from that 'en-lightened' perspective, it is not so difficult to put this journey into context.

I took the teachings to heart and I followed their suggestions and protocol. After a follow-up treatment from the Healer's Circle, I slowed down my efforts to get well and paid more attention to how I felt and what I could reasonably manage. At my next chiropractic visit I was advised that I would have to learn to live with the pain for the rest of my life, that my thoracic spine was my 'Achilles heel' and it would never function normally again. That was the message I needed to guide me to discontinue his treatments. I was going to get well, completely well.

It took about two to three weeks to notice an improvement and then it progressed exponentially from there. By the time six to eight weeks had passed the entire back pain episode was behind me and I was full steam ahead. I never forgot the words from the journey however. I became more careful with what I was asking of my body, taking into consideration what was also being asked of me by Spirit. And of course, I accepted their apology!

Chapter Forty-Five

Food and Medicine

Bear reveals the depth of her knowing about the rooted ones . . .

As I prepare for my morning practice it occurs to me that in recent journeys with Bear I have not asked what I can offer in return. "No time like the present," I say to myself while calling out to Bear. I greet her by telling her how much I love her and ask if there's anything I can do for her.

> I see Bear ambling toward the fire from the left. She rears up on her hind legs and gives out a big roar. She is not so gentle today. She is thick, sturdy, and powerful. I am struck by the clarity of the way her paws place themselves on the earth with each step. Today she 'appears' more like a physical bear than I have ever seen her. Her movements, her fur, the smell of having her near . . .
>
> She walks in front of the tipi and comes up behind me. She places her front paws on my shoulders and begins her kneading and pushing treatment. I can feel my physical body loosening and lengthening and am reminded of her influence in my work with patients. It is she who guides me through the nuances of body work.
>
> She turns and gets back down on the ground. Again, I ask what I

can offer. I receive the knowing that she is willing to work more closely with me in my plant studies. Now she is on the move again, swaying her head and neck back and forth, back and forth, close to the ground. I get it! It is her perceptions that can help me. How Bear perceives the plants, how she smells them, eats them, receives them, is so much different from me. Yes, there is much to learn from her. Wait a minute, I came into this journey to offer something back and here she is giving me more than ever! She hears my thoughts and responds in a way that lets me know this IS how I give something back. Recognizing and acknowledging her gifts is a form of reciprocity.

⁄ ⁄ ⁄ ⁄ ⁄ ⁄ ⁄

Several months later:

"Bear, I would like to ask you some questions about my learning of the plant medicines."

As Bear approaches, he looks very large and male today. He takes his usual path around the tipi then rears up on his hind legs, very imposing.

"Bear, you are learn-ed of the plant people and their medicines. Is this something we could speak of together?"

The scene changes and I am by the fire with Bear, this time much smaller and more feminine. She is cooking me a fish.

Bear, "You see this fish, it crisps and cooks as it sears in the coals. The flesh stiffens and the skin chars. It heats internally as well as externally."

Jaki, "Yes, I see these things."

Bear, "For you, how different is this fish to eat whether raw or cooked?"

Jaki, "For me, it is most palatable and delicious, and a pleasure to eat, when cooked. Raw it has no appeal."

Bear, "Plants are very similar. There are plants you prefer, ones you don't. Those you would eat raw, those you would cook. Medicines from plants are also food, in a way. There should be an instinctual and cellular attraction to that which we need, whether for nourishment or healing. However, your bodies are not clean. The tastes and perceptions

have been distorted. If you clean them first, the medicines will be received differently, more in keeping with the natural order of things. The ideal is no sugar, no salt, or anything refined from its natural state. That's it. It's easy. Those three things will re-calibrate the body, the taste buds and the cells. Spices are best avoided but herbs can be used liberally. This may seem like more than people are willing to do. Do they want to use plants as medicine? If the answer is yes, then those are the internal conditions required, just as your people need to fast for medical tests or consume certain potions for others. This is the first step. We can't really talk about plants for healing until this has been accomplished."

⁄ ⁄ ⁄ ⁄ ⁄ ⁄

Considering what had just been offered, and my love of working with the plant people, I took Bear's advice very seriously. I decided to embark upon a no sugar, no salt, all-natural diet. It was important to me that I did this before I returned to ask about a particular plant. I decided that seven days should be sufficient to reset my system. I found the diet remarkably easy. There were a few things I prepared ahead of time, including a seasoning mix of herbs and crushed, dried, vegetable flakes, to add flavour and interest to the food. As all cheeses contain salt, I made a batch of yogurt cheese from the sheep's milk yogurt that is one of my staple foods. I used it to dress up baked potatoes and to sprinkle on salads. I made a simple bread using the seasoning mix instead of salt, and baked it like a flatbread in a round cast-iron frying pan. I cut it into wedges and sliced the wedges horizontally for sandwiches or toast. I roasted cashews and almonds in the toaster oven, a handful at a time, then crushed them in the mortar and pestle to make nut butters. Surprisingly, they took only a few minutes to make and it was no inconvenience to toast the nuts while I was showering. I could then 'butter' them for my morning toast or use them later as a base for vegetable dips, with a little seasoning mix added. Meats and fish were cooked simply, then smothered with an herb paste. I found that meat was the most challenging food to eat without salt or spices, so the herb pastes were integral to my enjoyment of the process. Once completed, I returned to Bear.

"*Bear, what can you teach me about the medicine of peppermint herb?*"

"*Ah peppermint. Very soothing to the stomach and digestion. You see how the peppermint grows on a thin tall stalk? It is good for your people to regulate their appetite, so they too can be thin but strong. The peppermint stalk tends to dry out when conditions are not perfect, and so will the people who can benefit from this medicine. Take as a tea, prepared gently and mindfully. A little honey (less than ½ teaspoon) can be added but NO sugar. It is important to taste the tea as one drinks it, so it is best to drink it as the sole activity for those five to eight minutes. The taste importance cannot be overemphasized. The tea will also help people to relax and has a settling effect on their nervous system. For those who are uptight with bulging eyes, this is a good tea for them. Drink during the day though, not at night, as it can stimulate. It is also good to drink after heavy meals, but must only be sipped, and in this case, not sweetened.*"

"*Thank you. May I also ask about the essential oil?*"

"*Ah, a potent and beautiful medicine. Use this one gently, with care. It is best to befriend the plant first. You will understand her more. She is quite complex, this little one, but she will serve you well in many ways. Do not make her angry. In an ideal state she has a wonderful balance of force, presence and gentleness. If her force is encouraged she will not be friendly and there will be possible risks. Do not bring violent moods to her. Calm the person first. This one is not for children. Spearmint is better for them.*"

"*Thank you Bear. May I return with more questions another time, about other plants?*"

"*Yes you may. I like this engagement. I am delighted to teach you about the rooted ones. Be well. Go now. We will talk more another time.*"

Chapter Forty-Six

The Lake of Tears

*The wind had tried for two hundred years to free
the tortured soul. It needed able humans to lend a
helping hand.*

When the phone rang it sounded so normal. But that was an illusion. This was no ordinary phone call. It was a cry for help from a complete stranger, a woman forced to approach someone like me, who could perhaps provide answers that were not available by ordinary means.

It had started with the deaths of two healthy horses within the space of one year. Inconceivably, both had drowned in a small lake on privately owned property—a lake that was no deeper than four-and-a-half feet. One horse could perhaps have been accepted, even if the explanation didn't seem entirely plausible. One horse could have been filed away into whatever category mysteries eventually go. But not two horses. Two horses encountering the same strange fate was enough to instill fear.

The couple who owned the property felt stalled in moving forward—with any decision. Without knowing what factors contributed to the deaths, they weren't sure if they were responsible in some way, or if they could have done something to prevent it. They owned many more horses and were naturally concerned for their safety. They also knew they could drive themselves crazy trying to find the cause of the untimely deaths. Were the horses disturbed by the housing development at an adjacent property? Was it a reaction to their food? Had something or someone spooked them just as they were entering the lake? Their grief was overshadowed by the nagging fear that something was wrong on the land where they lived.

At the time of this call I was working with a private student who, in addition to displaying some remarkable journey skills, was an accomplished horsewoman. This was one of those opportunities where many people could benefit. If we worked together, I would have assistance and support, she would be able to take her skills and apply them in a practical way, gaining invaluable experience, and the owners of the land would have two of us working for the price of one. I invited Melanie to join me.

In preparation for our work ahead, Melanie began with a journey. In it, she saw the lake where the horses had drowned, but from a time long ago. Moving quickly toward it, carried by the wind, was a huge fire. Then she was in the water, she could feel the heat and it was hard to breathe. There were native people there, crying, and horses rearing and thrashing. Melanie saw and felt the death. She asked if the dead horses from that time had called out to the horses that recently drowned and was told "yes." It was not intentional. The confused and tortured spirits that had suffered in the fire were trapped there. Their pain had drawn the other horses to them, and once in the lake, they became held in the same trauma. They could not set themselves free and died horribly. She was shown a way to take the horse spirits and re-balance their energy, then dissipate it like dust into the wind. She also asked if she could help the people and came to understand that it was fine for her to help with the animals, as they were very clear and didn't hold on like people do. People could resist and she was to leave that work to me.

The healing had already begun, but based on these visions there was clearly more to do and we needed to assess the situation carefully. We drove to the site and parked the car nearby. As soon as our feet touched the earth, the first sign of distress was evident. Here we were, in a rural setting, with a lake nearby, surrounded by trees, shrubs, and natural grasses, and there was not a bird to be found anywhere. The quiet of the sky was eerie and disconcerting.

As we were walking around the circumference of the lake, looking for a suitable spot to enter, a mother moose and two of her young—only several weeks old—came out of the woods in front of us. We watched them make their way around the shore, cross the lake at a low point and walk over to the other side. It was as if they were showing us the ideal route. We did a slight detour to pick up a canoe, then followed their trail and started out onto the water.

We paddled into the center, where we simply floated for a time. Then I started to drum. As the sound of the tom hitting the skin echoed through the land, I saw a vision of native people, walking with children and carrying babies on their backs. I could see them trudging into the water up to their waists, but no horses, no fire, and no fear. They were coming to gather food, roots, and cordage. They were dressed in fairly heavy woven garments, predominantly red in colour. I surmised the season must be spring or fall. I recognized the lake as a valuable resource for these people.

I then directed my attention to the lake itself and immediately sensed conflicting energies. I started to feel anxious, fearful, even panicky. This was a type of panic where even the sounds of the earth, however relevant, only heightened the sense of chaos. Then calm—exquisite, dreamy calm—the water luring me into gentle daydreams and to sleep. Both feelings were held there, and what was most surprising was how quickly they shifted from one to the other; no catalyst was needed.

The canoe started to drift northward and immediately my head felt full of worry and turmoil. The sun went behind some clouds, yet a moment earlier the sky had been clear. I sensed a dark imposing presence, a stirring, whirling vortex. I realized this area would require some clearing and cleansing. I made a mental note that we would need to perform a ceremony there with tobacco and sacred plants.

The assessment was complete. Melanie and I made arrangements to return later in the day to begin the healing work. That way, the land, the nature spirits, and myself could all prepare for the changes ahead. When we arrived, equipped with supplies, I could sense pockets of disrupted energy beneath the surface of the lake as soon as we approached the shore. We donned our gum boots and walked into the water's edge. I offered tobacco, said a prayer, and let the nature spirits know that we came humbly, to serve in a healing way. I lit a piece of charcoal and burned juniper, to initiate the cleansing process. I drummed, feeling my way to the rhythm and tone that was required for the land there. I closed my eyes and opened myself to whatever energies and spirits were present. I called in the Circle of Helpers and found myself supported by a lineage of native Wisdom Elders, ones I had never seen or worked with before. They showed me a vision of medicine men gathered together in a council. I could sense the urgency. A wildfire was in their midst, their people and horses were suffering, and it was up to them to find the solution and the healing that was needed. As I watched I tried to understand their fear. There was something odd about the scene, something that didn't make sense. I thought to myself, "they would know that there are natural phases that the earth goes through, that there will be fires and lives will be lost." I waited for more guidance, more insight, but none came. I called upon Raven to take me into the unknown, and he did, but the answers didn't come right away. In the meantime the following detailed and complex story unfolded:

There is one medicine man who stands out from the others. His fear is tangible. Despite all his skills and experience he believes he is failing his people and that is difficult to bear. The wind becomes strong. I sense I need to help free this medicine man, that part of his soul is trapped in that scene and has been for a long time—perhaps hundreds of years. I reach my arms many feet beyond me and encircle him. I protect him and gather him to me, preparing to set him free. The wind grows stronger and speaks to me. It tells me that it has been trying to free this lost soul for so long, that it has tried blowing stronger and stronger but to no avail. It needed help.

Just then, another native man comes into focus. Whatever tragedy befell his people, he was ten years old at the time, and one of the few who survived. He felt fortunate beyond measure as his early years had been challenging. As a boy he was not chosen by the Elders to be a spiritual leader. He was not chosen by the medicine people to learn their ways. He showed no hint of skill in trapping and hunting. He feared for his

future in the tribe. He wanted desperately to be important, to be looked up to. But his talent, and therefore his contribution, had been uncertain. Now his fate was laid before him. He was the one who lived to tell the tale and it was a story that could be told for generations. He could craft it any way he chose for there was no one to refute him. And so, he claimed his position among his people. This young boy grew up to be a storytelling Elder and for the rest of his days the most prominent story he told was of the medicine man who failed his people. The ongoing repetition of the tragic events dishonoured the soul of the medicine man and kept it ensnared in that moment of time when he was haunted by his own blame and grief. This was the piece I couldn't see before. This was Raven revealing the mystery.

With the information laid before me I could now begin. I confronted the storytelling Elder and asked him about what he had done. He told me that the story was the answer to his prayers, that he didn't care about the misrepresentation that was placed in its telling. He wasn't concerned that he was perpetuating a trap that held the ancestral medicine man in turmoil. It was the opportunity that became his livelihood.

I waited for the wisdom of the healing solution to be shown and then I told him that he didn't need the story anymore. Couldn't he see? He had become a remarkable story teller, worthy of a special position in the tribe. Could he not share the stories of healing, wisdom, and culture? Could he not share the stories of the medicines, the dances, and the Sweat Lodge, the stories that would heal his people, both those in the past and those of future generations? No one would miss the other story, it was time to let it go and in so doing, release the trap that held the medicine man. Could he not see how holding on to that one story so tightly held him back?

He listened to my words and considered them carefully. He agreed to let go of the story and I watched as the wind was now able to set the medicine man free. Shortly after, more than one hundred other souls followed. They too, had been held captive, but I hadn't been able to see them before. The complex web of grief, suffering, and betrayal had become the twist in fate that confined them all.

In the meantime Melanie had been doing her own work and it wasn't until afterward we had a chance to share. She spoke of her experience first and I followed. A short way into my story she began to cry and she wept for the rest of the sharing. She was so moved by what had happened and how her story and mine were two parts of the same whole.

As Melanie described, "As soon as you started to drum a light wind came up and the noise around the lake became more pronounced, like a sort of chatter. When you said, "Here they are, can you see them?" I couldn't, but I closed my eyes and a native woman and two small children appeared, telling me that they had been waiting for so long, that they desperately wanted to be released and to go home. I was able to tell them that you were already working on it and that the healing had begun. And then an incredible sense of calm enveloped me. It felt amazing. I wanted to help, to do more, so I called on my spirit guides. I was told that this was not my journey, that I was here to gather the lost souls and put them together, that you were here to do the healing work, and that we each have our own path."

As we were leaving the lake that day and walking away from the shoreline I noticed flashes of dark purplish light in the grasses. I had never seen anything like it before. There were so many of them I thought I must be seeing things. To be certain I wasn't in some strange post-ceremonial state, I mentioned it to Melanie and tried to point them out. It was then I realized that they didn't move when my eyes moved, as I had originally suspected. They were actually fixed in particular locations. Once Melanie spotted one, she could see them all. I suspected they were accumulations of dark, condensed energy that were now able to bubble up to the surface and be released.

Once they were done, we both looked up at the same instant and saw the sweetest bird just ahead of us at the edge of the lake, in amongst the grasses. With gratitude welling up in our hearts, we found ourselves held there; something about the presence of this creature was so comforting, so reassuring. We had been able to make a difference. The land was already returning to its natural state of balance!

– – – – – – –

As the days passed I came to understand more fully the scope of what

had happened at the lake and what we were to take with us into our lives and our service. For several nights afterward, during my dream time, the land continued to teach me. There are many more places that still hold the trauma of the past. It is now time for our relationship with Mother Earth to be restored to the depths that has always been possible. We are to take better care of her, and in turn, she will be able to continue taking care of us. Those who are listening will be shown what needs to be done.

One of the most striking features of this story is that there were hundreds of people who had died in that fire, and many, many horses. The soul of the trapped medicine man, held for a seeming eternity, was the key piece that, once shifted, allowed all the others to follow. All that needed to be done was to set that one soul free. Nature, and the wind, could then take care of the rest.

Chapter Forty-Seven

Post-Concussion Syndrome

It's a sign of maturity to be comfortable with how little you know. It also keeps you on your toes . . .

I t had been more than two years since Rayanne received a concussion blow to the head. We had done our best, after the initial injury, to return the body to a state of wellness, and certainly improvements were made, but some of the after-effects still lingered, limiting Rayanne's ability to fully function in the world.

Rayanne was a very dynamic young woman who had worked hard to become a structural engineer and be respected in a male-dominated industry. The incomplete recovery from the concussion was devastating to her, professionally and personally. In her own words:

> "At the time, I was considering quitting engineering and my lifelong dream, to either spend the rest of my life on government disability or asking, "Would you like fries with that?" I was so tired, so beaten down, so overwhelmed by depression and anxiety by that point that I was very close to leaving everything I had worked so hard for."

It appeared Rayanne was doing all the right things. She had been to physicians, psychiatrists, and neurologists. She came to see me for regular treatments and we had explored a wide variety of possibilities. She had received several soul retrievals, both from myself and other practitioners. She maintained a healthy lifestyle and had tremendous support and acceptance from her partner and family. I asked myself over and over what I could be missing.

Out of the blue one day a memory surfaced, from years before, of a young infant patient who had been brain injured during birth. That experience had helped me to understand the connection, and the working relationship, between the brain/mind and the soul. This inspired me to look at Rayanne's situation in a different light. Perhaps there was some kind of disconnect between the brain and the soul that needed mending. I had no idea what medicine to offer or what approach to take, but when I mentioned it to Rayanne, she was willing to give it a try.

At our next session, as she lay on the treatment table, I stated my inquiry to the Mountain.

The first thing I saw were swirling, circular colours of light, moving counter-clockwise. Then momentary flashes of Rayanne in different situations and times of her life over the past five to six years. They were so quick I simply watched them come and go. Then a shocking image appeared, and stayed. It detailed the moments when Rayanne received her concussion and was laid out flat on the ice. I saw 'something' leave her body. It had no form, so the seeing wasn't really visual. It was like a wisp of air or breath that left her head and floated upward. I could tell there was a strong sense of disorientation within the wisp. It had an awareness, a thinking presence, yet in that moment all it experienced was confusion. It didn't know what it was, where it was, or why it was. Then I saw Rayanne get up, try to shake off what had just happened and get back to the game on the curling rink.

The images turned to present time and I saw what appeared to be an outer space phenomenon, a kind of black hole surrounded by an irregular, oval-shaped swirl of purple light, varying in thickness and intensity. It looked somewhat like a giant purple eye with a black

pupil. I stayed with this visual for some time with no change. Then a 'miniature Rayanne' climbed out of the inside. She appeared alert and happy. She told me she had been living there for about two years and that she was studying the universe, which she found fascinating. When I explained the situation, it was clear she had no awareness that she was related to another aspect of Rayanne. She expressed herself as a self-contained being. When I shared that the 'big' Rayanne had been missing her, she was quite distraught. She didn't like the idea that her presence there could be impacting another being in a negative way. I asked if she would be willing to return. She agreed, but only in the way of a scientific experiment, to see what would happen.

At this point, I didn't actually know how to retrieve a 'brain part' and had to ask for help. I came to know that I was to place my hand on Rayanne's lower abdomen and the brain part would enter in through my hand and be received by her spinal column and nervous system. When I did this, I could see the sinking down of an 'energy' that reached to the spine, then spread out in both directions, down to the sacrum and up to the top of her neck, in one rapid flow. When it reached her head there was a burst of light, looking like a light bulb that had just been turned on. The strength of the image at this stage and the intensity of the light took me by surprise.

A minute or two later, there was a sense of completion and I knew the treatment was over. When I took Rayanne's meridian pulses I could feel the magnitude the shift had created in her life force. She would be in a delicate and vulnerable state for a while, until everything settled in. I asked her to stay in close contact over the next 24-48 hours and if she needed a follow-up we would arrange one.

She phoned two days later. The day following the treatment had been very difficult, cognitively and emotionally. In fact she was unable to work and called in sick. She felt so low she advised her employer she would need to take the next day off too. Yet on Friday morning she woke up feeling surprisingly well and went to work after all. She worked her full shift, which included some intensive trigonometry, and found she was able to handle the calculations and sharp focus. She was still feeling well when she completed the work day and sounded alert and functional when we spoke. This was significant as she had been finding her work days very taxing, even with the reduced hours after her injury. She would often remark that it took the other 19 hours of the day to prepare and recover from the five hours of work. As a result she was able to manage her job, but not much of anything else.

After another six days Rayanne came in for a follow-up visit. She had a very unusual story to share. For a few days she had felt quite well, but then it started to fade. It was about that time she attended her regular yoga class and during a quiet meditation, found herself being inwardly screamed at by her newly retrieved brain part! "Your life sucks," this new inner voice declared, and went on to deliver a litany of examples of why her life was so lousy, sedentary, boring, and uninteresting. Her life was indeed quite different than it had been before the concussion. I suggested to Rayanne that she try to remember what she used to feel like, and bring that feeling state back into her awareness, so the brain part could experience more familiar territory.

Before our next scheduled visit, while out for a long walk, I realized I had asked too much of Rayanne. While it was necessary for her to reinstate some of the previous mental, emotional, and spiritual experience of herself before the concussion, any shift she attempted would only be temporary—she no longer felt like that! Her life and her inner way of experiencing had changed. But this understanding led me to the solution. She needed to be taken back in time. In that way she could return to the old way of feeling and being. The brain part would recognize the environment it had been estranged from and Rayanne would now have a present day experience of that state, something for her to hold on to. The Mountain had taken patients back in time before, so I knew I could call upon it for help.

At our next visit, when Rayanne lay down on the treatment table, I placed myself with the Mountain Spirit Beings and explained the situation as best I could. Then I waited. Again it began with scenes from other experiences in her life coming and going but this time staying long enough that I could narrate each of them fully. The scenes came and went and then settled on what was to be the final one: Rayanne outdoors, in the winter, in the mountains. In many ways it was an ordinary scene; Rayanne had just

stepped out of a car and was taking a look around, breathing in the cold, crisp, winter air. I could feel the warmth of the sun on her face, the solidness of the earth beneath her feet, and the inner feeling of awe and delight at looking up at the mountains, appreciating that she was back in nature. The scene was actually more feeling than visual and the two of us soaked it up, lingering in its lovely expression. We had found the moment—the moment in time that exemplified Rayanne when she was well. I stayed with the feeling experience and asked Rayanne to do the same. Still holding one part of my awareness there, I also went off to find the brain part. Oddly, I found her sitting on a chair. I approached carefully and before I was able to say a word she started to melt, slide off the chair, and become one with Rayanne, infiltrating her entire being. In the moments afterward I came to understand the full scope of what had happened.

The brain part that had separated from Rayanne due to the blow of the concussion was an anomaly. Brain parts do not usually separate. Unlike a lost soul part, which is frozen in time and unaware of its exile to a certain degree, this brain part, because of its cognitive ability, became aware of itself after the initial disorientation. It was, in a sense, independent and functional. It found itself in some kind of 'inner space' and proceeded to do what a brain part might do, become curious about its environment and want to study it, to again feel the capacity to learn and grow intellectually. It continued to exist in this way until I brought it back into a post-concussion Rayanne. The environment 'she' returned to felt foreign, so the brain part maintained its self-awareness. This is how it was able to tell Rayanne, once she entered a quiet meditative state, that she was displeased and frustrated. Once Rayanne had been taken back in time to a strong experience of being her old self, the brain part naturally returned, and without intention or thought, reintegrated fully.

A few moments later Rayanne spoke out loud, stating that she had just experienced a physical shift, like something loosening in her head. I continued to stay connected and slowly over the next few minutes, felt her internal vibrations shift, to become more alive, cohesive, and strong. In fact I became so tuned in to Rayanne's internal experience that I felt my physical body losing its sense of self. It was a privilege to be connected with her at such a deep level, but more than that, I felt the boundaries of form that normally separate us dissolve, allowing for a pure state of spiritual connection.

When Rayanne was ready, I removed my hand and felt myself return to normal awareness. Rayanne stayed resting on the table. A few minutes later she opened her eyes and we reviewed what had happened. She told me she had forgotten all about that state of being—getting out of the car in the mountains and taking a few minutes to soak in the gratitude for being there and the presence of nature all around her. That was something she used to do all the time and she had lost it. I felt a wave of awe that the Mountain Spirit Beings knew just what type of situation to return her to when we went back in time. This one had been perfect.

When Rayanne left she said she felt entirely different from when she had arrived. I looked at the clock. The whole thing had taken less than an hour. I advised her that there was nothing to do now. The brain part no longer had any separate awareness so it could no longer think independently. She was whole.

⁒ ⁒ ⁒ ⁒ ⁒ ⁒ ⁒

A few months later Rayanne was still doing well. Friends and co-workers often remarked that she looked like her old self and had her old spark back. Her brain and body now needed some rehabilitation to return to their previous level of function, but she was committed to a full recovery. In the meantime, she started being able to put in a little extra time at work, to manage several projects at once, and remain clear and sharp as to what was needed for each. She was on her way back to health.

Chapter Forty-Eight

Asking

Considerations of sharing ceremony and spiritual relationships . . .

I had been invited to visit a beautiful retreat centre in the Rocky Mountains in the hopes of establishing a relationship with the owners and possibly offering ceremonial gatherings and workshops there. It was an exciting time. The centre was located in a beautiful, secluded area, and I enjoyed spending time with the land and exploring possible sites for ceremony.

It turned out there was an abundance of well-suited areas and my initial suggestion was to host a Sweat Lodge. It seemed an ideal choice, as it was simply an invitation to gather, to pray, and to deepen our relationship with Creator. There is no prior experience required to attend one and it can be open to people of all ages and all walks of life. To help the owners understand the nature of the ceremony itself we decided to experience one together. Scott was willing to come out to the site and be Fire Keeper and it was literally only a matter of days before we held the first Lodge.

The ceremony was so well received that the land owners asked if we could have another one, opening the invitation to family members. So we did. And after that they asked if we could host one for all the staff at the centre. We did that too.

Everyone seemed to be enjoying themselves and quite moved by the ceremony. Our discussions for offering a Sweat Lodge to the public, as part of their program, were still moving forward and a few weeks later we were huddled together in their meeting room to finalize the details and plans.

They formally asked me, "Would you be willing to host a Sweat Lodge ceremony for a group of people that were all complete strangers?" I explained that as long as I felt they were introduced to the ceremony appropriately and participating through their own choice, I would be happy to.

They continued, "Well, we definitely want to go ahead then. There's just a few small details to work through. We'd like to ask that you use only half the amount of stones so it doesn't get so hot in there. Hold off on using the plant medicines—people won't get what that's all about and besides it creates smoke that fills the lodge. And most important, can you tone down on the prayer thing? It's a bit much."

Words cannot fully and clearly express how this request was received. There I was, a Western, white woman who had been given the gift of running Sweat Lodges based on the traditional teachings of a Cree Elder. The trust that had been placed in me was enormous. The care and consideration I brought to each Lodge was in honour of that gift and the accompanying teachings. While each Elder runs a Lodge in her own particular style, the lineage that has come before is of the utmost importance. The ceremony can evolve and grow in the same way that people and communities do, but the ceremony itself is a long-standing tradition spanning thousands of years. It was not to be dissected, have parts removed and then put back together, and still be considered a Sweat Lodge ceremony.

In shock, the tears welled up more rapidly than I could control. I excused myself from the room. I found a place outside, the retreat of the natural world, and I cried. I cried and I sobbed and I shook and the whole time I was having this breakdown I was also curiously observing my reaction. I was surprised to find myself affected so deeply that I would lose control. Minutes passed and while I was not yet ready, I had to get back to the meeting. I forced myself to resume my composure and re-present myself before the others. I apologized for needing a few minutes to gather my thoughts and tried to explain how disrespectful it was to ask me to change a traditional ceremony, hoping they would come to understand the gravity of the situation, offer an apology, and try to remedy the strain that had now been placed between us. As I spoke, I looked around the room and everyone there was openly staring at me. I felt like a complete outsider and the rift that had just been created grew larger. When I finished my response the owner of the centre casually spoke up, and in a condescending tone said, "It was just a question."

A few hours later I called Fishwoman and told her what happened. Again I was moved to tears. It was a much shorter conversation than I had hoped for. I wanted comfort. I wanted understanding. Instead she said, "That's why you have been trusted with this ceremony. Because you are not willing to be led off in different directions according to someone else's whims. You are going to be true to the teachings you have received. The ceremony cannot be bought and neither can you."

I replied, "But it means I have to walk away. I have to leave here. I wasn't expecting that. It's going to be hard." "Well, that's the way it goes." she said, and then dashing my hopes for any further reassurance, quickly followed with "Good night then."

⁄ ⁄ ⁄ ⁄ ⁄ ⁄ ⁄

Over the years of spending time with Fishwoman, I always make an effort to consider my questions carefully. It's not that she discourages questions. There's just a sense when I am with her that she isn't inviting them. I noticed that in our early years when this was a new type of relationship. As I was not walking on familiar territory, I made a point to be on the lookout for the nuances of what was happening when we were together. I was surprised to discover that she considered questions in an entirely different light than anyone else I had ever known. In fact there was a hint of suspicion when one individual asked a lot of questions. To Pauline that indicated they were either not paying attention, or they wanted to gain more knowledge and information than was naturally available through what was happening at the time. One of the sayings I've heard her share repeatedly is, "don't be greedy with the teachings" and I've taken that to heart.

Once, when my husband was working in Vancouver for a ten-day stretch, with a hotel suite all paid for, I took the opportunity to go and spend some time with Pauline. I paid for my flight and took enough money to gift her a generous donation. When we were together, I paid for everything—our meals, our parking, and all our purchases. I understood this was the protocol and I was comfortable with it. At least once I took her to dinner at a nice restaurant. Fine dining was not something she could afford to do and it felt wonderful to be able to treat her in that way. It also sent a clear message that I considered her special.

During the four days we spent together all she talked about was her family and the repairs needed for her aging vehicle. There wasn't one time that she offered a story, a teaching, or participated in a ceremony with me. We simply got together and she talked and I listened. We repeated the same pattern each day, until I returned home.

Was I disappointed? I would be lying to you if I said I wasn't. Yet truly it was only a hint of disappointment, a fleeting thought that the wind could take away anytime it wanted. I understood before I ventured out there, that while I had hopes, that was my failing, not hers. She never promised me anything. She never even invited me! I called and said I had an opportunity to visit and she said, "Come on down."

She was the teacher. I was the student. From my perspective, it was impossible for me to know what it was I needed to know, so instead of questioning her, I left it in her capable hands. If she saw an area where I wasn't following the tradition, or acknowledging Spirit appropriately, I knew she wouldn't hesitate to point that out to me. She had in the past, sometimes embarrassingly so. In that regard I knew I could trust her.

At other times she has been generous with me, and amazingly, she remembers everything she has ever taught me, right down to the smallest detail. We laugh about that. And if I ever feel the need to do a tally of the value she has brought into my life, I'm afraid it leaves me indebted. Certainly not the other way around.

✓ ✓ ✓ ✓ ✓ ✓

I understand now how difficult it must have been for the indigenous peoples when they were first approached by Western anthropologists who wanted to study them and learn their ways. We know from documented accounts that the anthropologists adopted the classic Western style—that of asking questions. They would follow the Elders around, asking what, how, and why. The answers were then noted, translated, and documented. Those indigenous people learned through relationship, and for them, it was the relationship that was most important not the facts that resulted from them. These relationships ran so deep that when a stranger approached to inquire, naturally it would be the most superficial aspects that were shared. To have a person of another culture ask questions repeatedly, prying for understanding and then wanting to refine the answers to aid in their accuracy, well . . . I'm quite certain it appeared heartless and cold. The scientists were more interested in what they could take away from these people than what they could give back. Asking became the vehicle that made that possible. The irony is that in the end, all that information was only the tip of the iceberg. The foundation, the wellspring that supported that knowledge, that provided the depth and broader applications, was left with the people who knew what was truly valuable.

It is difficult for me, and others in our spiritual community, to share our experience of Spirit and Spirit relationships for the very same reason. It's not that we wish to hold back, keep them secret, or feel a sense of authority over others. It genuinely feels disrespectful to place what happens in the spirit world into the physical world when you know it will immediately be regarded and treated as any other physical event. Even in general conversation there is not much opportunity for an experience born of spiritual connection to be honoured appropriately.

In our community we tend to save the sharing of our experiences with Spirit until we are gathered around a sacred fire. In fact, Scott and I host ceremonial fires for this very reason. In the presence of Spirit, of Grandfather Fire, a gentle, understanding, and sacred environment is created, and the bringing of the Spirit experience into the physical world can now be carried out appropriately and respectfully. It's a privilege to be one of the circle when such an experience is shared. We don't comment afterward. We don't ask questions to further our understanding. If there are apparent gaps or the sharing didn't seem as coherent as we would like, it doesn't matter. The importance in the sharing was for the person who had the experience to bring it forward from the inside to the outside, and allow it to be more real.

In the process each of us is blessed with an additional nuance of understanding of what is possible. If we want to learn more, we can place ourselves in situations where our own understanding and experience can be enhanced. We can do the work ourselves. We can walk the path.

At our Sacred Fire Circles anyone in attendance, even a first-timer, can offer me, as the Elder, a handful of tobacco and ask for a teaching. It is one of the protocols we follow. I hold on to the tobacco until the question is complete and when I am ready to respond, I offer the tobacco to the fire and begin. However, not all questions are to be answered. Some can be answered at a later date and others not at all. Sometimes the tobacco needs to be returned. Wisdom requires that some things are to be learned first-hand and I would never take away the opportunity for someone else to gain wisdom.

Chapter Forty-Nine

The Influence We Call Healing

I appreciate that Spirit offers these teachings according to my capacity to receive them. In the meantime I keep working on my expansion, not knowing what will be asked of me next.

"Please continue your teachings on the non-physical causations of illness and the healing work that can be offered."

As I enter the journey I am moved to kneel. I find myself in a state of reverence so profound I feel as if I am sitting at the feet of God. I state my request.

"Rise. You are worthy of these teachings. There is a critical next stage to begin. To receive more from us you must be more open."

"What do you suggest?" I ask.

"It is important you continue with the physical postures. Start to incorporate backbends to open the heart chakra more. Do not be discouraged. You have accomplished much. This is about going beyond what others are able to contain.

"You have learned that the grid system gives you access to the physical and removing the grids gives you access to the non-physical. You have also learned that healing is required in both of these realms of existence.

The light work will be more powerful when you are able to channel more light through you. You have been visualizing the light, trying to correct the nature, density, and colour. This has worked to a limited degree. If you can open up your being the healing will be more effective. Greater intensity and dynamics of change will then occur. Do this via your crown chakra, which must be kept open and true. Continue the chakra work and explorations. They are important here.

"*Simply see what needs to be done and call in the needed pattern, in the same way you call in the plant spirits. Then watch the healing process unfold. You don't have to rebuild the pattern, piece by piece. It can all happen at once. Just hold the image, see what needs to be done. Keep your focus and your spirit eyes clear and precise. This is important and necessary. 'See' the problem—'call in' the solution.*"

"*How am I to explain this work in a way that maximizes the patient's ability to receive it?*"

"*Your hands are the vehicle through which you receive information and effect change. This needs to be clear. Your inner senses help to reveal the nature of the problem and your strength of prayer and trust in God, along with your intention, create a specific pathway for that prayer to be answered. In these cases, your prayers are a dialogue with the sources of healing. They respond to your call because you are paying attention to your inner work and to all the possible barriers that would limit this ability. Prayer is not simply good wishes, not for you, not in this instance. Rather, it is a specific call to the forces of Spirit to effect change according to your directive. Do not be overwhelmed. It is quite simple for Source to respond to a call that is so specific and the outcomes limited to an individual. It is much more complex, and often impossible, for Source to answer a call where the outcomes affect many, and with conflicting positions on the results. Be clear in what you ask for, be clear in your intentions for the request, and be clear in your ability to channel the healing through you. This is your work.*"

Chapter Fifty

Plants as Food

Even in the kitchen the plants need to be treated with respect.

S everal years ago I had the idea to gather a group of people who were skilled in journeying, to explore specific topics and share their results. I was inspired by a desire to further an understanding of our role as humans in the grand scheme of the cosmos. When I don't know the answer to something I often turn to a journey to advise me. Having several people journey with the same intention was an exciting prospect and I hoped that it would take our learning and growth beyond what each of us could accomplish alone. Sadly, after a few journeys the group lost focus and was later dissolved, but my journey that follows has stayed with me.

"What is the role of human in the ecosystem of which we are a part?"

I jump down my tunnel to the Lower World. I reach the layer that I expect to stop at but continue going downward. Still falling, I go lower and lower, never seeming to stop. Then I realize that the tunnel around me is changing, shifting, and I am changing, shifting. The journey has begun.

I feel I am traveling deep into the earth itself. The tunnel around me continues to close in. I start to spin. My arms are now overhead and I am getting thinner and thinner. I am becoming molecules. I am in the core of the earth and I can feel its vibrational nature. I feel like I am 'essence', in stasis, waiting to be influenced by potential, thought, and flow. I will have no control, that is not my purpose, I will simply RESPOND.

Suddenly I am swept up, as if in a whirlwind of dust and moving air, and am propelled upward to the surface. Now I am outside. I am a bumble bee and have all the instincts and knowings necessary to that form. It seems bumble bees don't live very long however. All too soon, I find myself landed on my back, kicking and squirming as the life force leaves my body. The dance of transformation—it is frightening and exhilarating at the same time. The duality of opposites comes together and I am at peace. I am no longer a bumble bee. My form gets absorbed by the earth and once again I am molecules.

I become part of a patch of land that is planted with barley. I become one of the barley plant's molecules. Reaching toward the sun is the desire and fulfillment that drive my existence. There is nothing more. How could there be? The sun and the water are my bliss.

I get pulled from the earth by a giant tractor. I am being harvested and fed to a human. This particular human doesn't appreciate my essence, doesn't recognize the gift of the earth and sky that I am, and the perfect cycle of birth, growth, death, and decay, receives a jolt in its vibrational pattern. I contain nutrients so I am still a source of nutrition for this human, but a separation has occurred. Humans have removed themselves from the flow. It is very complex, because they are still part of the cycles of the natural world. But they are not participating in the dance of creation, they have excused themselves to attend to other matters. It has not been this way for long, and it is to their own peril that this shift has occurred. And there is a sadness in the ecosystem as a result of this separation, yet it is of no great consequence. It simply is.

This journey had such a profound effect on me that its potency has not diminished over time. It wasn't so much the teachings I received, but the experience of it. To feel myself as the dying bee, hissing and spinning, and at the same time feel the ecstasy as life and death meet. To feel myself as the kernel of grain that was not received in gratitude . . . If I had been received in gratitude the entire outcome of the journey would have been different, and perhaps the outcome of the human race as well.

Human beings struggle to let go of actions and thoughts and allow themselves to 'be', and in this journey I was blessed with the pure joy of 'being'. The feel of the sun—words seem inadequate to describe it. As the kernel of grain my entire existence was consumed with the feeling of the sun, and it was a full and complete existence.

What a tremendous gift life is and yet so often we don't experience it that way. Then when we remember, we isolate times and situations in which to feel honour, respect, and gratitude. It is, as the journey said, a hindrance to the flow and beauty of life. BE alive in every moment. NOTICE the energies and vibrations around you and inside you. Then the gratitude will rise up like a natural bubble, reaching to the surface, moving through your being, and it will become part of the energies and vibrations that other living beings around you are experiencing and noticing, and the perfect cycle will flow once again.

- - - - - - -

We cannot live without the plants—literally. They provide our food, shelter, medicines, clothing, cordage for rope and tools, and the air we breathe. I am only too aware that while my life and health are dependent upon the plants, their lives are in no way dependent upon mine. I am always on the lookout to bring a better balance to that exchange.

Even though I was already working with plants in a spiritual way, this journey created ripple effects that spread outward. It was only a matter of time until they entered the domain of the kitchen.

I have always enjoyed growing food, preparing it, and sharing it. When my children were young and I was a stay-at-home Mom, I explored the world of wholesome, natural foods, and couldn't get enough. Decades later, the enjoyment of the process involved in bringing food to the table has never lost its appeal. There is always 'something' going on in my kitchen, whether I am soaking and fermenting grains, growing sprouts and micro-greens, making seasoned oils, or crushing herbs into paste. Ever since I started to cook, I made everything from scratch, not just recipes but condiments even: mustard, mayonnaise, and seasoning blends.

Unknowingly, all that had prepared me for entering into a sacred relationship with food. The journey highlighted the one piece I had been missing: I hadn't been offering my acknowledgement to the food itself, and its source. I had been considering my needs but not theirs. When the journey stated, "This particular human doesn't appreciate my essence, doesn't recognize the gift of the earth and sky that I am," that human was me!

So I started paying attention to the food. When I picked up a green pepper and held it in my hands, I would see it for the gift that it was. I would notice what a marvel of creation—texture, colours, and flavour—each piece of food was. From there, gratitude was effortless. I entered into a sweet and silent relationship with the food I prepared. It wasn't about what I did with the food, it was about what 'we' were able to create. The food provided the raw materials and I worked with them as honourably as I could. The kitchen literally felt different because I brought myself to the activities there in a different way. This had some unexpected side effects. No longer could I put food into a blender. When I turned the switch to 'on', the sound and vibration instantly had an effect on me. It took me out of my reverie for the plants. I asked myself "If this is how I feel when I use the blender, how do the plants feel?" Those beautiful friends who give so much and I thank them by throwing them into a machine with a steel cutting blade that whirls at up to 600 revolutions *per second!*

The simple act of preparing food with appreciation and reverence became the new motto for the kitchen. The mortar and pestle crushed the nuts, seeds, and spices. My electric grain mill was replaced with a manual one and the sounds that filled the air as the stones ground and turned were a rhythm that felt in harmony with my soul. As I tossed the grain meal to separate the flour my spirit danced along with it. As I cut the vegetables with a hand-forged knife I thanked the plants for their friendship and their offerings. I came to understand that the plants knew how to nourish us when they were treated with respect. They were not unlike the other creatures. If we considered them 'our relations' we would hold our place together on this earth in a beautiful, loving, and supportive way.

In turn, my body, my cells, knew how to accept the food. My biology was still that of my ancestors and the history of the relationship with food was part of my inheritance. The plants knew how to give. My body knew how to receive. Now *there* was a relationship worth treasuring.

Chapter Fifty-One

The Way of Fire

There is no aspect of our lives; no task, no thought, no deed, that is not about relationship.

I see Bear ambling along the path. Then I see myself, sitting by a small fire with a blanket wrapped around me. I am shaking and appear quite ill.

Mother Bear comes toward me, then moves around the fire to where I am sitting. Without a pause, a word, or any teaching, she pushes me out of my spot (in the North) so she can sit there. I shuffle over to the East, still looking toward the fire.

As I observe me, I am shivering and cold. With the fire still burning, Bear puts one paw into the hot coals and swishes them about. This appears strange, as I wonder what effect that could possibly have. And then I realize she is tending the fire, for me. And by tending I mean that she is adjusting, coercing, manipulating the fire, to make it the most suitable one possible for my healing.

I come to understand that she is working with the medicine of fire, crafting it to be just right. And then I have the privilege of watching as the fire responds. It shifts and moves, rises and falls, it flares wildly then gently. I watch as Bear and Fire become One. I feel the deeper, subtle layers to this shifting, but I can't yet bring it up to the surface *to find the words to describe it.*

Fire can be a form of medicine. The way a fire burns affects its potency and the type of medicine it offers. Bear knows the Way with Fire. She crafts the fire as one would craft a poultice or a balm.

And it works. I stop shaking.

As I stay in the journey I come to understand how fire will hold an intention. In this way it can be a vehicle of prayer and of healing. Build a fire with a specific purpose, with specific prayers, and it will 'become' accordingly.

⁄ ⁄ ⁄ ⁄ ⁄ ⁄ ⁄

I used to think of journeys as an experience of sharing that were often accompanied by teachings. If I had undertaken this journey several years before, that is what I would have understood it to be. I would have marvelled at learning the ways of fire and that one of my guides, Bear, knew the way.

Often I have said to my students, particularly those just learning how to journey, "The experience of a journey changes you." I would even have gone on to explain the many ways that this was possible and some of the resulting effects. But as my understanding of the medicine path grew I was able to notice another layer that had previously eluded me, and this journey was a fine example.

Fire Ceremonies had been part of my life since 1999 when I first studied with Eliot Cowan. Each night after a day of teachings we would sit by the fire. The following year he put out a call for Fire Keepers, those who would be willing to host monthly fire circles in their community and consecrate the fire in accordance with his Huichol tradition. It was a way of offering ceremony to build communities, of bringing his teachings forward, and an opportunity for sharing from the heart around the warmth and comfort of the fire, as our ancestors had done. I was one of the first people to sign up.

From those early beginnings sitting with Grandfather Fire has become a regular and important feature of my life and spiritual practice, although the tradition I follow now is informed by the Mountain and Pauline's teachings. Grandfather Fire is the spirit of Fire. As in all encounters with spirit,

if one takes the time to develop a relationship, there will be mutual benefit. Grandfather Fire would sometimes speak to me, guide me, take my prayers to Creator, and transform my fears and suffering. In short, I thought I knew something about fire. After receiving the journey above I realized I had only scratched the surface. I had never thought about fire as medicine.

The journey teachings were still fresh in my mind a few days later when I was preparing for one of my regular fire ceremonies with Scott. This was to be a small one, just Scott and myself. I went outside to prepare the fire pit, bringing plain paper, tobacco, and matches. Then I reached into the wood pile to select a piece for kindling. As my hand touched it, the building of the fire as medicine began. That had not been my initial aim, I was simply intending to prepare ahead for when Scott arrived, so we could enjoy our ceremony together. But I had changed since the journey with Bear. The wood now responded to my touch, letting me know that was not the piece that would hold my intention the strongest. My hand moved to another and the feeling was much different. This one would be appropriate. As I chopped it into smaller pieces it was like taking a story and breaking it down into sentences, phrases, and even words. Each piece of kindling then held that word or phrase and would contribute it to the fire. As such, I was able to discern which pieces to add and which ones to leave in the pile, best left for another time.

The teachings continued to silently and gently erupt from my being as I brought the fire from intention to creation. With the appropriate 'wood words' selected, I could reunite them in a different way, a way that would place my prayers and intention into the fire itself. The next layer of larger pieces followed the same pattern: touching, discernment, selection, and placing them into the pit.

For the first time in my life when I lit the match and placed it to the paper bed, I wasn't simply starting a fire, I was completing a process of creation and beginning a process of healing, growth, and ceremony. The fire understood its purpose. It understood our need for that evening. Now we could experience the ceremony together, united not only in intention but in form. What I had held in my heart was now literally held in the wood and as it burned and more layers of my intention were added, Grandfather

Fire could respond to our need through his understanding. In a sense, we had begun with a conversation to go over what the aim of the ceremony was, what was expected, and what was hoped for as the outcome. I now trusted that not only would Scott and I be able to enjoy our time at the fire, but that we would come away from the ceremony restored and renewed. Grandfather Fire and I had worked together to develop a plan and the burning of the wood was that plan in action.

Chapter Fifty-Two

Another Layer of Wounding

It's not about being healed, it's about allowing your life to be your healing journey.

In the 1990s, while still working with medicines on a physical level, I became entranced with essential oils. After being introduced to the medicines of Nature and Spirit, I initially set that interest aside. But it didn't last long—I still enjoyed using the oils and found them a valuable medicine. So instead, I decided to bring them into the fold! I took the time to perform ceremonies and work my way slowly and individually to get to know each one. I followed the ways of my new teachings—I let the plants guide me to their uses. My training in aromatherapy did nothing to prepare me for what happened when I tuned in to their spiritual nature. What they shared was incredible! When an essential oil offers its medicine there is nothing like it. It's worth every moment of time spent in building the relationship and listening with your soul.

The following patient story is my own. I had dedicated some time to develop a relationship with essential oil of Roman chamomile, never suspecting that the plant had its own ideas for me!

I journey to the Lower World and meet Bellarina. Just finding her there makes me smile. I share with her that today I am meeting Roman

Chamomile. Immediately an image of the plant pops into my view but it looks like a picture or photograph, not a live plant. Slowly it begins to appear more real and the leaves start to move with the breeze. I become a fairy and hover over the plant. I seem to be remarkably attentive, very focused, and able to study the plant with great detail and care. I am in no hurry. The lure of its scent connects me to the deeper medicine. I rest myself on the stem and close my eyes.

I can feel the water and nutrients moving up through the stalk from the soil below. I can see the little tubes/channels inside the plant. I strangely feel like I've stepped outside my thinking mind but stepped into my awareness mind. Does this plant open up and heighten our inner senses?

I see a young girl, perhaps me, with a yellow floral skirt, dancing in a field of tall grasses. I am holding my skirt up a little so my knees and legs are free to move and express themselves. It is the bliss of a summer day with no need to go elsewhere and no pressing responsibilities. Freedom. I lie down in the grass and feel the warm sun on my face and body. I am happy; a calm, peaceful happiness, but at the same time I feel like I am holding a special secret inside and delighting in the fact that it is all mine.

I ask this plant about the medicines it holds. "I am a children's remedy. I reconnect them with their true nature, which is calm and happy, content to be alone. When they are distressed, I ease their mind of worries and excessive thoughts. I help you to remember 'play' and 'beauty', and how much we need both. I foster a playful, gentle heart. I soothe and soften rough skin. I help it to become smooth again. I calm redness, irritation and inflammation, especially red, hot swellings. I remind the cells involved in inflammation to calm and settle, to return the skin/organ to its original nature. I will help red, hot insect bites—mix with a little peppermint or tea tree oil. I will help calm bee stings. I settle an aggravated stomach. I can ease anxiety and am good to use in a relaxing massage blend. I can be used for meditation and concentration. Do not inhale too deeply or too strongly. Treat chamomile with gentle care and you will receive gentle care. Get out

of your stress. Get out of your head. Smell chamomile and return to who you are."

The inner vision continues to unfold, more details becoming available. I come to understand that there is a connection between chamomile and vibration. It can help to reestablish the ideal attunement or vibrational pattern in an individual. If the individual is still holding on to trauma, the medicine will have to break through first and this will create reactions of displeasure and discomfort. Best to tell people 'how' it works before trying it on them. When our ideal vibration is restored, tension falls away.

I see the skin of a drum that has chamomile flowers painted along the outer edges. I see a drumstick hitting the drum in the center. The sound reverberates and vibrates.

I remove myself from the trance to get up and reach for my drum. As I pick it up to play, I realize I must switch hands from my usual position, today holding the drum in my right hand and the tom in my left. I play for a while but I am strongly aware of the fact that my drum has no chamomile flowers drawn on it, which doesn't seem appropriate. As an alternative I take one drop of chamomile essential oil and dab it on the drum, in each of the four directions, then resume playing. Immediately I notice a difference in tone—surprising! I drummed as I felt moved to and had a strong sense that the vibration of the drum supports chamomile in its medicine, in its healing. Then I return to the journey state:

I see a vision of someone placing a drop of chamomile behind each ear. I hear "Combine with the drum to bring blocks and stagnation to the surface, to be released energetically."

I realize I have not yet met the plant spirit of Roman chamomile. In my relaxed, dreamy state I have not felt the desire to inquire, I have been content just to Be. But I am here with Chamomile now and it feels like the right time. Immediately Bellarina is hovering over one plant and activating it with her wand. A plant spirit emerges. I cannot yet see her clearly but I sense her femininity and I feel 'white and yellow' colours. An extremely graceful being glides up from the flower heads. She is regal, like a young queen in a white gown. She exemplifies poise and grace. She has not yet spoken. It feels intrusive to speak to her directly, without proper introductions. I ask Bellarina to do the honours. She introduces me as One Who Walks With Eagle Mountain. The plant spirit is immediately drawn to, and interested in, the child 'me'. Her manner changes. She becomes forthright, inquisitive. She comes toward the child me and starts poking me with a stick/wand, as if to see if my skin will bounce back, like I am a specimen. It is annoying. I feel poked and prodded like I am being studied. There is no respect for 'me'. She is so detached from my experience of this that it starts to feel creepy. I don't want to take it anymore. I want to push her away, tell her to leave me alone. I don't want to be studied. It's clear she has no regret at her actions or approach. She remains detached. She does what she needs to do, clear and simple. I come to understand. She needs to open me up to see what is inside, and when she finds it, she can work her magic.

"Oh beautiful chamomile spirit, will you speak to me of your gifts and medicines so that I may accurately and purposefully use them in service?"

"Well, I calm and soften. If there is a rough exterior or an artificial one, I need to probe into it and break it down first. Some do not like that about me. I think it is a small price to pay for there are greater gifts that await.

"I soothe the skin, as you have already noted. I can relax the internal organs when there is interior tension. Place a drop on the local area, have me available for inhalation, and drum your drum. Together we will open the person up and let vibration and healing enter.

"I can soothe the heart when its beat/pattern is erratic. Use my scent—breathe. Every internal organ in the body knows the rhythm and tone of the others. They communicate this way. When the body is healthy it is a symphony, and with each change in activity or thought the melody changes, but can stay harmonious if the conditions are right. It is like being hummed a lovely, lilting lullaby, over and over, then a different lullaby, all creating a soothing environment to bathe your

organs in. All organs must be part of the symphony. There is a great sense of loss when one is no longer present. In organ transplants the harmony is disrupted and the replacement part will never contribute to the same melody—the same song."

The journey, and the time I had to spend with Roman Chamomile that day was over but I felt I had barely scratched the surface. I looked for another opportunity as soon as possible and found an opening the following day. I began by simply reintroducing myself to its scent. I prepared beforehand, calming the mind, approaching my new friend with reverence, delight, and consideration. Slowly I brought the small bottle toward my face and with my hand, wafted its aroma. Smelling the essential oil once more, I came to know: Chamomile is a Touch of Grace.

I journey back to the field of chamomile flowers, all swaying in unison. I enter into their realm through an invisible doorway held by light and intention. It feels like a blessing just to enter here. I see a silhouette of myself as a being of light, perfection. Then I see the areas where the light is compromised, dim, and dull. The first is in the pelvic area, then the right shoulder. Next is my neck, below the ear on the right, in line with the jaw. As I gaze upon these areas I sense a sadness, a very quiet, deep, personal sadness. I am profoundly affected by this.

Now I see chamomile plants, several of them, driving up in cars. The troops have arrived. There is one who is clearly the leader, now directing the others on where to park and where to go. I am still a light being hovering in mid-air. Tears, holes in the fabric of my being open up and start to ooze. The first one I notice is on the left side of my abdomen, a split about two to three inches across. It releases a yellowish, creamy pus. Another one opens in my chest, by my right shoulder, and another at my anus. I feel hideous, diseased. I want to hide. I bow my head; I feel so exposed. It is not shame, but more like knowing that those who would gaze upon me in this state would find me repulsive. I am repulsive.

A circle of chamomile plants now surround me. They are on the earth.

I am floating above. There are about eight of them and as if they had thrown tethers that hooked into my light-flesh, they start pulling me down toward them. The light being that I am, as I watch, is struck by the resemblance to being burned at the stake. It is not the visual image that is so similar, it is the feeling of being held tightly while the pain of torture awaits. And yet, it occurs to me that at least being burned would evoke sympathy, I invoke disgust.

As my light-body gets closer to the earth it starts to puff out in certain places, like an inflammation, and I look more distorted than ever. Getting even closer I start to panic, to rebel. "I can't do this. Let me go. Set me free, even if it means staying like this." I squirm and wiggle. I feel like a trapped animal. I cry out, "You don't understand. You don't want me. You don't want me down there with you. I'm not worthy of the Earth. She is pure and loving and giving and I would poison her if I landed." The chamomile flowers all appear to have gone deaf. Oblivious to my plea, they continue to pull me closer. I don't know what to do. I feel completely powerless to stop them. I reason that they must have no idea what they are doing. Why would they want me down there? Why?

I'm going to explode. It's all too much. I can't hold myself together. I have lost my composure. But if I explode I will spray poisonous goo all over the chamomile plants and Mother Earth. I'm so desperate I start to moan and groan and sound like a wounded or tortured animal. I can't bear the pain of existing like this. I just can't bear it.

I keep getting closer to the Earth. 'Panic' doesn't even begin to describe it. Every piece of my insides is crawling, trying to break free, to get away from this fate. How long can this go on? How can I endure? I start to feel the auric energy of the earth reaching toward me, full of love, forgiveness, and compassion. I can't go there! Every part of my being starts to vibrate with tension. I am losing the fight. I haven't much resistance left.

As I get even closer, I cannot even hold my light-shape together. I start to melt, to lose my form. I become a blob of light, pathetic. The blob does not respond to my conscious mind. I have lost control.

The light that is me continues to pool. I am losing consciousness. The 'I' as I knew it is ceasing to exist. (In the physical world my body starts to vibrate and shudder.) I set that part of me free as the light becomes a liquid pool, unaware. There is a memory of me but I am no longer me. I am an ooze of primordial goo. I am liquid energy. (My body continues to shake.)

Then, without warning, a sudden transformation—a burst of light/beginning/manifestation. In an instant, the pool of light is moisture soaking into the earth's surface and dozens of chamomile plants spring up in that particular spot, full of life (my body gives a big sigh and my breathing slows considerably). I want to run and play. I want to feel movement, I want to flow, flow, flow. I want to be a river or a channel (body now in fetal position). I want all my molecules to move, to rush, to slow down, to 'respond'. I want to enter the dance of life.

I am the Earth (deep breath).

I have just begun my journey.

I am a small child-like being, innocent, cautious. I want to go and explore and I feel safe enough to do so. I want to taste the leaves of the plants. I want to feel the cool running water of the creek on my feet and legs. I want to listen to the bird song and try to sing back. I want to talk to the sun as if it was my companion and I want to sleep on the earth, cradled in my mother's arms. I am alive.

It took a while for this journey, and the healing I received, to sink in. I lay down afterward with a warm blanket and allowed myself some time. Part of me was surprised to learn that deep down inside I felt that I was hideous, repulsive, and a damaged specimen of a human being. Yet another part of me was so relieved. I couldn't have moved forward in my life, in the ways that I wanted, if I was still harbouring those feelings unconsciously. Now they have been both revealed and released, all in the same transformative journey. The panic I felt! It was so real. Afterward I felt soft, slightly vulnerable, but safe. Once again I could be tender and child-like, instead of carrying around the emotional armour I assumed was needed to protect me. I had a reinstated sense of innocence and the gift of that feeling felt new and unfamiliar, it had been absent for so long.

On the outside, and to others, the shift was also obvious. I not only approached other people and situations more softly, I actually looked softer, felt softer to be around. I could more easily let go of little things that annoyed me. I could sit with others in a more relaxed manner. Before, I was often told that I approached people and events as if I was on a mission. Now, they were encounters, and an opportunity for new relationships to unfold.

Chapter Fifty-Three

Hard Times

I am only human—some things are still hard . . .

I find that dedicating my life to being in service to my people and all our relations is an enormously satisfying way to live, particularly when the focus is on healing and spiritual wellness. There are times however, when walking this path presents challenges that can literally stop me in my tracks, knock me down, and give me pause.

Those are the hard times, the most difficult times, and the anguish I feel lures me downward even further, leading me to doubt. As a Pipe Carrier and Spiritual Elder there can be no room for doubt. If I am not standing strong on my path of service, if I am not fully trusting the healing gifts of Spirit, then the pipe must be returned and I must step back from my duties. Just the thought of it adds another layer of despair.

More than twelve years ago now, when I was still a novice on this path, preparing for a spiritual pilgrimage with one of the significant teachers of my life, Eliot Cowan, I was asked to conduct a very detailed fast for six weeks, many facets of which needed to be shared by my husband, Chris. It was a difficult fast as it touched on many areas of my life at the same time: my food choices, the times of day when I ate, my method of bathing, and the physical intimacy Chris and I shared. As it turned out, as we were hitting the home stretch and I was packing for departure and checking off the list I had been sent, we realized we did not follow the instructions precisely. We had made one small error. This meant I had to call Eliot and alert him. It was a very difficult conversation. We had embarked upon the fast willingly, and despite the restrictions, felt dedicated and committed. I also tried my best to approach the fast with gratitude and joy, for I was genuinely excited for the opportunity it afforded me. To fail, if only in one small matter, felt enormous.

Chris had a different take on the situation. This was my path, not his, and he was willing to stand beside me all the way and do his part, if it was important to me. But there was a limit. When Eliot learned of our transgression he felt we needed to make amends and asked us to continue our sacrifice longer than the others, which included some time after my return from the pilgrimage. Chris felt his intentions were strong and pure and the extended fasting felt like a punishment we didn't deserve. He was angry.

After it was behind us we rarely spoke about it again. When Fishwoman arrived on the scene as a lifelong teacher, Chris breathed a gigantic sigh of relief. Fishwoman always acknowledged that she was merely human and that sometimes we made mistakes. Those mistakes were not considered failures—they were part of the path of learning through experience. I confess that I too felt relief. Following the mandate that Eliot had asked of us was indeed challenging and if I had become his apprentice, the level of expected commitment would only have increased.

Entering into Elderhood and being seen as a spiritual teacher and guide myself has led me to experience the other side of those challenges and it is humbling indeed. Being the bridge between the world of Spirit and the world of matter may sound noble but at times it feels more like 'piggy in the middle'.

Being the bridge means being responsible to both sides, and on this path, where relationship and reciprocity are the cornerstones, there is also a component of accountability. When Spirit advises there is an expectation of following through with attention to detail. While Fishwoman is in many ways a gentle Elder, some of my lessons have been delivered quite harshly. This particularly applies to following protocols at ceremonial events. There have been many times when her words have been sharp and cutting, leaving me feeling torn to shreds. At these times, a pure heart and good intention were not sufficient. They were a good start, an important foundation, but I still needed to pay attention, listen carefully, and follow through appropriately or the blade came down.

It is easy to take advantage of Spirit; in fact it requires discipline and diligence not to. We are given far more gifts than we can offer a reciprocal exchange for. But that doesn't negate the importance of trying our best to balance the scales. One of the ways we do that and show our gratitude and reverence is to pay attention to the small things, and if we are not certain at any turn, to ask for guidance and not forge ahead anyway. Walking a medicine path and maintaining its integral relationships is unlike any other relationship in our lives and it requires a special attention to flourish.

Now that I am the one conducting the ceremonies and teaching the protocols, I see my students presented with the same challenges I had, and sometimes they are not as considerate in their response to me as I was to Eliot and Fishwoman. They fall back on the same premise that Chris and I did all those years ago, feeling wronged by the sting of accountability when their intentions were true.

When I am teaching I often feel the need to remind my students, "I mean what I say and I say what I mean." As a culture, so many of our words are not thoughtful and considered. They are chatter, filling the space between us. We respond by tuning in and out, effortlessly, paying more attention when our interest is piqued, and when it is not, secretly and silently moving on to something else inside our heads. When we walk a spiritual path it is important to make an effort to change this.

I feel strongly that my approach is valid, as it is guided by my spirit teachers, but every day I meet the challenges it presents for others. All it takes is a few moments of distraction, of letting the mind chatter take over, and they can miss something important. Then it is my job to bring the omission to their attention. When the omission is in regard to ceremonies it is important that the message be received loud and clear. Their natural defense mechanism, their desire to protect themselves, leads them to counter, "But my intentions were good! I didn't mean to make a mistake. That's not fair. I was doing the best I could." It's a tough lesson to learn that good intentions are not enough. One more thing is being asked of you: your commitment and presence in the moment. How well are you paying attention to what is being asked?

There is the additional consideration that students are often in the midst of a healing journey themselves and therefore coming from a place of need. When illness and distress have a strong hold it is not possible for them to be objective, to be as considerate of others as we would like them to be. It is only from an internal state of abundance that we can keep giving and giving. Otherwise we compromise ourselves in the process.

There have been many times when I was the one who didn't pay attention, who didn't follow through, or who had my own idea about my spiritual practice. There were many times that the Mountain was stern in its telling that I had made a mistake, or been neglectful. But when the Mountain teaches, even when the messages are difficult to hear, I feel loved and accepted. I can ask for no better Teacher. While the pain of embarrassment may be still present, I offer my gratitude. The path before me is now more clear than ever and I know the areas within myself I need to strengthen. With the Mountain as my mentor and guide I try to do the same for my students. I point out where things have gone astray. I let the people know what is important by being as efficient as I can in offering corrections.

The relationship between individuals, their teachers, and Spirit is not a chain of command, it is a chain of regard. It is an acceptance of the differing roles and involvement that each has in your life. If a teacher isn't willing to point out where you have strayed, how will you know when your footsteps are true? If a teacher isn't willing to ask more of you than you are inclined to give, how will you know what you are capable of? If a teacher isn't willing to risk the bliss of the moment to invest in your spiritual future, how will you find the depth of meaning and purpose that you are looking for and is the reason you began this journey?

An unfortunate reality in the outcome of these encounters is that students go away in judgement of me, and perhaps even the path itself. They want it to be nicer, easier. They question whether this is what they signed up for.

This is where the most difficult challenges come in. I am human. The Mountain Spirit Beings are not. While I understand how important it is to honour every student's journey and to recognize that they are still in need, they are still learning, sometimes the human part of me wants to scream out, "What about me? What about the way you are treating me? How do you think it feels to be the brunt of your anger when you lash out that you have done nothing wrong? Of course you did something wrong or we wouldn't be having this conversation!" The human part of me wants them to respond to my teachings the way they respond to Spirit's teachings, with respect and honour, recognizing that they didn't offer all they could, and promising to do better, to be better.

I've had many years of spiritual training from the Mountain to help me during these difficult times and I am still here doing my work, day after day. I have learned that whenever I am in the presence of someone else, it is no longer about me, it is about us, and I need to take the 'other' into consideration for every moment of our time together. For the most part I have no trouble rising to the occasion, putting my 'spiritual teacher' hat on and taking whatever toxic thoughts and emotions are being poured out toward me and transforming them into kindness and love. But some days I don't feel I have it in me. Some days I don't have the strength. I am tired and depleted myself, or am already giving all that I can and regrettably, can't find more to offer. These are the hardest times.

It is a fine line to walk, giving all that you can and taking good care of yourself at the same time. Spirit, particularly Bear, helps me tremendously in that regard. I must remember to take the time to rest, to replenish, and simply 'be'.

It is difficult for all of us to accept our shortcomings, particularly when someone else brings them to our attention. But it is through alerting us to those gaps in awareness that we are able to grow and flourish. We *need* those teachings, however difficult to receive. As a student, I can now accept this for the gift that it is. It is another way that Creator brings forward into my life that which I need. As a teacher, I remind myself that it is an act of compassion that I offer to others by repeating what they have forgotten, or did not make the effort to receive. No matter how painful the encounter, it will ensure that their feet are headed in the right direction, that they are walking the path in a good way, and the spirits watch over, pleased to be heard.

Chapter Fifty-Four

A Mountain in Distress

Sometimes it requires the bringing forward of everything you know, everything you are, and then trusting that it will be enough . . .

A few years ago, when a student discovered my intimate connection with mountains, she shared a story with me about a friend's mountaintop business that was experiencing strange and inexplicable events, some of which had resulted in dire consequences. This was a tourist-based business that had been erected on the side of a mountain and had been in operation for about ten years. It was open to the public during the winter months and had a staff of about twenty. Many of the buildings and facilities there had been anchored, literally, into the stone walls.

Over the years so many odd things had happened there that even those who didn't believe in metaphysical phenomena or ghosts knew that something was very wrong. Machinery would fail with no physical cause. Staff members would increasingly experience mental difficulties and depression, proportionate to the length of time they worked there. The final straw had occurred only a few weeks earlier. A man had died while hiking on the mountain. An avid climber in his 30s and a picture of health with no pre-existing medical conditions, he was found dead on one of the lower trails, with no evidence of trauma. No sign of a fall or heart attack. On his body was a working cell phone that had minutes before taken photographs of the area, but no attempt was made to call anyone.

I knew a few things about angry mountains from my time spent with medicine people in other countries. There, the consequences of violating a mountain were clearly understood. Any dramatic, man-made change to a natural landscape opened up the possibility of distress, particularly when no ceremonies were performed to engage the nature spirits and no action taken to mitigate the trauma and stress forced onto the environment. In learning about the history of this site, and its previous ownership, I knew that no considerations had been given to the land or the mountain. All decisions were based on potential success and profit.

I also knew, from previous land work I had been involved with, how mountains felt about the giant man-made machines that burrow into solid stone beneath the earth's surface, shredding and spitting out whatever was in their way.

When this student, Michelle, advised the management team that I had experience with healing land areas that had once been traumatized, I was asked to help. Over the weeks of meetings, discussions, and finally, a decision to move forward, Michelle began to feel quite strongly that she wanted to be involved. This was unexpected. She had known the people who operated this business for several years and had been to this mountain a few times in the past, never feeling particularly drawn to it. In fact, it had so little appeal that she admitted to actually avoiding it. But now something had changed. Neither of us knew what it was but there was a hint of authenticity and appropriateness that we couldn't shake. We made arrangements to go to the mountain together.

The evening before we were to begin, I drove to the nearest town and settled into a hotel room. I wanted to spend some time just being close by before the work began. As the darkness fell and the quiet of the night opened, I journeyed to my Mountain to ask for guidance.

"My child you must be careful. You do not know this mountain, nor has it reached out to you and asked for your help. There are many imbalances there, some from deep inside. Did you notice how still it

looked? When you first arrive, find a place to offer a generous amount of tobacco. Sing the Little People song. This will advise the mountain of your skill and your intentions. While all mountains are one, we do not relate to this mountain in the same way as others. This mountain is no longer proud. Just as a child feels ugly and awkward with braces that everyone can see, this mountain has been enduring these cords and cables for many years and does not hold the feeling of majesty that is its right and inclination. As your people have been scarred and maimed in an area that is visible to others, so too has this mountain. It has been defiled."

I ask, *"Grandmother, who is it that the mountain wants to show its majesty to? Is it not the two-legged who offer adoration and acknowledgement? We do not see the mountain as scarred or defiled, we continue to see it as magnificent."*

Grandmother responds, *"Your thoughts may be helpful. We do not hold any promise of your success there. Do what you can, do the best you can. We will hold in our hearts that the mountain will receive you well. That is all we can do. Please be careful. If the mountain threatens you, you must leave at once."*

Day 1 - Laying the Groundwork

Michelle and I arrived at the mountain and followed the instructions exactly as given. We found an isolated area, away from the structures and people so I could listen to the mountain. I asked Michelle to create a small medicine wheel and make additional offerings. Before we began, I talked briefly about the importance of the next few hours. We were there because the mountain had a wounded spirit. In all likelihood it was very angry and capable of causing harm. We were simply to introduce ourselves and see if we could get to know her a little, then move toward building a relationship. We were not to ask anything of her. We were not to presume that because we believed we were there to help, that the mountain saw it that way. She was not the one who approached us. On the other hand, the increasing number of dramatic and unexplainable events could indeed have been a cry for help. I reminded Michelle that assumptions can be dangerous.

I lay down so my body could have full contact with the mountain's surface and my immediate sense was that there was a barrier between the mountain and those who walked and worked upon it. As I tried to know more, I could almost feel a pushing from the inside to the surface, as if at the slightest provocation, this mountain would be inclined to throw people right off.

It was then I realized that the mountain had noticed me. There was a subtle shift, as if someone was peering out a window from the deep walls inside and wondering, "Who is this two-legged who is actually listening to me?" I sensed the mountain was now a bit interested, a bit curious. This was not her usual experience of those who walked upon her. This was a good sign. I felt hopeful about the possibility of developing a relationship.

We sat on the mountain at this same spot for several hours, asking nothing, expecting nothing; simply being there in a different way than the other humans. Our intention was to listen, notice, and feel.

We then ventured upward to get closer to the peak. As we travelled we could see the enormous machines and generators which created the continual noise and vibrations through the rock. As soon as we arrived and stood at the top, I could feel the wound. I felt the sense of embarrassment and vulnerability, and how, after all these years, it still felt strange—all the structures and cables. In my journey the night before I had learned of the loss of majesty. Up there, I was struck by the reality of it. I felt its impact. There was also a feeling of resentment and spite, of, "I'll get you back for this." I saw an image of an angry, mischievous child, one who tried hard to be creative in his ways of vengeance. At the same time, I sensed a softer side, more feminine, frightened, withdrawn, with not a lot of hope left for a brighter future.

I introduced myself, "Grandmother and Grandfather. I am One Who Walks With Eagle Mountain. I am here to listen, if you will speak with me." Almost immediately a change occurred in my physical body—I felt the vibration of the pulleys and machines, but no longer from my feet being planted on the earth, from the perspective of this mountain! She was showing me what she had to endure. And in the same way that I experience 'my'

mountain as several different aspects or beings, I noticed there was a part of this mountain that had gone slightly mad from it—it never stopped. This part of the mountain was confused and had lost touch with reality—it had to. That was the first hint of the healing that was needed.

I then saw a vision of a Grandmother at a sewing machine, obviously exhausted, hands chapped and cracked, working as hard as she could to mend the tears, to put things back together. I saw a Grandfather figure. He appeared like a prisoner of war, defeated, numb, and silent. Finally the nature spirits came into view, many of them in a suspended state or frozen, unable to bring their life force and their spirit forward. They were cut off from their source.

The long-standing and continuous assault had inflicted a disorientation and the mountain had never been able to reclaim its rhythm, its natural pulse. This increased its suffering and the isolation it felt from the other mountains. It was no longer in harmony with the earth.

Michelle's experience was quite different from mine. She tuned into a sad, weeping, female mountain—one that appeared to look to her for help. I realized that this mountain was actually desperate for a relationship, the one thing it was never given, that was never considered important, and it had chosen Michelle. At one point when she was lying against the surface and listening, she felt part of the mountain reach up and grab her hand, holding it tight, not wanting to let go. The experience had quite an impact on her.

This was another unexpected development and it was important for Michelle to consider carefully what was involved in establishing a personal relationship with this mountain. It would require a commitment, some training in working with mountains, regular visits to perform ceremony and offerings, and a continual holding of it in her thoughts and prayers. She was interested and intrigued that it could become part of her apprenticeship and our work together. She didn't live very far away, so physical distance was not a problem. And so, what mere hours before had seemed unimaginable was now being placed in her lap. She was asked to befriend a mountain. I knew what that felt like.

It appeared the mountain already knew who we were and what we could offer. I was there as an outsider, a visitor, but hopefully one skilled enough to help repair the damage and create a new beginning. Michelle was needed in a very different way. The mountain needed a guardian and a friend, someone who would come to know her intimately, watch out for her and protect her. She needed someone who would bridge the world of business, people, machines, and the deeper more intimate needs of a mountain. She needed someone who was physically available. Michelle accepted the challenge. She offered a promise to be the spiritual guardian of this mountain for six years. In return, the mountain told us her name. It was Helen of the Mountain People.

Day 2 - An Offer of Help

I was on my own today. I began with a slow morning. It was the only pace I could manage. I felt I could not, or should not, rush into a meeting with the mountain. That would not be well received. Once I was all set to leave the hotel, the thought popped into my mind to stop along the way for a muffin and coffee, which I actually didn't want. I had already enjoyed a nutritious breakfast and felt good. Perhaps some procrastination was being asked of me, so I stopped, although I ate less than half the muffin and had only a few sips of the coffee. I wanted to show that I was listening and I understood the mountain's apprehension to my arrival. I had seen the same features so often in my healing practice, particularly with patients coming in for soul retrieval work.

When I arrived at the mountain I went to the edge of the parking lot to offer tobacco and acknowledge the features and elements present—the plants, the stones, the creatures and wing-ed ones, the waters, and the weather beings. I offered tobacco for each one and then found my way to a secluded area, overlooking the valley below.

I lit a coal and offered juniper to Helen of the Mountain People. Then resin. I lit a cigar (tobacco) and spoke out loud of my willingness to sit with her. I could still sense her hesitation but she showed no hint of rejection.

I waited, to let the mountain prepare. I closed my eyes to check in with her. All of this mountain's energy felt at the surface, a coat of armour, a barrier to her inner nature, protecting her from further injury. Without

warning, I experienced a rush of emotion from her and I recognized the feeling. I too had closed myself off, hidden myself away, and shut out the rest of the world. I understood some of this mountain's suffering! This was our place of beginning, our opening into relationship. I realized how uniquely suited I was to help there. I was One Who Walks With Eagle Mountain, a Mountain Spirit Being in a human body. I knew about the nature of mountains and after all my years as a practitioner, I also knew about the nature of wounds and the process of healing.

Remembering the image presented the day before, of the Grandmother at the sewing machine, I reached out and respectfully asked "Grandmother, may I help with your repairs and mending?"

She replied, "There is nothing you can do."

"Please look at me. Please notice me. I am a mountain too. I can be of service. Will you let me help you to heal?"

She started to cry but did not back down. She had to hold it together—always! She could not even speak of her needs or respond to my request. I continued, "I would like to honour you. I would like to do something nice for you." I could tell she felt she was beyond hope, beyond help. I understood that she needed a little time. I settled in on my blanket prepared to wait for hours if need be. I hoped she would accept me, particularly now that she knew she would not be deserted. Michelle would be there to offer ongoing friendship and support. Helen of the Mountain People would be well taken care of.

The hours passed, until I felt an immense sadness come over me. It was consuming. Helen had let down her guard, her shield of protection, and was willing to show me her pain. I needed to be careful. It could easily overtake me. My mind flashed back to the movie, "The NeverEnding Story," and the scene when the young warrior's horse, Artax, was sinking in the swamp. Warrior Atreyu was pleading, "Artax! Artax! Don't let the sadness of the swamp get to you," over and over. Yet Artax was helpless in the grip of that sadness and was overcome. He sank until he was no longer visible. Then I thought of the two horses that had drowned in the small lake on the property I had been privileged to work on, the story I shared with you earlier in "The Lake of Tears." That lake was full of trauma. That lake was full of sadness. The horses were overcome.

I called on my Mountain Spirit Beings: Grandmother Mountain, Grandfather Mountain, and Wizard, to be with me. I needed to Be Mountain. It was the only way I could be strong enough. I lay down to be as close to her as possible. I heard the noise of the machines anchored into the mountain. I heard people's voices.

Every wound that is allowed to fester will generate anger. This mountain was no exception. I offered my support simply by acknowledging her pain. I knew that she wanted me there and yet at the same time, she didn't. What was she going to do with me? Interspersed with the feelings of connection were those that I should leave. The wounded animal retreats from the pack sending a strong message to 'leave me alone'. This mountain had never received such respite. The perpetrator of her wounds remained firmly attached.

Again I felt myself sinking and again I strengthened my mountain nature. Then I realized another layer to my service. I could show Helen of the Mountain People the inherent nature of mountains! I could reintroduce the experience of healthy *mountain* in the same way I could reintroduce function and flow to the meridians of my patients. I could present the memory of wholeness. I closed my eyes. I saw the energy pathways of the mountain like rivers of light. I saw the bolder and more predominant ley lines, less numerous. I saw a stagnant red energy where each of these channels extended beyond the base of the mountain and I knew how this mountain had isolated herself from the others. I saw two concentrated areas where the light was reduced to a trickle. Already I felt so tired, so small by comparison. Being exposed to this, being face-to-face with another feature of her wounding, felt almost overwhelming.

I shifted my awareness from my mind to my heart and instantly felt held in the family of spirits that watch over me. I felt their strength and resolve and it infused me. I stood up and planted my feet boldly on the surface of that mountain and allowed myself to be the portal that opened her once again into the archetypal nature of Mountain. I held it as long as I could.

When I opened my eyes I saw a little gnome peeking out from behind a stone that was three times his size. I could tell by the way he surveyed the area that he was checking to make sure the way was clear and safe. He

seemed satisfied. With a circling motion of his right arm he signaled for the others behind him to come forward. The nature spirits had returned! I sang to them and welcomed them back to the mountain. Helen had received the gift and accepted me.

Day 3 - Building Relationship

Michelle and I headed up to the mountain about 9:30 a.m. As an apprentice of mine, I had accepted responsibility for mentoring her. There was so much to learn and this angry mountain was a difficult way to begin. But she was brave and committed. She too could feel the pain. We found a nice spot in the forest. I asked her to introduce herself and call in the four directions. She stood on top of a large boulder as she did so. We made offerings, starting with juniper, then frankincense. We kept gently checking in with Helen, assessing her relative strength/weakness, her distress or ease at our presence. She was very quiet and unresponsive. Undaunted, I suggested we share stories with each other, knowing that Helen would be listening and getting to know us too. We would behave as if we were having tea with a frail, old friend, one who had very little energy to contribute, but was enjoying the company and the conversation.

By 2:30 in the afternoon I felt the need for Helen to rest. Michelle and I went into town for some food. I really needed some fresh fruit so we bought blueberries, a pineapple, and a cantaloupe. We went back to Helen about 3:30 and offered her a spirit plate of the food, placing four offerings, one in each direction, and then a different sacred plant on each: sage in the West, copal in the North, spruce resin in the East, and frankincense/myrrh in the South. We lit the resins to burn them and release their scent, and the aromas combined in an intriguing way as they wafted upward. We felt that Helen was pleased. I had asked Michelle at different times throughout the day to keep checking in, both as to how Helen 'was' and to how we were being received. I felt she was accurate in her assessment each time.

Near the end of the day I asked Michelle to draw a picture of Helen. She drew an outline of a mountain with a woman's face inside. I then asked her to add the man-made structures, in the same the way they were placed in the physical world. I did this on purpose, to show how grotesque it was. As we gazed at the completed image we found ourselves in a discussion about the nature of disfigurement and handicap. We talked about people we knew who had experienced similar adversity. Some were able to overcome the challenges. Others were not. We explored the differences. Love, support, and acceptance were critical for the handicapped person to resume the desire and willingness to contribute to society.

I asked Michelle to modify her drawing, to thin some of the strong lines, and to be creative to find a way to keep the cables and structures present yet allow the beauty of Helen's face to predominate. She did a wonderful job! When finished, Helen looked radiant and a hint exotic, with a strange dangling earring down one side of her face.

It was time to go. Helen had been quiet the entire day, but she had gotten the chance to know us better, and we now had a new image of her to hold on to. Building relationships takes time and patience.

Day 4 - The Day to Begin.

I slept in. I couldn't believe it, yet at the same time recognized my level of tiredness. It had been a full three days so far even though they didn't look busy in the usual sense.

I took a leisurely hour to have breakfast and get ready for the day. I began by typing up the notes of everything that had transpired so far. It didn't take long, maybe half an hour, and it all began to sink in. As I reviewed the depth of this mountain's wounds, her different aspects, her self-imposed separation and isolation, I realized the complexity of the task before me. This was likely the most challenging task I had ever been asked to do. The thoughts generated in my mind became physical and my body responded: my heart rate increased, my breathing became quicker and more shallow. I was a mere human, a white woman who unexpectedly found herself on a spiritual path and had been running as fast as she could ever since to keep up. I came to recognize that it would take all the skills I had, my own connection with Mountain, everything I knew about how to facilitate healing in a 'living' system and an enormous amount of care and consideration to use

only the most appropriate approach and methods. And I had approximately eight hours left! A wave of humility washed over me. Who did I think I was that I could do this? It was entirely possible that no other human being had ever been asked to accomplish such a feat in four days. I was forever changed as a person simply by holding that awareness.

Where could I begin? What was my first step? If I didn't start at the beginning, at the root cause, even otherwise well-chosen medicines would not produce the desired results. I could not allow her symptoms to distract me, to lure me off course from the fundamental imbalance. I was not there to offer symptomatic relief; I was there to restore the heart and soul of a beautiful, precious mountain, to reconnect her to her mountain brothers and sisters, and to allow a community to support and continue the healing that had begun, with the help of Michelle.

A crack of thunder temporarily distracted me and brought my attention back to the physical world. Within seconds it was pouring rain—a storm had begun. I was in the midst of my preparations. I knew I couldn't stop what I had started. I would have to continue the work at a distance. I could see Helen from my hotel room. Perhaps this was a gift from Creator. Perhaps the geographical distance and the weather beings would provide some additional protection.

I picked up my drum and started to play. I called in all those who support and guide, teach and heal. I approached Helen of the Mountain People and declared, "I have returned. I have come to offer my help." In response she allowed me to see her as a person, a human. She was standing at a kitchen counter cutting an apple into sections. He hands were old, wrinkly, and very dry. She had no joy, no light or sparkle. She was going about her tasks, feeding the creatures that inhabit her surface. She had no song in her heart. She placed the filled plate on a bare table, sat down in a stark wooden chair and placed her head in her hands. She was functional. She had always been. She took care of the others. From the outside no one could see the wounds, the suffering, the limitations. I placed myself in the scene she was showing me and put my hand gently on her left shoulder, then took a chair beside her. I solemnly offered my help and support.

At the same time that I was with Helen of the Mountain People I was with the Mountain Spirit Beings from my own special mountain. I began communicating to her who I was and where I came from, through the connection, not with words. I had no specific intention, other than to offer a most thorough introduction.

Like filaments of light that are infused with knowing, spreading from my fingers into her body, she began to remember how she once was. It filled her with sadness, but also a longing, a longing to be like the other mountains once again. She had not dared to have this thought for more than a decade. It would only have increased her pain. I had the distinct sensation of the clouds parting, revealing a small break in the cover where the rays of the sun could shine through. In that moment, feeling relatively safe and no longer alone, she allowed herself to feel the warmth.

Helen then slumped her head down onto her crossed arms and began to cry. I felt her pain and was flooded once more with the complexity of the problem. All my thoughts of healing methods, approaches, and considerations now felt irrelevant. Somehow I knew that anything I had planned to offer would be received as interference. I stayed with the emptiness, the hopelessness, for a few more minutes, letting it sink in completely until I knew what to do. And there it was—something that hadn't occurred to me before. I could introduce her to the state of pure Love that I knew my Mountain could give.

I worked to find that state of being within myself while I maintained my focus on Helen. I let my spirit find its way to my mountain viewpoint and as I gazed upon the other Mountain Spirit Beings, I reached out my hands to them. We joined as One. I closed my spirit eyes so I would not be distracted by their presence and allowed myself to feel, truly feel, what was happening between us. Then I made my request to feel the Love that they had shown me was possible, the Love that is the light of the universe. And in the same moment I found it, Helen and I experienced it together.

That state of pure bliss informed me what the next step was to be; Helen needed a sincere apology for what had been done to her. She couldn't move forward without it. So I began: "Helen of the Mountain People, on behalf of my fellow humans, I acknowledge the harm we have done to you. We violated your body; we broke through your stone surface, hooked you up

and anchored our structures inside, without any right to do so, without permission, and without regard for you. To deepen the graveness of our error we remained ignorant of what we had done for many, many years. It is only through a kindness of heart and the desperate need for balance and peace on the mountain, that one man dared to look up and consider what had been done to you. In credit to him, he did what no one else had been willing to do. He engaged a plan of action to resolve it and establish right relationship once again."

It was a good beginning but she needed more. Someone had to take responsibility and that person was me, because there wasn't anyone else around who could do it. Being human, I was part of the problem. I had to find the place within myself that resides in all of us, that allows such things to happen. It had to be genuine so that Helen could feel the sincerity. It wasn't the words that were going to make the difference, it was my repentance. I began by recognizing the desire within myself to have everything on my terms. How insatiable was our human list of wants and how arrogant we were to allow our will to dominate and force nature and other people into submission! I recognized that *what I wanted* became the driving force behind every decision I made and every action I took, from what I wanted to eat for breakfast, what my home and garden looked like, to what schedule I kept in my work and practice. The list went on and on. I then remembered a particularly sensitive topic. I wanted new wooden cabinets for the kitchen, which involved the sacrifice of trees. I wanted a granite counter top which involved tearing into the structural integrity of a mountain . . . that was it! I found what I was looking for! I was no different from the ones who had drilled into this mountain, who had erected their steel structures upon her. I, Jaki Daniels, One Who Walks With Eagle Mountain, had considered my desires above others and caused harm by implementing the steps to manifest those desires. I had violated a mountain. I imposed my personal will and created suffering. I accepted full responsibility. I saw clearly the error and inconsiderateness of my ways. I had done wrong.

"Helen of the Mountain People, will you forgive me? I accept responsibility for your suffering and your pain. I will make no excuses. When you look at me, you look into the eyes of the one who has wronged you."

She screams out, "You are one of them? I thought you were different!"

"I am no different. We are all part of each other. I am one of them."

She received my words as a knife thrust directly into her pumping heart and she staggered backward in horror. I knew she was close to her limit. But I watched her expression change as the shock and the pain faded and she came to her own awareness that she was face-to-face with the one who had caused her suffering. She could now focus all of her rage and pain at me. She could take her revenge. She had the power to kill me in an instant.

I had no choice but to surrender. I couldn't possibly be the victor in battle. I had done my best. I stayed absolutely still and quiet. All had been revealed and there were no other thoughts that felt relevant.

Through my vulnerability and open heart she saw into humanity. She glimpsed the totality of who we are. She realized she could see us as a self-ish, confused people, desperate not only for our survival, but something we call success. Yet there I was, doing the unthinkable, confessing my sins and asking for forgiveness. She knew why I was there. I was there to create a new beginning, to close the door to the past and start again.

I sensed an opening and spoke up. "This time it will be different, Helen of the Mountain People. I cannot tell you how—the awareness and the changes are still in their formative stages but they have been set into motion. What I can tell you is that we will love you, we will honour you, we will consider you whenever possible. And we will make every effort to create and nurture an environment where you can feel that love. Words are only the tip of the iceberg. Trust us. We will show that we are worthy of it."

Helen accepted.

/ / / / / / /

I returned home the following day with the gift of my life, the full awareness of the risks and dangers I had taken on, and the relief that Helen of the Mountain People was willing to give us two-leggeds another chance. I could not control what happened at the resort, whether more structures would be built, whether more defacing would be done. But between Michelle and I, we could offer something that would at least bring the two sides into a better balance, one that was hopefully sustainable.

Helen could begin to heal now and she needed some time and space to do it on her own. I left her in peace.

- - - - - - -

Based on the first three days of assessment and relationship building with Helen of the Mountain People, it would have been so easy to structure out a 'course of treatment'. There was obvious soul retrieval work. There were blocks and disruptions to the rivers of light through which her life force flowed that could have been corrected. There were re-connections that needed to be made between the different aspects of the mountain. It appeared there was much to do. All those thoughts, all those well-laid plans, would have come from the mind and were not what she needed most. What she needed was an apology, and the right to reclaim her majesty in her own way.

- - - - - - -

It was almost a year before I received a progress report from the management of the mountain business. That may seem like a long time, but at what point can you gauge success when it's a mountain you are dealing with? We needed to go through a year of cycles and seasons to compare the level of chaos and disruption that had occurred in the past with what this recent year had shown.

They noticed the difference! While there were still problems, in every occurrence since the healing work a cause could be found and a solution implemented. It was still a challenging business, but that was normal, and to be expected.

Chapter Fifty-Five

Ways of Healing and Being

The Mountain's trust in me was enormous. It kept nudging me to be all that I could, and more than I imagined . . .

I call out to the Mountain Spirit Beings. "One who is known to you, Sasha, has asked for our help. She is suffering and requests the healing light to restore her, back to her true nature, the health and vitality that are her destiny to achieve. I stand before you, your humble student, and respectfully ask, how do we begin?"

The Mountain Spirit Beings are moving very slowly and the tone is sombre. I see Grandmother Mountain more strongly than the others. They are gathering wood for the fire, for Sasha's fire of transformation, for healing. Being present to their focus and sense of purpose creates a shift in my physical body, a deepening, a slowing down, a preparation.

"Only from a place of One-ness can you bring someone into the One. Then your preparations are complete and you are fully established in the Union. Then all striving, all effort, all intention, will necessarily cease. As an aspect of the whole, reach out and touch her, allowing her to synchronize and adapt to your state of being. That's all there is.

"In the past we have shown you methods, nuances of light, focus, and

intention. *These help the human mind to understand what is possible and how it is possible. In the same way that you place your hands on a patient and call in the plant medicine, you have become One with the light and the light will heal.*

"As Mountain, our highest teaching has been to help you grow, expand, and evolve so you can hold the Light of God and the awareness of its presence momentarily within you, as it passes from us to them, your people. There is no higher accomplishment, although it will take a lifetime to perfect.

"The daily practice we encourage is not merely to practice, don't you see? It is the way to develop the art and it IS the art. It is all you have to do and all you have to BE. Yet this is a difficult task for humankind and requires much training. You need to shed the layers of your pain, your experiences of separateness, your surrender to the mind. To live from the soul is to live in continuous alignment with the light that shines from above and within. As a way of life this is near impossible in the man-created world of high speed vehicles and high speed thought. But you can choose it, you can call it back when you are safe in the arms of Nature and your patients are safe in yours. The best you can hope to achieve while living in the city is to always recognize what state of being is required at any moment and consciously participate in it. There are many, many, missed opportunities for bliss. There are also the distractions you perceive as enjoyable. It is all relative. When you have experienced the true Joy of Being many of your distractions will lose their appeal.

"Continue your practice. In fact we say to you, develop your practice, heighten your practice, expand your practice, BE your practice. Your mind knows all that it needs to. Now your soul needs to be the light that will guide you on your way forward."

Chapter Fifty-Six

Turning Back Time

The teachings become the basis for the healing work and the Mountain transcends the boundaries of form . . .

Sasha first came to see me in January 2011. Formerly she had been working as a manager in an engineering firm but had been on disability for almost two years. Her primary complaint was persistent and debilitating chronic pain, but her condition was very complex. Over the past 18 months she'd received what she described as "fairly severe intervention" by the medical profession, including prolotherapy, botox, and trigger point injections into her back, abdominal and pelvic muscles, ligaments and sacroiliac joints. There were also a multitude of spinal nerve block injections and a procedure to cauterize some of the peripheral nerves in her lumbar spine. She had received more than 40 injections in the past month alone and in the process was exposed to abnormally high levels of radiation. The medication she was prescribed, including opiates, anticonvulsants (for nerve pain), anti-inflammatories, antidepressants, and sleeping pills, had created a wide variety of side effects. Not only were these treatments invasive, they had made her condition worse in many ways and did not result in either a definitive diagnosis of her problem or any relief from her symptoms.

Sasha had considerable pain and discomfort in her mid and low back areas, as well as severe hip, thigh and buttock pain on her left side. She complained of pain in her lower abdomen and pelvic regions, as well as a great deal of neck and jaw pain on the right side. She had difficulty both standing and sitting and could not walk any appreciable distance. She described her nervous system as "being on fire most of the time" to the point where she was rarely able to breathe in a normal, even pattern. Before her illness had compromised her life to such a degree that she was essentially disabled, she had been very athletic and enjoyed a variety of physically intensive sports, including mountaineering and mountain biking. Here are some of her words from our initial session:

> "I recognize that healing is a process and I'll have to go through a lot of stuff."
>
> "My nervous system is really wrecked. The end of my tongue and some of my face is numb. When that happens on my body I can handle it, but when it happens on my face I start to think of paralysis and get afraid."
>
> "I'm scared to stop moving. I'm afraid I'll end up in a wheelchair."
>
> "Being still and letting go of the mind are difficult for me. I can easily process and re-process events."

After Sasha's initial clearing and balancing treatments I asked permission to visit her soul. Once the connection was established, I immediately found myself at her heart, her physical heart. I saw a square red box lying on top of it, tied with a red ribbon. It looked brand new—suspiciously new, and I was to open it. The ribbon released easily and before I removed the lid I could see inside. There was an adult Sasha in a beautiful baby blue shirt, but she was obviously suffering. Her body was tight and tense. She appeared like a wounded animal trapped in a cage with no light and no exit. Her fingernails clawed at the sides, trying desperately to set herself free. I expected that when I removed the lid she would dash out as quickly as possible, but instead, light poured in and her body softened and released. She

collapsed to the floor of the box. I received an understanding about light and vibration and sound, and the relationship between them. Then the box started to dissolve, leaving Sasha resting openly on her heart.

As I stayed with this image, my mind began to make sense of the two different types of suffering she had been experiencing. One was the suffering of being trapped. The other was the physical pain. The dissolving of the box that held them separate meant that she could now come together as one whole person.

During a session about six weeks later another soul story appeared. As I touched her I saw swirls of light energy, mostly white. I felt as if I was looking into the heavens. Then below the swirls I saw a tiny planet with both Sasha and I standing on it. It was so small we could visually see the curvature of the surface. It felt like Home, that we belonged, and that the two of us 'came from' the same place. There was some connection between this little planet and the power of manifestation, with the result that we were both able to hold that ability in a beautiful and reverent way. We understood that it was not a source of personal power and neither was it a burden. The scene changed and we were running on a beach. We were laughing and playing and the mood was light. This too was a teaching of how to hold that knowledge, of who we are and where we are from, in a humble way.

On March 25th, two and a half months after we first met, Sasha shared with me that the day before she had experienced two hours of absolutely no pain. She described the bliss of just 'being' inside her body. She cried when it happened and she cried again while sharing it with me.

Over the next year there were many ups and downs in her healing process. In the meantime she had learned how to journey and was receiving deep and detailed insight into the physical, emotional, and spiritual causes of her pain. She was committed to working with spirit medicines and changing her life as needed to accommodate receiving them as gifts in the most respectful way. She dedicated herself to wellness and spent hours each day doing breath work, visualization, qigong, sound healing, and other internal energy balancing techniques. She came weekly for treatments and was offered a combination of soul exploration work to help her understand who she was and why she was here, meridian balancing work to improve the functionality of all her organs and systems, and other spirit medicines that came forward to help calm the chaos and soothe her being so it could heal.

One year later, in March 2012, I did a journey to ask for guidance on what the next steps in her healing were, and how I could be of service. The following is an excerpt from that journey:

I find myself in a storm with howling winds and a rapidly changing sky. In contrast, the earth appears frozen, stuck in time. I have a sense of someone behind me, breathing loud and hard.

I see a plant, about 14-inches high, that has just shot up from the parched, cracked earth. I know it wasn't there a few moments ago. Then, as if underground tendrils were spreading rapidly, more shoots sprout up in the vicinity, all looking like the same plant. They look strong, vibrant, green and healthy, yet there is no water source nearby.

I see Sasha, in her kitchen, she is humming and nibbling on bits of food. There is a distinct air of ease. Then I see a direct, sharp, piercing pain affect her. She literally recoils backward forcing some of the food to be ejected. And then I see Sasha in a bathtub—a big, old-fashioned claw foot tub. She is surrounded by candles and there is a floral scent in the air. The water is warm and comforting and she is relaxed and at peace. In her mind she is preparing, or reviewing, a presentation/ lecture she is to give the following day. She is confident and looking forward to the opportunity to share her experience and insight.

Everything dissolves and I find myself at the primordial energies of Creation. My heart skips a beat. I always need to be so careful when I am here. I must be sure to stay focused.

Wait. Something is not right. The energies here are not moving as they should. It is as if I have entered a 'freeze frame'. Am I the only source of animation here? Then things start moving, but much too slowly, as if there were some opposing force, a resistance that was limiting it.

Grandmother Mountain appears and steps forward, addressing Sasha directly. "Sasha we have heard your plea. While we have not yet been

officially introduced we know it is just a matter of time in your world and therefore quite irrelevant. You are with One Who Walks With Eagle Mountain and therefore you are with us."

(Now speaking to both of us.) "Time can stand still. Time can change its course and speed. Time can defy the expectations you have of it. Can you see where this is leading? Form can follow. Form can operate outside the physical laws of time and linearity. Sasha has touched upon and experienced this truth, but it is hard to hold on to. Yet this is what she must do and you must do it together. One Who Walks With Eagle Mountain knows how to go back in time, Sasha knows how to support and encourage this process internally. We will work together to restore appropriate form and function to the left hip."

"You (Jaki) must go back in time, capture the physiological 'imprint' of when the hip and associated muscles were healthy, then bring that imprint forward into present time and reintroduce it into Sasha's body/ being. This is the next step in your work together and will help to determine the new course of action. The universe will experience a temporary 'stop'. The laws of energy, light, and form are highly complex. We will help you. We will serve to create another freeze frame to allow you to bring Sasha's past imprint forward. We will stop time for you. The work must be highly focused however. As much as we have the ability to interrupt and temporarily cease the flow, we cannot hold it or sustain it. That would be contrary to the natural laws.

It will take up to three months for the full results of our combined efforts to be complete and therefore understood in their totality. In the meantime however changes will be felt and noticed.

Do not think of this work as exceptional. That will limit you. Understand that we are playing with the boundaries of what the physical world and its laws consider possible, yet remarkably, that is what we have been doing all along."

For both Sasha and I this journey was a lot to take in. It took some time for us to prepare. Two months later, on the first day of May, we were ready. The journey was all we had to go on. Neither of us knew what to expect, how the work would be done, or what condition, physically and otherwise, Sasha would experience afterward.

I lit some copal and brushed Sasha down with my eagle feather. Then I drummed around her body, taking care to allow the resonance to sink in. I tried to listen and feel what rhythm and pattern were needed in each moment, as I moved from head to toe and side to side. I then found myself placing one hand near Sasha's left hip and one hand on her shoulder, while I stood at her left side. With my inner sight I could see Grandmother Mountain continue with the drumming. I began feeling the pain within Sasha's body, but it wasn't so much the physical sensation of pain, it was the experience of 'experiencing pain' and what that does to a person. I immediately felt so ill I wasn't certain if I could continue. I held on as best I could, knowing it was just a matter of time before the sensations would shift.

And then I saw the incident that was the catalyst for Sasha's hip problem! I saw her fall from a mountain bike. She was in a wilderness area and the soil was slightly reddish. I noticed she fell on her right side, not her left, and the fall itself did not look severe. It was clear however that this was the incident that knocked her internal pattern askew as I saw 'something' leave her body, signifying that from that moment on she was no longer whole. And then I noticed that her breathing had been affected. It was now uneven and erratic.

In the following half-hour or so I found myself being witness to certain life events that Sasha had experienced, some more detailed than others. These flashes or vignettes each told a story of physical, emotional, or spiritual pain. I was able to feel the ways in which her life had been difficult. I could feel the emotional drain of living with the burden of every movement being so excruciating, relentlessly. Some of these insights affected me deeply, helping me to understand Sasha, what she had endured, and how she came to be the way she is now. Yet there were others I had no context for. They came through me but they were for Sasha's understanding alone.

Then it came. The pivotal time in her life, in her history, where she was well and strong and her left hip, muscles, tendons, ligaments, and bones were all in the proper state of function and alignment. It was a scene when

she was ten years old. I was able to see it so clearly—the exact hue of her denim jeans, the weave of the wool on the sweater she was wearing. But it was how she stood on her own two feet that was the key. We had gone back in time to where her skeletal system and associated muscles were completely healthy. And we needed to stay there, feeling how she stood, how she moved, how she felt inside her body. We needed to experience that more strongly than any other feeling or memory so we could carry it forward into present time.

While Sasha was staying with her ten-year-old self, I placed my hands gently over her hip area, one on top of her abdomen and the other underneath. Inside her body I could see a 'pocket', an area of flesh and bone that was so compromised it simply appeared as a void. I could tell that the skin, tissue, tendons, etc. that were on the far outer left were the most compromised, as they were not getting the full amount of blood, energy, nutrients, and waste disposal that they required.

The assessment felt complete and I settled in and waited. Then I watched as the empty void filled up with light, a particular hue of indigo-violet that was exquisite to behold. It took me a few minutes to realize that the colour I was seeing did not exist in the physical world. This was not a dense colour. It was pale, open, and airy. It held within it an aura of perfection. The light stayed for quite some time, until I noticed energy starting to shift and change inside the hip area. I followed it on the outside with my hands. I was not moving the energy, clearing it, or supporting its presence, I was simply following what was happening. Slowly, the shifts became physical and the structure of the body began to respond. The entire hip and pelvic area started moving and changing—on the inside! Staying with the perfect hip of Sasha's ten-year-old self, we experienced her body remember what that was like, then adjust itself accordingly! Sasha was not directing this. There was no way she would be able to change the placement of her hip inside her body while lying perfectly still at the same time. We experienced it as it was happening *to* her.

A few minutes later we were done. There were no more images. The connection to the Mountain slowly faded and I removed my hands from Sasha's body. I sat down and waited for her to return to this time and place.

It didn't take long. We talked about what happened for a few minutes, then she hesitantly got up from the table. We had no idea what to expect. We didn't know if her muscles would go into spasm from the dramatic structural shifts, if she would need to use crutches to walk (she had brought a set in her car, just in case), or whether she would need to train her body to work with the new alignment. We had tried to anticipate some of the possibilities beforehand so we could be as prepared as possible.

Sasha stood up, then bent forward at the waist, toward the floor. I turned for a moment to put something down on my desk and when I turned back she was standing again. "Did you just touch your toes?" I asked, hardly believing what I thought I saw in my peripheral vision. She bent at the waist again and I watched in awe as her fingertips did not stop at the floor but kept going down until the back of her hands rested lightly on the carpet, her head almost touching her knees!

Shortly afterward she walked out of my office and went home. It was slightly awkward. What more was there to say? What more was there to do? How do you transition back into the physical world after an experience like that? How do you hug and say goodbye after what we had just been through together?

A few days later Sasha sent me these notes, so we had a documented record:

> "I felt unsettled prior to the appointment. I didn't quite know what to do with myself. I had no idea how much the healing would involve, how much would actually change, and what would be required of me to embody the treatment. Jaki began the healing in a ceremonial way: she put on a skirt, lit a candle, smudged us with copal, and called in the seven directions with her rattle. As she drummed, I could feel the vibration in my spine and bones—a slow, quiet rhythm. When she stopped and Grandmother Mountain continued in Spirit world, I felt it in my hip, it was faster but still a gentle rhythm, not hurried or insistent. Jaki narrated as she went back in time to the mountain bike crash. She used the word 'disequilibrium' and

described the creation of two patterns, one above the waist and one below, with little connection between them. When she placed her hands on my hip, it was exactly where I intuitively felt the source of the problem was, but I did not share this with her. She went on to describe the state of my bones and their porosity. Then she was somehow experiencing toxins being released from the bones and being replaced with light. The toxins were so vile she wanted to vomit. Jaki spoke of my preparations, the transformational breath work, the emotional work, and how they had led to this one moment of time. I would not have been ready to receive this before now. Then, I felt my foot rotate outwards as it was resting on the table, felt my femur shifting in my hip cavity, and could tell there was now more space inside my body for it to move! Jaki described how this healing was being given as a gift. No specific being spoke. It was odd in that it all seemed to happen with ease. I was puzzled by this. When the healing was finished, I lay quietly on the table, giving myself permission to accept the changes, to embody them (that might have been the hardest thing of all) and to love myself. In debriefing afterward I realized it would be hard to know what to do with myself, after pushing through things for so long, enduring the suffering, always running on an energy deficit. I didn't remember how to feel any different.

That night I had a dream, a snake dream. A grey rattlesnake had somehow got inside the house where I was living. I don't remember the plot but woke up completely soaked in sweat. Snakes have always been a sign of healing and rebirth for me. The next morning walking my dog, I had full range of motion, and afterward I stood on the sidewalk realizing I was not experiencing any pain . . ."

Before I saw Sasha for her follow-up appointment, scheduled for six days later, I received an email containing the following: "I rode 21 km on my bike yesterday. No worse for wear . . . except that I noticed I am really out of shape. I'm free!!!!!"

On July 30th, the day before the completion of the three-month recuperation period that Grandmother Mountain had advised, Sasha came in to see me. She had just returned from vacation and felt overdue for a tune-up. She had been very active while away and perhaps pushed herself to the limit. However, she excitedly shared that her holiday was full of physical activity, including surfing and kayaking. She also mentioned three separate 40 km bike rides where she not only left the rest of the group in her dust, she was riding like the wind, full of energy and glee. In fact, she described herself as having the boundless energy of a ten-year-old.

In no uncertain terms, the healing she had received was a miracle.

Chapter Fifty-Seven

The Inner Workings of the Brain

The missing pieces of Todd's story, continued from Part I.

The first six months of Todd's healing journey had, more than anything, helped him to participate in his own life again and feel good about himself, which was wonderful. But I disagreed with his declaration on September 2nd that he was "better" and no longer needed treatments. At the time, I wanted to show my support for his newfound independence and confidence so we agreed to take a break from our sessions until just before Christmas, then give him a tune-up in time for the holidays. At his December 17th appointment I learned that he had been doing really well until the beginning of December when he started to vomit again, and from there, declined rapidly. Even his handwriting began to deteriorate. Molly had been called to his school twice the previous week to pick him up because he was pale and dizzy and thought he might fall. It took three treatments within the span of eight days to return Todd to a more stable state.

While Todd's progress had been remarkable in many ways he had not yet achieved the calm and articulate mental state that was shown when the Mountain first revealed his internal story. I knew I would not have been shown this if it was not possible for him to achieve it. The time had come for some much deeper work.

I called out to the Mountain. I closed my eyes and waited. It didn't take long before I found myself in a highly detailed inner vision experience, with some scenes revealing themselves in a practical manner suggesting a diagnosis, while others were startlingly fiction-like, in the style of metaphor, myth, and fantasy. As the first scene came into focus I saw Todd lying prone on a flat table and there were beings of light all around him, including me. I was one of the circle. My heart skipped a beat as I realized that these beings intended to perform some sort of brain surgery on him. Using their hands to radiate a beam of light they cut across the top of his head, from mid-ear to mid-ear, and pulled open the skull to expose his brain. I could easily discern which areas were healthy and which were not. I had a sense of when the tissue was the appropriate texture and colour and had the optimal amount of blood flow. I could see where the surface undulations were in the ideal location and reached the appropriate depth as they entered the tissue. One area, just above Todd's forehead and over his right eye, emitted sparks of a blue-ish colour. Once this was shown, I was able to notice other areas that were sparking—the erratic light revealing that the 'wiring' in his brain was malfunctioning. Accompanying the distress at seeing the extent of the compromised areas was an overwhelming feeling of sadness. I realized in that moment that the sadness Todd had been experiencing wasn't a response to his illness—it was integral to it!

The scene blurred temporarily and when it resumed I had a small, thin wand in my hand. I knew I was to place it over the affected areas in Todd's brain. When I did so the excess light and energy were instantly drawn into the wand, then dissolved. This approach worked well until I moved over the most intensely sparking area, the one with the blue light. As I held the wand I felt a sharp, pulsing current being drawn upward, then stop. The power of it made my hand shake. More important, the light it now held was not dissolving. Something was wrong. I took my awareness further inside the tissue and followed it deep into the brain to the source of the problem. Imagine my surprise when I found myself face-to-face with a troll-like being, standing at the end of a severed 'wire'. Beside him, under the exposed tip, was a blazing fire, sending shock waves of pain and distortion along it.

The story had changed from physiology to metaphor but the meaning was clear. I had found the source of Todd's problem and knew what needed to be done. The troll had to be removed and the exposed wire repaired. Using the only tool that had been given to me, I carefully held the wand above the troll and asked that he be dissolved and any remaining light essence be released upward and taken out of Todd's body. Within a few minutes all that was left was the frayed end of the wire, still hanging. I took it in my hands, smoothed it out and connected it to an adjacent open wire so a continuous circuit was restored. Within seconds I could feel the brain starting to heal and I realized I needed to get out of there, quickly! I found myself back at the surface, at the area of blue light. I placed the wand above it and the light started to enter, then dissolve. I smiled. Then I realized how utterly tired I was.

Before I closed the connection I saw one more scene of Todd. His eyes were shining brightly, hinting that he was holding on to some kind of secret and it delighted him to do so. I could feel his life force and his will and knew that he was going to be fine. This was his story and he was going to hold it close to his heart so it could fuel him and be a source of strength. He had what he needed to move forward now.

The healing work was done but we weren't out of the woods yet. As could be expected after such a dramatic shift, Todd went through all the stages of a classic healing crisis, beginning with the return of his symptoms.[19] He had been ill for about nine years so it was natural to take a few months for his body and brain to process the effects of the changes. During that time he was unable to attend school. He was too ill to come for treatments—he couldn't manage the car ride. At its worst Todd began regressing in other ways. He rebelled against the dietary changes that had been so helpful. His behaviour became more infantile—he wouldn't accept responsibility for his

---

[19] The Law of Cure in Chinese Five Element Healing states that all illness leaves the body from the inside out, from the top down, and in reverse chronological order. A healing crisis is actually a positive sign showing that the illness is being released and the process of healing has begun.

actions. He didn't want to play with his friends. At times, it was hard for Todd and his family to stay positive, but we trusted the Mountain's gifts and I made regular house calls.

Todd's health and emotional poise fully recovered, and when it did, his stability of function was more independent than ever. He was able to manage well with only occasional treatments. Once this phase had begun, he progressed and matured quite rapidly. When he returned to school he not only received good grades, he was able to manage the distractions and annoyances in the classroom without effort or comment. He became a physically active child, riding his bike, playing sports at school in the daytime and street hockey at night. The crowning glory came in the fall of 2012 when Todd secretly auditioned for the lead role in the school play—and got the part! He was growing up, gaining confidence, and taking charge of his life. He was able to behave and function like a normal, healthy child.

Initially, Molly had approached me (and the Mountain) to help relieve Todd's depression and lift his spirits. She had not actually expected, or asked for, a healing of his physical condition. But the medicine of the Mountain was able to reach deep inside and correct the imbalances that underlay his diverse symptoms. The Mountain found the story that was his illness and presented him with a new one, which he embraced.

Chapter Fifty-Eight

The Dawn of Knowing

Dare I say—"I get it."

It was the evening of the crescent moon and therefore time to offer gratitude to the Mountain Spirit Beings. I built a small fire in the back yard. When the coals were ready, I had my juniper at hand and looked into the night sky seeking Grandmother Moon. It had been overcast all day and was just now beginning to break. I walked around the yard, approaching from several different directions, but where I imagined the moon to be was still obscured in heavy cloud cover.

I stood beside the firepit and offered my prayers. I sprinkled the hand-ground juniper into the cooler parts of the coals and wallowed in the aroma of the smoke wafting upward. So much had happened in the past month. The Mountain had been very generous. My heart was full of gratitude and awe for the blessings she bestowed.

I took a moment to glance skyward once more, fully acknowledging the moon's presence even when I couldn't see her. As my eyes lifted, the clouds parted and revealed a most beautiful crescent moon, directly in my line of sight. I gasped with surprise and delight. Seconds later, she was again covered and did not reappear.

There was something about this showing that felt personal, like a special gift had been offered. The perfect timing—it didn't seem possible or probable to be mere coincidence. That awareness created a unique feeling inside. When I came back into the house it was only 9:30 p.m. but I went to bed instead of finishing up the dishes and the kitchen chores as I had planned. It was the only way I knew for certain I could hold on to what had just happened.

As I crawled into bed I allowed the feeling inside me to linger. I knew how precious and important those feelings could be. I knew I could 'carry them forward' in the same way my patients did after a particularly moving healing session, and that they would support me in whatever goals or ideas I focused on. Thoughts were more than mere thoughts when they were accompanied by a certain feeling! I held onto the gift of the night and the blessing of feeling loved while I acknowledged and gave thanks for my good health, vitality, and strength.

Sometime during the early morning hours an understanding blossomed. I now knew what medicine was, what healing was. Our state of health is based on how we live and feel and breathe. What is the nature, the quality, of our life force energy? Aliveness is a relative state. All true medicines are agents that can create a change in how we feel and how we experience ourselves from moment to moment. Healing is the result of being introduced to an internal sensation different from the one previously carried. In that sense, my sighting of the moon was a healing. Something precious had been given to me and it changed me. It was now my job, my responsibility, to acknowledge the shift and be open to the myriad ways it might influence me: my growth, my maturity, my learning, and my compassion for others. It is the same with journeys and the healing stories that are told. Through direct engagement with Spirit, a different internal sensation is introduced. We can all feel it, yet so easily we become distracted and the 'regular' world comes crashing in. This is where we take responsibility for our own health and well-being! It is not that we need to become our own doctor, or that we need to become experts in the fields of health and medicine. No, there are specialists for that. It is the responsibility of the patient, the recipient, to take the seed that has been planted, allow it to germinate, and to nurture its growth.

My mind danced and ran in this newfound understanding. My soul

rejoiced in the knowing. It was so simple. It was how I always knew it was, but now it was no longer a definition I held in my mind, it was a knowing I held in my heart. This was how a hug could be medicine. This was how plant spirit medicine worked, how mountains healed, how love healed. In every example I could think of, the change in internal experience and the feelings that were generated were the signs of healing presented by the medicine. This even explained the few patients over the years who did not respond well, who did not seem to improve. In every case I could think of, these were the patients that the medicine, and myself, were unable to shift. They were never able to sink into the experience and receive it. They simply lay there on the table, completely absorbed in their own thoughts, expecting me to offer something to heal them and turn their situations around. But they were not involved, they were not engaged.

And then I remembered a Vision Quest several years ago, where Fish-woman and I were sitting around the fire after dinner one night and she said something that completely captivated me. I don't think anyone else even noticed but I was so grateful for those few words, for the sharing of that teaching, that I went into the tent, grabbed a one-hundred-dollar bill and a pouch of tobacco and brought it back to gift her. What she had said was, "Anytime someone tells me that my medicines don't work, I say that they need to come and spend three days with me." She knew! She knew that it was not any inability on the part of the medicine but on the part of the patient to receive it. By spending time with her, whether or not she literally meant three days, was to be introduced to how she lived in the world, how she experienced relationship with the elements and other forces of life, how Creation was alive to her. She lived in the world as a participant in a constant interchange, or exchange, and when she took a medicine she didn't just take it as a thought, she took it as an active agent of change, an ally to support her intention. If a patient wasn't getting better, it could certainly be the case that he was blocking the ability of the medicine to be felt, to be truly received.

Our current pharmaceutical medicines are not about healing. They don't make you a better person, a happier person, able to live in the world with a renewed sense of hope, meaning, and purpose—a state of wellness that influences everyone you meet. Those medicines are about relieving symptoms—they often don't even attempt to get to the cause of the problem. Once the symptoms are neutralized they no longer distract you from getting on with your life, so you can have things be the same. In the system of medicine I'm taking about, you'll never be the same!

To be so stubborn as to believe that you don't need to change anything and that someone else can make you well is naïve. Yet you also don't need to self-diagnose and treat. When we are struggling and suffering we cannot see ourselves clearly. We can only see through the filter of the dis-ease or the dis-function. It is far better to place yourself in the hands of someone who not only holds the medicines but has the skills to see you as you really are.

Healing is a process of growth. It takes time. The patient stories shared here reflect that. Other than the removal of the residue of trauma, most patients work for months, if not years, to get well. Most illnesses are not born of the body alone, they develop over time and reflect an internal conflict brewing and building. To heal, all parts of you, every layer, needs to be involved in the process. That's why it can't be instantaneous. My teacher Eliot used to say, "You can't plant a garden today and expect a harvest tomorrow." Those words convey the truth about healing.

To receive the gifts the medicines are willing to give, you need to be open to influence. You need to allow yourself to be shifted and changed. And you need to be aware of the nuances of those changes so you can guide your practitioner to help in the most effective and efficient way possible. If you get up every day thinking the same self-deprecating thoughts, still hating your job or your relationships, hating the way your body looks or how it works, wishing your life was different but not willing to do anything about it, then wellness won't come. You have locked yourself into feeling a certain way. You have to be willing to feel differently to live differently!

The beautiful medicines of the natural world can introduce you to that new way of being. They can literally enter into your body and be felt. They are the agents of change, all you need to do is be grateful, to recognize them for the gifts that they are and hold on. Hold on to them with your very life.

Chapter Fifty-Nine

As One Door Closes, Another Opens

This is not the end, I will keep walking this path.

When I came back from Peru in 2004 and knew I was ready to commit to this path, I initially thought I would revisit the teachings the Mountain had offered to date, ensure that I understood them all, and then incorporate them into my healing practice, my life, and my understanding of the ways of the world. But when I went back to the Mountain and shared that I was now ready, we kept moving forward. New teachings were continually offered, regardless of whether I felt I had learned and applied the previous ones. There were no reviews.

I can see it clearly now. There is no going back. There is only going forward. All those lessons, all those mountain teachings, the dreams, the ceremonies. I was not in a process of learning. I was in a process of becoming.

So many times the Mountain Spirit Beings asked me to 'be' with them. When I was troubled and seeking answers I would turn to the Mountain and they would invite me to 'be'. When I was struggling with the teachings, trying to understand, they would again invite me to 'be'. The teachings were not meant to be learned, processed, remembered, and practiced. They were the narration that accompanied the changes that were happening within me at the time. They were offered to provide something for me to hold on to, to feel connected with, and to gain a sense that I was progressing. I understand now how it all works.

Teachings are to be received. They are to be taken into your being. And the more teachings you receive the more your being will expand to accommodate them.

If the Mountain had said, "Spend time with us and we will help you to experience the one-ness of the universe," I would have been striving for that particular goal. I would be sitting in stillness but my mind would always be on the lookout for when I had found it. Instead, the Mountain didn't provide an end goal, only a direction to pay attention to in the moment. By continually asking me to 'be', by encouraging me to be aware and expand, by gently pointing out the human limitations I kept bringing forward and helping me to release them, the Mountain did, in effect, take me by the hand and show me I was not separate. I was truly part of the One.

Because I didn't know what to expect from the expansion process I had nothing else to focus my awareness on except what was happening within me, what I was experiencing, and how others experienced me. It was gradual and subtle. I knew I was able to hold more and more in my awareness as the synchronicities that were once rare in my life became commonplace. I began to have experiences of knowing, not from a process of gathering and refining data, but just 'coming to know' something that was happening around me or to others close to me. When we allow our awareness to extend beyond the confines of our form we naturally become aware of more than that which affects our limited selves.

As the gifts which Spirit offers are integrated, and as we come to be in service with them, we further expand. We expand from the experience of allowing them to move through us, to be a vessel of divine will. We begin to see how subtle shifts can have profound results. We begin to understand what medicine, and what healing, really is.

Many years ago my friend Marilyn did a journey for me and in it she was told, "Jaki's garden is a garden of lost souls." I accept the job of gardener. I will tend to those souls—those people. I will care for them and in the process offer the medicines that can help them become whole again.

That medicine could come from the Mountain, it could be a soul retrieval, it could be a story that enters into the fabric of their being and starts the process of mending the tears. It could simply be the act of spending time with someone, to create an opportunity for them to be known for who they truly are, wounds and all, yet feel loved instead of judged. Maybe all I need to do is hold on to the vision of their wholeness until they feel ready to hold on to it for themselves. Others have done it for me. I am willing to continue the practice.

* * * * * * *

I have often wondered why the Mountain chose me. I have written about it, talked about it, and dreamt about it. I kept looking back to 1999 and who I was when the Mountain first spoke to me. I was not interested in shamanism, not looking for a teacher of the spiritual ways, had no yearnings for ceremony. I could not even speak to a deep and abiding love of the natural world, or a sense of awe at the mysteries of the Universe. I wasn't looking for answers to the BIG questions.

I came to accept that I may never know the answer, that perhaps it was not within my ability to grasp. Then one day I saw what I couldn't see before. Every time I asked the question, "Why - did - the - Mountain - choose - me?" I was looking back in time, looking back to what I might possibly have done to deserve this. That was the wrong question! The Mountain didn't choose me because of who I *was* or who I had *been*. It chose me for who I would become! The Mountain reached out to me fourteen years ago and ever since then I have been reaching back. I have been doing my very best to work with, integrate, honour, and appropriately share what was given to me. My entire life has changed and there is no doubt that I will never go back to who I was then. I will continue walking this path. That is why the Mountain chose me. The Mountain needed someone who would receive the gifts it could give and create the space and purpose in her life to accommodate them. Somehow, I don't know how, I was a person who could recognize the precious nature of such a gift and hold on to it with the regard and reverence that it deserved.

Each of us can choose to walk a medicine path, a path where all we do and all that we are contributes to the process of healing for someone or something. I can tell you from my own experience, it's a beautiful path to walk, and there's room for many, many more footprints.

The Legends Say

Oh, and one more thing . . .

There are many teachings today about creating the world that we want for ourselves. There are movies and books that speak to what is described as the Law of Attraction, the goal of which is to help people understand the true nature of the world we live in and how what we bring forward through our thoughts and emotions influences what we experience. I believe we all feel that basic truth at some level. We know that if we are grumpy, irritable, and out-of-sorts, it is likely our day won't go so well. At the same time, we've all felt on top of the world, where nothing could possibly go wrong.

If there are natural laws which can support our physical and financial well-being, take the guesswork out of what is possible, and ease our struggle to achieve our goals, we should certainly figure out how they work! The Law of Attraction provides an invaluable tool in that regard and helps us to see clearly how much of the time we get in our own way. It's exciting to play an active role in the creation of a future that is the stuff our dreams are made of.

There is one problem I have encountered with this teaching however. Some people take it too literally and simplistically, not considering the deeper implications or how to apply it thoughtfully and responsibly. While the teachings can be directed toward material abundance, the more important possibilities are the opportunities for personal and planetary growth, improving the quality of our lives by recognizing that the needs we have on an emotional and spiritual level are the ones we need to fill, and that as we become more conscious of who we are and how our actions and choices affect others, our influence can be far reaching.

In my experience, the greatest blessings I have received have not only been unplanned and unexpected, but literally beyond what I could have imagined for myself. I could not have asked for something that I didn't know existed!

／／／／／／

A few years ago I came across a book, *The Indian Legends of Canada* by Ella Elizabeth Clark. It is a book of legends that have been passed down through First Nations people across this country, a compilation of stories that have been told for hundreds, if not thousands of years. In this collection they are presented as told by the descendants of those Elders and tribal peoples who received the experiences or heard the stories, first-hand, and then translated into English.

I opened the book to have a look inside and found myself at a page detailing a Seneca legend called "The Origin of Stories." I had originally intended to merely glance through, to determine if the book was an appropriate addition to my waiting room. But I found myself reading the story. It begins by describing how a young orphaned boy was raised by a woman who had known his parents. When he reaches a certain age she encourages him to learn how to hunt and he begins by leaving the village to bring back game birds. Initially he is focused and successful in his hunts and brings back an abundance of birds. One day however, as he stops to repair an arrow, he finds a high, smooth, flat-topped stone and climbs on top of it. As he is sitting there, he hears a voice say, "Shall I tell you stories?" He looks around to see who is there, who is speaking. It turns out it is the stone itself! He offers the stone the string of birds he was going to take back to the village, as a gift in exchange for the stories, and the stone begins. Each day after that he returns and each day the stone tells the young boy stories. After a while the people in the village become suspicious as to where the young

man is spending his days when the hunts are no longer profitable. Word gets out about the teaching stone and all the people of the village want to join him, each bringing a gift to the stone. In the last lines of the telling the stone instructs the people to keep the stories, to remember them, and to share them, generation after generation. The Seneca people came to believe that this stone knew all that had happened in the world before them, and passed along that knowledge to their people.

When I turned the page to the part where the stone said "Shall I tell you stories?" I felt as if the world itself started to slow in its turning and that a 'pause' had been created in the universe. There I was, with the book still open in my hands, flooded with questions, thoughts and feelings. A legend! What happened to me was the stuff that legends were made of!

When I first stood on the Mountain and heard its voice, I could have turned away. I could have ignored it. Instead I created an opening for it in my life. Now, one of the teachings I offer to others is, "Always leave room for God." Never be so focused, or distracted, by what it is you think you want, that you don't notice when something else is actually happening. That 'something else' may be a gift greater than you ever imagined.

About the Author

Jaki Daniels lives in the foothills of the Rocky Mountains with her husband of thirty-six years, Chris. Their two grown sons, Colin and Jay, live nearby. Based in Calgary, Alberta, she has been a natural healing arts practitioner for 27 years. While originally focusing on herbalism, aromatherapy, and natural foods, her practice has grown and evolved to embrace the indigenous medicine-woman healing ways. Having apprenticed in ceremonial protocol with Cree Elder Fishwoman for 14 years she is a Pipe Carrier and Lodge Keeper (sweat lodge), hosting community ceremonies on a regular basis, including an annual Vision Quest with Fishwoman. Jaki offers her unique gifts through her healing practice, teaching, and writing. She released her first book, *Heeding the Call*, in 2007, and is currently working on her third, tentatively titled *The Tranquil Kitchen*.

www.jakidaniels.com

Correspondence may be sent to:
Hearthlight Publishing
18 NORTHMOUNT CRESCENT NW
CALGARY, ALBERTA, CANADA T2K 2V5 OR
info@hearthlightpublishing.ca